Evaluating and Improving Written Expression

A Practical Guide for Teachers

JANICE K. HALL

ALLYN AND BACON, INC.   Boston   London   Sydney   Toronto

Library of Congress Cataloging in Publication Data

Hall, Janice K
    Evaluating and improving written expression.

    Bibliography: p. 197
    Includes index.
    1. English language—Composition and exercises.
I.   Title.
LB1576.H22   372.6'23   80-22787
ISBN 0-205-07276-3

Printed in the United States of America

10 9 8 7 6 5 4 3   86 85 84 83

In memory of my father
Adam E. Kroelinger, Sr.

Contents

Preface   ix
Acknowledgments   xi

1 **Introduction   1**

THE COMPLEXITY OF THE WRITING PROCESS   1
EVALUATION OF WRITING SKILLS   2

2 **How Are They Doing?   9**

INFORMAL EVALUATION   9
INFORMAL EVALUATION COMPONENTS   10
    Ideas/Content   10
    Organization   18
    Vocabulary   21
    Sentence Structure   25
    Spelling   30
    Handwriting   32
INFORMAL EVALUATION PROCEDURES   34

3 **Get Them Writing!   47**

CREATIVE WRITING ACTIVITIES   51
PRACTICAL WRITING ACTIVITIES   85

4 **Build Their Skills   95**

ORGANIZATION   95
VOCABULARY   113
SENTENCE STRUCTURE   135

5 **Tackle the Troublespots**   **153**

      MECHANICS   154
      SPELLING   169
      HANDWRITING   177

Appendix A **Resources for Classroom Use**   **187**

Appendix B **Resources for Teacher Use**   **193**

Appendix C **Reference Bibliography**   **197**

Appendix D **Publishers' Addresses**   **203**

Index   208

List of Activities

Creative Writing Activities

Picture File 53
Storybooks 54
Storyboard Sequence 55
Creatures, Monsters, and Dragons 58
Comic Strips 58
Slide-Tape Show 59
Scene I, Scene II, Scene III 60
Story Starters 61
Titles, Tcpics, and Twisters 63
Alligator Antics 64
Telephone Conversations 64
Journals 66
Autobiography 68
Zany Stories 69
Fables 71
Characters I 72
Characters II 73
Character Moods 74
Cartoon Characters 75
Points of View 75
First Person Point of View 76
Settings I 78
Settings II 81
How Do Stories Begin? 81
Eye Witness News 82
New News 82
Pro and Con 83
Ads 83
Targets 84

Practical Writing Activities

Telephone Messages 85
Writing Letters for a Purpose 85
Teen Job Ads 87
Want Ads 89
It's My Opinion! 91
Complain, Complain, Complain 91
How Do I Get There? 92

Organization

Grocery List 96
Jumbled Jokes 99
Irrelevant Sentences 100
Sentence Sort 101
Mixed Up Stories 101
Sequence Words 102
Spotting Details 103
Task Analysis 104
Time Machine: Past 105
What's the Big Idea 106
Questions 107
Listen for the Details 108
Outline Match 108
Prove It! 109
Broad and Narrow 109
Hasty Generalizations 110
Fact or Fiction 111
Is That So? (Fact or Opinion?) 112

Vocabulary

Using Specific Nouns   114
Using Specific Verbs   115
Synonym Call   120
Synonym Pass and Sort   121
Antonym Concentration   121
Substitution   124
Repetitive Words   125
Mary Had a Little Lamb   126
Descriptive Words   127
Make It Real   128
Strange As It Seems   128
Happy As a Lark   131
The Sun Is a Golden Earring   132
Sound Poems   133
Alphabet Antics   134

Sentence Structure

Kernel Sentences   136
Dogs Eat   138
Building Simple Sentences   139
What's Going On?   141
Zany Sentences   143
Reducing Expanded Sentences   146
Pass It On   147
Building Compound Sentences   148
Sentence Combining   149

Make It Parallel   151
Help!   152

Mechanics

Capital Contest   154
Run-on Sentences   156
Sentence Fragments   157
Sentence Collage   157
Hidden Sentences   158
Sentence Scramble   159
Foolish Questions   160
Ask Or Tell   161
Ask, Tell, Exclaim!   161
Conversations   162
Punctuation Dictation   163
Add the Ending (Verb Tense)   163
Sports News (Verb Tense)   165
I, We, He, She, They, It   165
Mixed Up Stories   168

Spelling

Spelling Interviews   171
Visual Dictation   171
The Bare Bear   171
The Hoarse Horse   175

Preface

This resource manual presents a structure for the informal evaluation of writing as well as activities for teaching writing to students in grades four and above. The concepts and activities are designed for use by regular classroom teachers, resource room teachers, and others who work with students who have writing problems.

The Introduction reviews the factors that cause writing to be difficult, then surveys methods and specific tests currently available for evaluating writing ability. Chapter Two outlines three performance levels of writing ability in six skill areas: ideas/content, organization, vocabulary, sentence structure, spelling, and handwriting. Specific step-by-step instructions for evaluating student writing are explained.

The activities presented in "Get Them Writing," Chapter Three, provide an integrated language arts approach to improving writing skills. Emphasis is placed on thinking, listening, speaking, and reading as well as writing and rewriting as interrelated components of the total writing process. The teacher has a dual purpose: to encourage an increase in student writing productivity and to set and prioritize specific manageable objectives that will help students improve their writing skills. Total correction of daily writing assignments is de-emphasized as students follow goal-setting procedures and focus on improving one aspect of writing at a time.

"Build Their Skills," Chapter Four, presents activities that focus on the development of vocabulary, sentence structure, and organization skills. In most cases, sample words, phrases or sentences are provided at several levels of difficulty so that the user may gear specific activities to different ability levels.

The emphasis in "Tackle the Troublespots," the last chapter, is on building proofreading and editing skills. Goal-setting, gimmicks, and games help direct attention to frequently made errors: sentence fragments, run-on sentences, awkward sentence structures, and improper capitalization and punctuation. Instead of working on textbook exercises, students proofread their own writing to identify and correct one specific error pattern at a time. When students have difficulty identifying errors in their own writing, activities from this section which isolate error patterns can be used. Increased student awareness and responsibility for identification and correction of errors help to eliminate some of the persistent problems in writing.

Ideally, the total writing program should provide positive reinforcement for *all* student writing, regardless of errors. Written expression will improve gradually as students have more experience with writing, setting goals, isolating error types, proofreading, and rewriting.

Acknowledgments

Although only one name appears as author on this book, many people have contributed to its development and publication. The initial impetus was provided by my students in the Learning Center at Lincoln School in Brookline, Massachusetts, who were having a difficult time with the basic skills of reading and writing. Betty Baum, a fellow teacher, and I recognized the need for a collection of activities for teaching writing to reluctant readers and writers. Don Maietta of Boston University provided additional encouragement through his class on writing problems, which he held in my Learning Center. Many teachers who have attended my workshops have provided valuable feedback on the evaluation techniques and the writing activities. Regina Nysko, Mary Moses, and Regina Moss carefully typed the manuscript.

Finally, Gene McCann, Series Editor at Allyn and Bacon, provided the encouragement to keep going on the project; and Valerie Ruud, Production Editor, provided superior editorial assistance. Thank you all!

1

Introduction

Why is writing such a complex process? This question has been the topic of a large number of studies in recent years. Cooper and Odell (1977) have described the writing, or composing, process in the following manner:

> Composing involves exploring and mulling over a subject; planning the particular piece (with or without notes or outline); getting started; making discoveries about feelings, values, or ideas, even while in the process of writing a draft; making continuous decisions about diction, syntax, and rhetoric in relation to the intended meaning and to the meaning taking shape; reviewing what has accumulated, and anticipating and rehearsing what comes next; tinkering and reformulating; stopping; contemplating the finished piece and perhaps, finally, revising. This complex, unpredictable, demanding activity is what we call the writing process. [Page xi]

Written language is humanity's highest verbal achievement and it is only achieved when all of the preceding levels of language arts skills (listening, speaking, and reading) have been established (Myklebust, 1965). The student must have intelligence, motor ability, sensory capacity, and socio-emotional maturity to learn the skills of writing. An inability to write, on the other hand, may be the result of any of a number of breaks in the sequence of learning, or a lack of integrity of the peripheral nervous system (as in hearing and vision impairments), central nervous system impairments (as with learning disabilities), emotional disturbance, or a lack of opportunity or training. Students with any of these specific handicaps may produce writing that is deficient in content, vocabulary, syntax, organization, and spelling skills. Writing samples from these students are generally shorter in length than those written by students with no handicaps.

Many other factors contribute to the complexity of the writing process: the high level of abstract thinking required, the increased level of self-responsibility, the maturity of self-motivation, and the completeness that is required in the written form of language (Lundsteen, 1976a). Difficulty with these may result in a lag in writing skills of as much as six to eight years. In writing, students must translate their own inner language (which is often condensed and abbreviated in a form of verbal shorthand) into appropriate words, sentences, and paragraphs, which accurately convey an intended message. Writers do not have the benefit of immediate feedback in the form of questions or other verbal or body language from a listener. Instead, the writer must anticipate the questions and other responses and account for them during the actual writing process. In other words, students must analyze their writing and clarify their ideas as they go along.

A large number of constraints must also be satisfied at the immediate time of writing. The writer must deal with content constraints (purpose, ideas, organization) and structure constraints (sentence and paragraph construction), all the while keeping in mind the need for comprehensibility, enticingness (keeping the reader's attention), persuasiveness, and memorability (writing so the key points will be remembered) (Bruce, 1978). The necessity for keeping all of these constraints in mind at one time increases the difficulty in writing.

Different purposes for writing and different audiences require different styles of responses (Britton, et al., 1975; Kinneavy, 1971, Moffett, 1968). Writing styles and purposes range along a continuum on which distance and time between the sending and receiving of the message increase. For example: The shortest distance from a message sender to a receiver is a *speaker* talking about a *familiar subject* with a *listener.* The longest distance is a writer writing a message about an *unfamiliar or theoretical topic* for a person who will *read* the message at a much later time (as in published writing) and who will provide no feedback. As the distance and time from the message sender to the message receiver increase, the demands placed on the writer increase: vocabulary, style, allusion, rhetoric all have to be geared to the intended audience (Moffett, 1968). A personal note to a friend, for example, requires different style, vocabulary, and organization than does a theoretical paper on the effects of nuclear warfare.

Table 1-1 is presented here as a summary and graphic display of the complexity and interrelation of the skills required in the writing process. Writing truly is not a linear process as the task analysis suggests. It is one of many stops and starts, of many readings and rereadings, of much movement back and forth from the first stages to the last as ideas are crystallized, reformed, and revised, and the structure is shaped, modified, and polished until, at last, the writing is done.

EVALUATION OF WRITING SKILLS

The development of an efficient and reliable method for evaluating written language has been a concern of researchers and educators for many years. One controversy has centered on the analysis of the qualitative versus the quantitative features of writing. Quantitative measures such as vocabulary knowledge, usage, capitalization, punctuation, and spelling can be measured with machine-scored, standardized measures; but qualitative features, especially style, organization, and level of abstraction in writing cannot be measured so objectively. The analysis of qualitative features of writing requires the use of actual student writing samples. However, even the use of student samples has not solved the problem of evaluation, since there are numerous approaches to analyzing writing ranging from simple error counts to any of the many forms of holistic scoring.

Different types of testing and scoring procedures are needed for different purposes. The selection of a particular test or testing process will depend on the kind of results desired and how these results are to be used. Generally, test results can be used in the following ways:

1. To report student progress to administrators;
2. To report progress to parents;
3. To identify the progress that students make over a period of time;
4. To determine levels of student ability in order to place students in appropriate classes;
5. To diagnose specific strengths and weaknesses of individual students as a preliminary to providing individual or small group remedial instruction;
6. To determine the effectiveness of a particular program or instructional method that is used; and
7. To identify the actual steps that students use as they prepare to write, then write, and revise their work.

Table 1-1   The Complexity of the Writing Process

Stage	Skills	Tasks
Prewriting	Thinking	decide to communicate in written form
		explain the matter to oneself
		form tentative plan for writing
		identify target audience
		identify style or writing necessary for purpose (narrative, expository, persuasive)
		discover ideas, generalizations, theme, topic
		narrow topic appropriately
		develop topic sentence or main ideas
		select relevant facts, examples, details from experience or research
	Organization	sequence general content of message
		group related ideas
		omit irrelevant ideas
		sequence ideas (chronological, spatial, logical, etc.)
		state conclusion or summary
Writing	Language Skills (Vocabulary and Sentence Structure)	choose appropriate vocabulary for purpose and audience level
		arrange vocabulary in meaningful sentences using correct grammatical relationships
		vary selection of sentence types
	Spelling Skills	discriminate the sounds and sequence of sounds in words
		recall the shape and form of letters
		recall the shape and form of non-phonetic words
	Handwriting	sequence the appropriate motor movements to write letters and words
	Mechanics	include proper punctuation, capitalization
Post-Writing	Editing and Revising	*content editing*
		read the written message
		identify gaps in presentation
		identify need for additional facts, details, examples
		clarify main idea and relationships between ideas
		delete irrelevant material
		add appropriate transitional phrases
		refine word choice
		structure editing
		revise awkward sentences
		combine simple sentences
		correct tense use

Most authorities on writing express discontent with the type of evaluation measures used in the past. Even so, several different kinds of assessment strategies and devices have been used with varying degrees of success: formalized evaluation, such as in standardized achievement tests and diagnostic tests; informal teacher evaluation; rating scales; peer evaluation; and self-evaluation.

Standardized Achievement Tests

Standardized achievement tests measure discrete subcomponents of writing, most commonly vocabulary knowledge, grammatical usage, capitalization, punctuation, and spelling. Occasionally, achievement tests will include items on topic sentences, sequencing sentences, and eliminating irrelevant sentences. These skill areas are tested by proofreading and editing tasks in multiple-choice format. Students are asked to pick the correct word to complete the meaning of a sentence, to choose the best sentence from a group of sample sentences, to supply the correct capital letter or punctuation symbol, or to choose the correct spelling of a word. These subcomponents of writing have been selected because they can be easily standardized and scaled in relation to representative populations. Test results, therefore, are provided in the form of grade equivalents and percentiles, and allow the teacher to compare each student's performance with standardized norms. Results are used to compare students' progress in specific subskill areas from one year to the next and to report progress to parents and administrators.

Currently there is general agreement that standardized achievement tests do not provide enough information about students' actual writing ability (Cooper, 1977). Furthermore, achievement tests are considered inadequate measures of writing ability because students do not produce a complete writing sample using their own choice of words, sentence structure, ideas, or organization; nor do they produce writing for different purposes or different audiences. (Braddock, Lloyd-Jones, and Schoer, 1963). A final weakness of achievement tests is their failure to provide diagnostic information about specific strengths and weaknesses in student writing ability. Any useful testing program should provide information to help the classroom teacher develop individual or group lesson plans that meet specific needs of the students.

Standardized Diagnostic Tests

Standardized diagnostic tests attempt to identify specific strengths and weaknesses of student writing ability. Although these tests provide more specific information than standardized achievement tests, they do take longer to score and interpret because they require the use of student writing samples. Three tests for intermediate students that fall into this group are the Myklebust *Picture Story Language Test*, the *Test of Written Language* by Hammill and Larsen, and the *Diagnostic Evaluation of Writing Skills* by Weiner.

The *Picture Story Language Test* (PSLT) uses a picture stimulus to elicit writing samples from students aged seven to seventeen. Scoring on the PSLT requires the use of three scales: the Productivity Scale (to measure and compare the length of the writing sample, the number of sentences, and the number of words per sentence); the Syntax Scale (to measure correctness of word usage, word endings, and punctuation); and the Abstract–Concrete Scale (to measure the level of idea content). The evaluation of spelling and handwriting is not included in this test.

Reviewers have generally criticized this test for its complicated scoring procedures, its low interest picture, and its standardization information (Anastasiow, 1972; Hammill and Larsen, 1978; Poteet, 1979).

The *Test of Written Language* (TOWL) was designed for students in grades three through eight. The test has two evaluation components: a spontaneous student writing sample and three objective subtests in the areas of spelling, word usage (measuring such skills as forming tenses, using correct word endings), and style (measuring the correct use of punctuation and capitalization). The writing sample, based on a sequence of three related pictures (a group of people preparing to leave a parched, barren planet, the space flight, and finally the settlement on a new planet), is analyzed for thematic maturity, vocabulary, and sentence structure (thought units).

The TOWL is a relatively new test and as such has not received extensive review. Because it gives results in terms of scaled scores and grade equivalents, the authors suggest that additional informal diagnosis of student writing samples be completed.

The *Diagnostic Evaluation of Writing Skills* (DEWS) uses the assigned writing topic "My Favorite Activity" as the stimulus for writing. Each writing sample is assessed on forty-one separate items in six categories of writing errors: graphic (handwriting), orthographic (spelling), phonologic (spelling), syntactic (grammatical), semantic (vocabulary), and self-monitoring skills. The examiner reads the student writing sample and tabulates the number of errors made in each category. This test has been used to select students requiring special remediation in both reading and writing (Weiner, 1980).

Two additional diagnostic tests that use student writing samples have been developed for use with older students. *DI-COMP, A Diagnostic System for Teaching Composition for Grades 10–14*, uses a checklist to tally errors in ten categories concerned with spelling organization, punctuation, grammar, and sentence structure. The *Test of Everyday Writing Skills* (TEWS) contains both objective and subjective measures. The objective measures utilize practical writing samples (e.g. letters, telephone messages) as stimuli for multiple-choice questions. The student is also asked to write an eyewitness report of an accident. This writing sample is then scored by the holistic procedures described later in this chapter.

Teacher Evaluation

Teachers seldom realize how commonly and seriously they disagree in their judgment of writing ability (Diederich, 1974). One study, which included the use of fifty-three evaluators, pointed out that at least five distinct factors are considered in the judgment of writing ability: ideas (the richness, soundness, clarity, development, and relevance to the topic and the writer's purpose); mechanics (errors in usage, sentence structure, punctuation, and spelling); organization; vocabulary (the choice and arrangement of words in phrases); and, finally, flavor (the personal qualities revealed in writing—style, individuality, originality, interest, and sincerity) (Diederich, 1974). The evaluators in this study received no specific training in grading procedures but reacted to the papers using their *own* standards. The results of this study point out the inconsistency of approaches used by persons evaluating writing samples.

One variable that occasionally influences teacher rating of writing ability is bias. Frequently the information that a teacher knows about a student, such as whether the writer is generally a poor, average, or gifted student, affects the student's grade (Diederich, 1974).

Traditionally, informal grading practices have varied significantly from teacher to teacher. Assignments have been given which have emphasized content and ideas, yet students' papers have been returned filled with red marks for poor spelling, punctuation, and grammar. Braddock, Lloyd-Jones, and Schoer (1963) summarize the results of a number of studies of teacher evaluation of writing with the following statement. "It has *not* been proved that the intensive marking [of student writing samples], with or without revision, is the best procedure to use with upper elementary or junior high [students]" (p. 36). Other researchers, in fact, have noted that only positive comments written on students' papers produce any positive effects (Beaven, 1977; Lundsteen, 1976b).

Holistic Evaluation of Writing

Holistic evaluation uses actual writing samples to get an overall impression of student writing ability, rather than a detailed analysis of errors. This technique gives a school district a reliable method for evaluation of large numbers of student writing samples by trained school personnel. It is most often used on a school-wide or district-wide basis at the secondary level, although it can be used at elementary and junior high levels as well.

In this process, students in all grades to be evaluated write on an assigned topic in a supervised writing session for a specified period of time. Evaluators, generally teachers excused from classroom responsibilities for the day, are trained to quickly read each paper (at the rate of approximately one paper every two minutes) and score the papers according to a previously discussed rubric, scale, checklist, or graded series of samples. The reader does not take time to identify or count errors, but rather reacts to the writing based on overall impression, then quickly moves on to the next paper. Two evaluators read each sample. If their scores differ substantially, a third reader is used to obtain a balance or consensus.

Holistic evaluation provides a rank ordering of scores. These results can be used for placement purposes and for reporting to administrators. Teachers receive the scores of students in their classes, but not the actual writing samples nor the reason a student received a particular score. In some cases, the students with the lowest scores are identified for remedial services and their papers may be returned to teachers for detailed analysis. Otherwise, there is no other feedback to the classroom teacher. However, teachers trained in holistic scoring usually have internalized the features of good writing and use this evaluation method on a daily basis.

An excellent summary of the variations of holistic scoring is provided by Cooper and Odell in *Evaluating Writing: Describing, Measuring, and Judging.*

Rating Scales   A rating scale is an organized list of factors to be considered when evaluating student writing. Diederich (1974) developed one scale after the completion of the study mentioned earlier. He included four of the most commonly identified factors (ideas, organization, wording, flavor) on the scale and subdivided one other factor, mechanics, into usage (which includes sentence structure), punctuation, and spelling. Since most teachers emphasize ideas and organization in their classes, these two factors were double-weighted. Diederich provided a written description of three levels of performance (high, middle, and low) in these categories. The resulting scale is a means of systematically evaluating the qualities of writing without having to make detailed notes. After teachers had received training in the use of this scale and had used it over a period of time, they found that they could judge papers more quickly on general impression.

A second scale, the Carlson Analytical Originality Scale, focuses exclusively on the creative aspects of story writing. This scale contains five major categories: story structure, novelty, emotion, individuality, and style of stories. Each category is defined

Table 1–2   The Carlson Analytical Originality Scale

SCALE DIVISION A–Story Structure		SCALE DIVISION C–Emotion	
1. Unusual title	0 1 2 3 4 5	22. Unusual ability to express emotional depth	0 1 2 3 4 5
2. Unusual beginning	0 1 2 3 4 5	23. Unusual sincerity in expressing personal problems	0 1 2 3 4 5
3. Unusual dialogue	0 1 2 3 4 5		
4. Unusual ending	0 1 2 3 4 5	24. Unusual ability to identify self with feelings of others	0 1 2 3 4 5
5. Unusual plot	0 1 2 3 4 5		
SCALE DIVISION B–Novelty		25. Unusual horror theme	0 1 2 3 4 5
6. Novelty of Names	0 1 2 3 4 5	SCALE DIVISION D–Individuality	
7. Novelty of Locale	0 1 2 3 4 5	26. Unusual perceptive sensitivity (social and physical environment)	0 1 2 3 4 5
8. Unique punctuation and expressional devices	0 1 2 3 4 5		
9. New words	0 1 2 3 4 5	27. Unique philosophical thinking	0 1 2 3 4 5
10. Novelty of ideas	0 1 2 3 4 5	28. Facility in beautiful writing	0 1 2 3 4 5
11. Novel devices	0 1 2 3 4 5		
12. Novel theme	0 1 2 3 4 5	29. Unusual personal experience	0 1 2 3 4 5
13. Quantitative thinking	0 1 2 3 4 5	SCALE DIVISION E–Style of Stories	
14. New objects created	0 1 2 3 4 5	30. Exaggerated tall tale	0 1 2 3 4 5
15. Ingenuity in solving situations	0 1 2 3 4 5	31. Fairy tale type	0 1 2 3 4 5
16. Recombination of ideas in unusual relationships	0 1 2 3 4 5	32. Fantasy-turnabout of characters	0 1 2 3 4 5
17. Picturesque Speech	0 1 2 3 4 5	33. Highly fantastic central idea of theme	0 1 2 3 4 5
18. Humor	0 1 2 3 4 5		
19. Novelty of form	0 1 2 3 4 5	34. Fantastic creatures, objects, or persons	0 1 2 3 4 5
20. Inclusion of readers	0 1 2 3 4 5	35. Personal experience	0 1 2 3 4 5
21. Unusual related thinking	0 1 2 3 4 5	36. Individual story style	0 1 2 3 4 5

Source: Carlson, Ruth Kearney. Sparkling Words: Three Hundred and Fifteen Practical and Creative Writing Ideas. *Geneva, IL: Paladin House, Publishers, 1979.*

in a descriptive listing of samples in Carlson's book *Sparkling Words* (1973). While this scale focuses only on creative writing, it helps teachers pinpoint specific indications of originality in student writing.

Peer Evaluation and Self-evaluation

Peer evaluation has been used successfully by a number of researchers and teachers and is popularly used in writing workshop settings. Sager (1973) developed a program called *Reading, Writing, and Rating Stories* in which students learn to evaluate short samples of writing using descriptive scales for vocabulary, elaboration, organization, and structure. Sager's research, as well as others', indicates that improvement resulting from peer evaluation techniques may equal or even exceed that resulting from teacher evaluation (Beaven, 1977).

Peer evaluation techniques require that students read their stories or reports to small groups to get reactions and suggestions for improvement. Students may use rating scales or specific guide questions at first to help them focus on relevant concerns in writing samples. After students receive feedback from other students, they incorporate the suggestions in revised drafts. These techniques encourage students to think of writing as a multi-stage process.

Self-evaluation of writing places responsibility for improvement on the student. Most often the student uses guide questions suggested by the teacher to review his or her own writing. Beaven (1977) asks the student to respond to questions related to the amount of time spent on the paper, the strengths and weaknesses of the paper, and how the paper will be changed in the next draft. Rating scales, such as Sager's (1973), have also helped students in the evaluation of their own writing.

Conclusion

If writing is a complex process, the evaluation of writing is even more complex. Of the many methods available for evaluating writing skills, none provide enough specific, relevant information for the teacher to prepare appropriate lesson plans. Currently there is increased interest in gathering student writing samples under test conditions as a replacement for generalized achievement tests. The use of holistic procedures to evaluate these writing samples is a positive step since this technique emphasizes the identification of student strengths rather than just weaknesses. In terms of motivation, evaluation techniques that use an error identification approach often have the unfortunate by-product of lowered student self-esteem. Unfortunately, too few school systems are pursuing the holistic method of evaluation and, as a result, too few teachers are receiving specific training in analyzing student writing.

The evaluation procedures in this manual are designed to help the individual teacher evaluate and identify levels of performance in student writing. Although the informal evaluation activities do take time, the resulting information will be valuable as an aid to planning specific teaching strategies relevant to students' individual needs.

2

How Are They Doing?

Informal evaluation of written expression focuses on six general areas of performance:

A. Ideas/Content (level of abstraction)
B. Organization Skills
C. Vocabulary Usage
D. Sentence Structure
E. Spelling
F. Handwriting

Each of these general areas is subdivided into three levels of performance (Limited, Growth, Mastery) as summarized in Table 2-1. In general, writing at the Limited performance level is *unfocused*. Students do not have a clear sense of purpose, a sense of audience, or the skills and techniques necessary to write stories or reports that are coherent, complete, and interesting. Usually written productivity is quite low—sometimes less than five or six short, simple sentences.

Writing at the second level, or the Growth level, *focuses* on the purpose for writing and the audience for which the writing is intended. Students at this level explore and experiment with different styles of writing, different writing techniques, more specific vocabulary, and a variety of sentence structures. Overall productivity (total number of words and sentences) increases as students write with more fluency. However, because students are experimenting with new styles, structures, and vocabulary, they may make more sophisticated kinds of errors, such as awkward sentence constructions and inaccurate word choice. These types of errors indicate that the writer has some grasp of writing skills and a basic understanding (conscious or unconscious) of different purposes for writing.

Mastery writing is *clearly focused*. The student has a clear sense of purpose and audience and consistently chooses writing styles and techniques that are appropriate for the purpose and audience. These writers have mastered the skills and techniques for producing writing that is coherent, complete, and interesting. This includes the use of precise vocabulary, varied sentence structure, and careful organization of ideas appropriate for the style of writing.

Mastery writing is rarely seen in the student's first draft, but it emerges as students proofread and revise; adding precise vocabulary; selecting appropriate details, facts, examples; varying sentence structures; and generally avoiding grammatical or structural errors.

9

These three levels, Limited, Growth, and Mastery, represent *broad* levels of writing performance. Growth in writing does *not* necessarily occur evenly across the six skill areas (content/ideas, organization, vocabulary, sentence structure, spelling, and handwriting). Rather, evidence of varying ability within the six areas is often seen. A writer may exhibit evidence of higher levels of abstraction, yet continue to use limited vocabulary or faulty sentence structure. Furthermore, writing may exhibit characteristics from more than one level of performance within a particular skill area. Thus, it becomes quite evident that it is necessary to look at writing performance in all six skill areas to identify particular strengths and weaknesses.

The writing samples in this manual were collected in resource rooms for learning disabled students and in regular classes. Errors are *not* identified in each sample, rather, emphasis is placed on identifying levels of performance and signs of growth in writing skills. Levels of performance in the six separate areas of the informal evaluation must be identified before a total educational plan can be developed.

INFORMAL EVALUATION COMPONENTS

Ideas/Content

Of all the facets of writing, ideas, content, and level of abstraction are the hardest to measure. So many variables (such as language experiences, school opportunities, personal interests, motivation) affect the student's actual written output that it becomes almost impossible to collect hard data on student progress. A number of writers have suggested characteristics which indicate growth in writing. Lundsteen (1976b) has summarized some of these characteristics:

> ...there appears to be progression in plot construction, characterization, choice of revealing detail, sequencing, support of main ideas, ability to make choices in forming and arranging sentences, coordination, subordination, and use of transitions (Burrows, 1960; Hunt, 1965). The compositional thought of children moves from memory of direct, sensory experience to pictured images of concrete objects held in inner speech thought (Vygotsky, 1962). The child's written thought moves from a few words to whole incidents and finally to the complex ordering of experiences through various forms of literature, such as the folktale, fable, myth, and fantasy (Nebraska Curriculum Development Center, 1966). [p. 24]

Thought development in oral and written expression progresses on a continuum from little or no control over the topic to total control of the topic. The degree of thought development depends on the writer's ability to use, expand, and elaborate on a given stimulus—such as a story starter, a picture stimulus, or an assigned topic—by making generalizations and/or judgments about a given topic or title, and select relevant supporting details, examples or facts, to develop the generalizations and/or judgments.

Moffett (1976) summarizes this idea in his Growth Sequence in which he explains that the goal is to generalize more broadly and to elaborate more finely, all the time moving away from egocentricity. He explains that generalizing and elaborating are opposite practices and both are needed in writing. In generalizing, students pull together a number of facts, note their similarities, and make a statement regarding this similarity. In elaborating, a generalization is explained or defined through the selective use of facts, details, or examples that prove the generalization.

In summary, generalizations are abstract, while elaborations are concrete and specific. The accuracy of the generalization depends on the *experience, knowledge,* and *attitude* of the person making the generalization. One problem immature writers have is making hasty generalizations—generalizations formed too quickly without sufficient information or generalizations based on opinion rather than fact.

This next section reviews three levels of performance in the use of generalization and elaboration.

LIMITED LEVEL

Writers at this first level of idea development are very often "stimulus-bound." They simply make lists of words, phrases, or simple sentences which relate only to obvious aspects of the stimulus or which focus on irrelevant details. These students do not make generalizations or elaborate on the given stimulus or topic.

The man is walking on the moon. He walk around the moon. He had some moon rocks. Then He take a picture from the moon. He went back into the rocket. He go back to the earth.

Grade 4

This is The Zoo. The giraffe is ripping the zoo keepers Coat. The Zoo keeper is fixing the hole. The two giraffes are alone.

Grade 4

Occasionally, a paper will be almost totally incoherent, as in the following example.

The wiet pebl kel The Indians to tak The besrbawuy

(The white people kill the Indians to take the buffalo.)

Grade 4

Writing at this level is very often self-oriented, presenting reports of single-event, personal experiences. At times, students transcribe their own spoken language and produce rambling stories which have no true beginning, middle, or end. The writer merely states a simple sequence of events without suggesting a generalization which would integrate the ideas into a meaningful narrative report.

The next day I got up and had breakfast and then I went to school and we did some work and played a game. Then we went outside and played some games and then I went home and then I went to bed.

At other times, limited writers transcribe conversations with other imaginary or real persons without identifying the participants, and often without including appropriate punctuation.

I want to play No you can't go out to play You were a bad girl You have to stay inside OK I'll stay inside

Stories written at the Limited level are frequently very short, generally comprised of only a few sentences, and generally do not show any originality of thought. Probably the greatest weakness of writing at the Limited level is the lack of a plan for writing. The student begins to write without formulating a plan and stops when tired or when enough paper has been covered. Occasionally, an inappropriate ending is tacked on as the student nears the bottom of the page. Trite endings such as "And then I woke up" and "They lived happily ever after" are frequently used to finish the story.

Two little Black Grils

There was to grils. They were playing. They were jumping up and down. They playing whit a rhope. It was a grimy green rhope. I hate Jump rhope. It really stinks. They were cute. But the rhope was ugly. They lived haply over after.

Frequently, writers at the Limited level add irrelevant details as they lose their original story thought and move on to a totally unrelated topic.

A Mother and her child.

There is a mother walking her little daughter in the park. The girl is really enjoying. Her mother loves her a lot and cares. That is why she took her to the park on a nice day. I sometimes go to the park with my auntie and her baby. At home I baby sit for her while she is doing something. And it will be her Birthday on Nov. 11, 1977, will be 1 year old.

Table 2-1 Informal Evaluation of Writing Skills

	IDEAS/CONTENT	ORGANIZATION	VOCABULARY

LIMITED	Writing is basically immature and exhibits one or more of the following characteristics:
	• unintelligible responses
	• "stimulus-bound" writing:
	  simple naming and/or describing
	  no original ideas
	  lists of words or phrases
	• single event personal experiences, or groups of events with no generalization
	  rambling, "on and on" stories
	• simple thought sequence
	• egocentric
		Writing lacks a specific organizing theme or purpose; overall organization is poor and sequencing is generally inaccurate or absent.
		• simple thought sequence
		  ideas may be out of order, or written as they occur to writer
		  unrelated ideas may be grouped together
		• irrelevant details
			The writer OVERUSES the following kinds of words:
			• general nouns: the man, the thing, something, the dog, people
			• general verbs: is/was, are/am, go/went, do/did, see/saw/look, want/have, get/got, make, said, like
			• general adjectives: good/nice, big/little, funny, pretty
			• general adverbs: many, some, very, really, too
			• articles, prepositions, conjunctions

GROWTH	Writers *begin* to relate and classify experiences and/or facts and make generalizations. A definite story line or theme is evident although it may not be completely developed.
	• relevant generalizations included
	• descriptive detail added:
	  character, setting, mood detail
	  sensory details: sight, sound, smell, taste, touch
	  character interaction
	  character dialogue or monologue
	• sequence of events is clear
	• personal style evident
	  original ideas expressed
	  use of humor, imagination
		Organization skills show improvement—but inconsistency in handling generalizations, details, and conclusions is evident.
		• lack of overall planning
		• paragraph structure may be inadequate
		  overgeneralizations and unsupported opinions
		  abundance of detail without summarizing statement or appropriate conclusion (main ideas omitted)
		  poor introductions to paragraphs or reports (lack of topic sentence or topic paragraph)
		  inappropriate or omitted conclusions
		  poor transitions between paragraphs
		• topic development may not be complete
		  content may be copied from one source
		  topic choice may be too broad or too narrow
		  shifts in point of view
		  shifts in train of thought
			The writer *begins* to play with words and introduces *some* of the following elements in the writing:
			• specific nouns, verbs, adjectives, adverbs
			• topic imposed words
			• imaginative use of words
			  invented words
			  alliteration, rhyming, repetition
			  original similes, metaphors, analogies
			As students experiment in vocabulary use, the following kinds of errors may be made:
			• word selection errors
			  word form substitution
			  preposition errors: "regardless to" "pretty as a picture"
			  cliches: "pretty as a picture"
			  overly elaborate, flowery words/phrases
			  excess words/phrases: "the reason is because"
			• word formation errors
			  prefix/suffix errors: "beautifulest"
			  inflectional ending errors

MASTERY	Writing is CLEARLY and CONSISTENTLY purposeful. Ideas and details are selected for specific purposes and generally involve analysis, synthesis, or interpretation.
	• judgments made: stated or implied
	• morals suggested: stated or implied
	• consistent point of view supported by facts, reasons, examples
	• deliberate selection of information:
	  some points emphasized, others ignored
	  appeals to reader's emotions
	  persuasion
		Writing is CLEARLY and CONSISTENTLY organized. The writer organizes his work for specific purposes and carefully selects relevant information.
		• topic appropriately narrowed and focused
		• adequate planning and preparation
		  use of notetaking and outlining skills
		• accurate paragraph structure
		  generalizations and summaries with relevant supporting details
		  opinions supported by relevant facts, details, examples
		  appropriate paragraph breaks and transitions
		  appropriate conclusions
			The writer ACCURATELY and CONSISTENTLY selects words which convey the intended message. Word selection is appropriate for style of writing.
			• precise vocabulary: deliberate word choice
			  abstract nouns: truth, hope
			  cognitive verbs: understand
			  judgmental adjectives: adequate

	SENTENCE STRUCTURE	SPELLING	HANDWRITING

LIMITED	The writer does not have good "sentence sense" and is unable to arrange words to form complete sentences. Some of the following characteristics may be seen.
	• lists of words and/or phrases (no sentences at all)
	• sentence errors
	  run-ons: overuse of "and," "and then," "and so"
	  sentence fragments
	  syntax errors: words omitted or word order inaccurate
	• overuse of short, choppy simple sentences
	• omitted punctuation, or totally inaccurate punctuation
		Comprehension of story or report may be difficult due to frequency of spelling errors. Possible error patterns may be:
		• Errors on both sight words and phonetic words. spelling may be bizarre and totally unrelated to either phonetic or visual elements
		• Errors primarily on basic sight words (e.g., went, want, where, work, walk, play, etc.)
		  spells words phonetically, or
		  adds, omits, substitutes, or inverts letters
		• Errors primarily on phonetic words:
		  adds, omits, substitutes letters, inverts letters
		  errors mostly on vowels; or
		  errors mostly on consonants; or
		  errors on both consonants and vowels
			Handwriting at this level does not present a neat appearance.
			• poor or inaccurate letter formation; letter substitution
			• poor spacing between words and/or letters
			• poor spatial organization (inconsistent letter size, or inconsistent use of guidelines; letters may be too large or too small)
			• smudged erasures or write-overs
			• illegibility
			• letter reversals, inversions
			• writing laborious and slow

GROWTH	The writer experiments with different types of sentences:
	• expanded sentences: when, where, how phrases added
	• compound sentences, complex sentences
	However, awkward constructions may appear with the use of longer sentences:
	• verb errors
	  subject-verb agreement errors
	  shifts in tense in sentence, paragraph, story
	  non-parallel constructions
	• noun/pronoun agreement errors
	• punctuation errors
		There are some spelling errors, but the words are readable. Errors are made on longer words and may be due to misapprehension or incorrect pronunciation.
		• phonetic spelling of misspelled words
		• word endings added or omitted incorrectly
		• syllables in words may be omitted
		• homonym substitution
			Overall handwriting is adequate, although there may be some awkward letter formations, especially if the student is just learning cursive writing. Student may need to work on overall neatness and use of margins.

MASTERY	The writer has clear "sentence sense" and manipulates words to form all types of sentences ACCURATELY and CONSISTENTLY. • variety of sentence structures and lengths used consistently • all forms of punctuation are consistently and accurately used	There are relatively few errors and the student is working at or above grade level in spelling skills. Errors are generally made on difficult words (multi-syllable words, or words with unusual spellings). Only a few errors are found in first drafts of longer compositions and reports.	Overall writing is carefully done and is quite readable. Completed papers are very neat

Another pattern seen at the Limited level is the use of lists.

> If I won a trip I would go to Africa because I have a spe-
> cil interest in African animals like the lion, elephant, cheetah,
> Giraffe, leaperd, Rhino, Hyena and so on. Well I also like to
> go there to see natives how they survive and I just like to be
> out in the wild and I like to Study animals.

Personal narratives are simple in nature, usually a rather straightforward list of events without the benefit of added descriptive detail or emotional emphasis. The writer relies almost exclusively on simple present or simple past tenses and provides a report with limited action and little originality of presentation. Each sentence in this next example could be elaborated on and developed into a separate paragraph.

> On Saturday mom, Dad and I went to the circus. The ring
> master announced the acts. We saw a lion tamer put his head
> in the lion's mouth. Then some acrabats swung on the trapeze
> up in the air. My favorite act was the one where the clowns
> ran around and tripped each other.
> The End

Overall, the limited writer lacks planning skill, which includes the ability to make relevant generalizations and to select the appropriate supporting details which would help develop the personal narrative or story. Ideas are handled in expected patterns and little, if any, originality or personal style is evident. Once the story is written, the writer feels that it is complete and does no further work on it (Bruce, 1978).

GROWTH LEVEL At this second level of idea generation, students begin to focus more clearly on the purposes for writing. They generally experiment with different types of writing and their individual styles begin to develop, as evidenced by increased use of imagination and attempts at originality. However, the stories and reports written at this level are not completely developed or free from error.

Several specific factors mark the transition from the Limited level to the Growth level. All of these factors will *not* be found in each piece of writing. However, the presence of more than one factor will indicate a greater degree of progress.

1. *Writers include relevant generalizations in their writing.* At first these generalizations are simplistic; but later, with more writing practice, they become more sophisticated. The following example is basically limited in content, however the student does insert very simple generalizations in the story. In other words, the writer has included information not evident in the stimulus (It is in the summer. The men are cold.) but does not elaborate on those points.

> There are two men on a raft. One men is in the raft. the other
> is in the water. The color of the water is green and white. The
> color of the raft is yellow   They are on the ra pids It is in the
> summer The men a recold
>
> *Grade 5*

2. *Writers provide descriptive details.* Information not readily apparent in the stimulus is added. This includes expressions of feeling or emotion, compari-sons, opinions, or additional examples which support their generalizations. Details are added to the story or paragraph, using perhaps, materials from personal experiences and memories or factual details and descriptions.

> *Sun Beginning to Set*
> The sun is beginning to set. The sun looks like a diamond
> with a glowing halo around it. The sun set seems to be going in
> to the mountains. There is a rushing river in front of the moun-
> tains. As the sun is going down it makes the river sparkle and

gleam. Trees sit behind the river. The delicate leaves are blowing off the thin branches. The sun adds a glow to everything on earth.

3. *Writers include clear sequences of events.* Clear beginnings (often an introductory topic sentence, or the identification of a problem or a goal), clear middles (the sequence of events lead to some kind of resolution), and clear endings (the resolution of the problem or achievement of the goal) are evidence of progress in writing skills. While some endings may be resolved quickly, they do not include the stereotyped "and then I woke up" variety.

Lost

It was a hot dry day and I had been walking for hours without Food or water when I saw a well. I ran as fast as I could go. When I got there I almost jumped in. I looked down the hole and it was all dried up. By then I was dying for a drink but all of a sudin I thout about last sumer when we were in a helicopter and I saw a little streem a round hear. So I walked 10 feet. There was no water except drib sand but I started to dig with my hand and water came up in the hole. I started to drink it. I thout it was the best water in the world. That night I had to stay ther be couls it had water. I had to wait for some plane to come By. I started to make a fire and I heard a sound like a plane. They had seen me. The next day I was home and safe and glad to get home.

The End

Grade 7

Occasionally, students will have a fairly well developed idea, but in their haste to get started writing they do not summarize or identify their topic to the reader. Instead, as in the next example, they jump right into the middle of the story. Even so, because this writing sample focuses on a single theme and uses all relevant examples, with perhaps some originality of thought, it shows evidence of growth in writing skills.

I am sick and tired of being thrashed around and forgotten places.

Everybody takes advantage of me.
and when people don't eat their lunch yukk it gets all moldy. And my handle my handle is just awful it rattles.

And what realy tops it off is my best friend got taken to the recycling company.

It's tough to be a lunch box aspecialy when the teacher yells.

She's murder on my ears

The End

Grade 5

At other times, the writer has a fairly well developed story beginning, but because of time limits or lack of interest, the story is ended abruptly.

The Angry Newspaper reporter

There once was an angry newspaper reporter in a haunted house who knew a sad balloon who lived at the zoo. One day the angry newspaper reporter who's name was Grump went to visit his friend. The balloon's name was Unhappy but it was to long to remember. So everyone called him Pop. Well Grump said to Pop, "Boy am I curious today." and Pop said, "Not me, I feel lonely."

Then the two Friends walked away together angrily.

The End

Grade 5

4. *Writers begin to develop a personal style* and show more originality in think-ing. This is seen in the use of invented words or names, the use of humor, dialogue, and original use of punctuation for added effect. Although the next writer has difficulty with consistent tense use, he does exhibit growth in writing skills because he has chosen a style appropriate for the topic (announcer style) and he does complete a clear sequence, even though he could expand the story by adding more details.

Babe Ruth

Here we are at yankee stadium. The players are taking their positions. The first pitch came in—strike one! The pitcher got the ball. He takes a puff of air, he throws the pitch—strike two! The crowd has a puzzled look on their face because they know it was going to be a strike or a home run. He throws the baseball in for a foul ball. The next pitch is a blazing fast ball. He rips a home run. The yankees are now the champions.

Grade 5

MASTERY LEVEL   Idea development at the Mastery level is marked by *consistency* between purpose and content. At this level, the student has complete control of the writing process, has a distinct point of view, and uses information to support that view.

Ideas, generalizations, and supportive details are deliberately selected for a specific purpose—to entertain, to present an argument, to persuade, or to build upon a specific theme. The selected generalizations are consistently appropriate and are sup-ported by sufficient relevant examples, facts, or other descriptive details. This also implies that the writer consciously selects, eliminates, and possibly manipulates infor-mation in an attempt to influence the reader. The writer has also developed a personal style which is reflected in originality of thinking, use of humor, effective use of struc-tural and mechanical elements (sentence and paragraph structure and punctuation), and mature vocabulary choice.

In story writing, plot development is very clear and effective: the main character is faced with a crisis or challenge which requires specific planning and action to re-solve. Information which develops character personalities and provides background for the crisis or challenge is included. The writer may also interject judgmental ele-ments, with a moral that is either stated or implied. Story endings do not follow an expected pattern and sometimes even have unusual twists.

The next sample represents a more advanced level of growth in writing skills in the Content/Ideas category since there is clear evidence of writer involvement, specific vocabulary, some variety in sentence structure, clear statement of problem, clear se-quence of events, clear resolution, and originality of ideas. However, a number of small problems prevent it from being an example of Mastery writing in all categories. The sample contains several awkward sentences (1, 4, 5, 6), fragmented sentences (2), and some unclear pronoun referents (3). Because there is definite evidence of writing skill, it is to be suspected that this student did not bother to proofread. An oral reading of this story to a classmate might have helped to identify the errors.

The Frog War

It was May 24, 1978, when the first hints of a frog versus toad war was started. It had been a hard winter for the toads and they had stooped to stealing rations from the frogs and the frogs suspected it. The frog king, a tough old army sergeant from the anteater wars, was preparing to declare war on the toads. The toads were not prepared.

On May 27, the frogs declared war on the toads. At the toad village there was near panic. It was a pell-mell of prepar-ing for an attack. In the king's underground mansion, there was a meeting being held between the king and the heads of the war department. The king was young and inexperienced. (1) He had the throne heired to him when he was young and evil toads had corrupted him.

And now, the meeting. (2) The young king's name was Paul and his evil advisor, Ivan (the terrible) who directed him to do dastardly deeds. (3) They were sitting at the head of the table, smiling menacingly, for they had an ingenious idea. They and their evil war department had bribed a king cobra snake into fighting for them in the war, which they *thought* would solve all their problems. Note, *thought!*

The food messengers sent word out all across the kingdom which relieved all the toad's tensions about losing the war. By and by word got around to the wizard who all his life wanted to be a frog, but alas, he was a toad. So the wizard got an idea. He set off across the toad-frog border with his hands up. Some frog soldiers captured him and took him to the king. The wizard told the king about the snake.

(5) The king promised to make the wizard an honorary frog if he would tell him how to get rid of the snake and also give him a magic ticker-tape machine which would give reports on the toad's battle manuvers. The toad thought about it for a while and finally agreed. Then the wizard said some mystic words and the magic ticker-tape machine appeared. Then the crafty wizard told the king of his plan to get rid of the snake.

The plan was to have the best ax-man in the kingdom come and stand behind a tree while a frog would be set out for bait near the ax-man. When the snake stuck out its deadly tongue, the ax-man would come and chop it off. Whact! Meanwhile, tree frogs above would be dropping razor sharp spears directly through the snake and lodging themselves directly in the ground, rendering the snake powerless.

And so, the plan was carried out, and if I do say so myself, it was executed quite well. Then the wizard suggested that the frog king send a note of terms to the toads by carrier-mosquito and they did.

The note read:

June 6, 1978

Sirs,

We have rid ourselves of your so-called menace. We will let you surrender. We do not want to have a war. We will send a treaty over to be signed. We will help you during the winter. These are our terms. Take them or leave them.

Sincerely,

Jack Ribbit
King of the Frogs

And so the note was delivered and it came to the toad's palace. There was a great festival following the signing. The evil Ivan the Terrible skulked away when the festivities started, never to be seen again. (6) After Ivan left, formerly wicked toads saw the light, and the two kingdoms came together and formed the Kingdom of Croak, ruled in joint throne by Jack Ribbut and King Paul. Their relationship grew strong and their reign was a long and happy one. As for the wizard, he became the royal alchemist and wizard. And they all lived Happily ever after. Ha, ha.

Grade 7

The next sample shows originality in approach as well as other features of the Mastery level. In addition, other mechanical elements have been mastered.

Hello Mirror. It's me again. You know that you are the only friend I have, so I know you will be honest with me. Tell me. Why don't other worms like me? Is it because my skin is brown? Lots of worms like me have brown skin. Do they hate all of us?

I thought Myrtle liked me. She's green. She's a nice shade of green. She looks something like a lily pad. I liked her anyway. But today, when she was talking to her friends and I went by, she looked the other way like she didn't even know me.

You know mirror, even worms have some kind of feelings. If old green Myrtle walked by and I was talking to Felisha, I would stop and talk to her.

Maybe Myrtle doesn't like me because I have a long tongue. Long tongues are good for catching flies though. I can't cut it!!!

Some days I just feel like getting eaten by something! I must be different in some way. I have got it!!! I must have bad breath! I will go use some *SKOOPE*. (That's Scope in our English). *AHHHHHH*!!! (blows on mirror) Hows that smell???

Well, if it's not that, what can it be? My skin is brown, but that doesn't matter. My skin has grooves, but that doesn't matter. My hair isn't long, but that doesn. . . .I don't have any hair at all!!!

Oh mirror, I just can't understand it. Once, when I was little, a wise old man told me to treat others as you want to be treated. I guess nobody ever told Myrtle that. Her friends too. I suppose if I told her, she would just say brown worms don't know anything! *IT'S NOT TRUE*!!! Is it???

Well, mirror, I guess I will just have to be satisfied with just having you for a friend. You still like me don't you? By the way, mirror, why don't you ever answer me?????

The End

Grade 6

Generally, writing at the Mastery level involves the conscious selection, manipulation, and interpretation of information for specific purposes and for specific styles of writing. Some students include morals or make judgments (opinions) in their writing at the Growth level and this is evidence of interpretive thinking. However, their writing cannot be judged as "Mastery level" unless it is clear, cohesive, and consistent in purpose and total content.

Organization The main concern of this section is the way students arrange their ideas in writing. Ideally, students should have well developed topic statements; an adequate number of appropriate supportive facts, details, or examples; and relevant conclusions. Each paragraph should contain a separate idea and there should be smooth transition between paragraphs. Paragraph indentations should be used to indicate the transition to a new idea. The result should be a story or report that is coherent and cohesive.

Three broad levels of organization skills will be reviewed next.

LIMITED LEVEL A student with limited organizational skills has generally not identified a theme or purpose or planned how to develop that theme. This may result from an inadequate understanding of the assignment or from the inability to identify a topic and select relevant information to support that topic.

Student responses may vary on this level. The student may simply list a group of totally unrelated sentences such as in the following example.

I Learn Math.
My friend Bob learns tricks.
People all over the world love
to shoot deersI like to see
sound of music. Theres a lot of
danger of going over train tra-
cks. Wene I go to school I
go through the front door.
A bird stood there.when I g
ot home I hid in my bed r
oom.I kept my turkey in the
cage Do you know anyone thats
af raid of a dead animal?

Grade 5

In some cases, students may be unable to identify the facts, details, or main ideas or other important considerations necessary to respond to assignments with complete information. Others can identify the information but present it in awkward fashion (e.g., sequence of ideas out of order, irrelevant details added, some important information missing).

My friend John is afraid because he thinks that, the boat
will crash on the rocks.Big waves are sending the boat to the
rock.When he's scared he walks around. the boat.and his face
turns red. His crew as afraid to.He has a large boat.He loves
the sea so much, he fishes 4 times a week.

Grade 7

Poor writers have difficulty in planning their writing. As a result, they do not always write clear topic sentences followed by appropriate, properly sequenced, supportive details with relevant summaries or conclusions. Main ideas and details are improperly handled and are frequently unbalanced—either a generalization is given without supportive detail, or an overabundance of detail is provided with no generalization or statement to show their relationship (e.g., time sequence, cause and effect, comparison). Because poor writers lack planning skills, they have difficulty identifying a good starting point, keeping to their topic (they change their line of thinking as new thoughts occur to them), and covering their topic completely.

The Crash
One day in Paris a Plane was flying and in the Plane Was
nixon, ford and kiss inger. they were on ther way to Egipt
they were in the mittel of the Adlantic ochon and a big lining
bolt hit the engen and started to fall   nixon said help help.
Thend

Grade 6

GROWTH LEVEL Movement from the Limited level is seen as students begin to sort and group information, and to sequence ideas and details appropriately. However, overall lack of planning at this level still results in a written product that is not totally complete or well developed. While the organizing theme or purpose may be sufficiently clear, it is generally not well developed. Basic paragraph structure may be missing as students forget to indent and fail to sort and group related ideas in separate paragraphs, although grossly irrelevant details have been eliminated.

Whales
There are many different kinds of whales. For instance, sperm
whale, blue whale, humpback whale, and Right whale. They
are different shapes and colors. Whales are the largest living

things in the world. The largest of all whales is the blue whale. The blue whale is 80-100 feet long. The smallest whale is 9-13 feet long. Its name is pigmy sperm. Whales are warmblooded. They can swim in cold water. Warmblooded means that the inside of the Whale stay the same temperature no matter what's the temperature outside. Some whales are different from each other. Only the sperm whale has teeth on the bottom. All whales eat their food whole. All whales are harmless except for the Killer whale. Killer whales like to eat whale, blue whales, dolphins, sleas, porpoises, Penguins, peoples, any thing that moves. Lots of Killer whales circle around the prey so it can't move. One Killer whale goes in and Kills him. They bite the mouth, the tongue and the fin, making him lose blood.

Grade 8

Book reports, essays, and larger papers (the most common assignments in the intermediate grades) present considerable difficulties for poor writers. Reports tend to be uninspired because students include only obvious, superficial information.

Field Trip

At 8:35 Tuesday morning room 2 and 3 were Planning for a bus to be at school, because both rooms were ready to go to Audubon Cayon Ranch. But some paper work didn't go through yet.

Finally at 9:30 the bus came. So at 9:45 we left. It took us an hour and a half to get there, the ranch is in marin. Both classes were divided up into groups, then our guides were assigned to us.

Then we started the long climb up the hill. We climbed for about five minutes then we came to a look out on the marsh. After we looked at the marsh we started climbing again. As soon as we took about 15 steps we saw poison ivy, everyone said that They're not going to let any leaf of Plant tooch them. About five minutes later we saw a woman with a camera running down the path. Then we found a strange looking Plant and our guide said "You can eat this it's minors lettuce, it tastes just like lettuce." Everyone ate then we hiked to a lookout point with binoculars we looked at the birds called Egret Then we at lunch after words we caught a snake, then we hunted newts in the marsh after five mins. we came home

Grade 5

The report of this class trip does show a clear sequence of events and clear paragraph structure, but it also includes many irrelevant details. A general statement of the importance of the trip is never made. Audubon Canyon Ranch is a sanctuary for egrets, yet the poison ivy and the woman running down the path received as much attention as the birds. The problem results from a topic that is far too broad and not focused on the importance or relevance of the ranch.

On tests, students frequently respond to the question without restating the topic—assuming the teachr will remember the topic. Outlining and notetaking skills are noticeably absent as students rely on copying information from one or two sources. Proofreading and editing skills are also weak since most poor writers are so relieved to have their report finished that they do not bother to check for errors. Introductory material and conclusions may be weak or even absent.

The National Assessment of Educational Progress (1972) reviewed paragraphing as one element in their analysis of writing samples in the First National Assessment of Writing and concluded that even the writing samples of seventeen-year-old students contained paragraphs that were *not* well developed. The judges reported that the papers exhibited a "stream of consciousness" quality and that ideas were not totally interrelated.

The major problems, then, in organization of ideas are a lack of sufficient detail to support generalizations, superficial ideas, the inclusion of irrelevant details, poor transitions between ideas, and lack of cohesiveness of ideas. However, students at this level generally use the basic paragraph structure, as evidenced by separation of ideas into separate paragraphs and indentations. The final report, though, may be adequate but not well developed.

MASTERY LEVEL   Writing at this level is clearly and consistently organized. The writer shows evidence of notetaking and outlining skills in the preparation stage and is able to select and narrow a topic appropriately, and to state relevant generalizations (topic sentences) about the topic. Facts, details, and examples are carefully selected to provide sufficient support for all generalizations and opinions. Proper paragraph structure is consistently used.

Vocabulary

Accuracy, specificity, variety, and appropriateness of word choice are the primary concerns in the analysis of vocabulary use in student writing. In the past, studies of vocabulary use have been limited to word frequency counts, word choice error counts, and differentiated word counts (the total number of different words in a writing sample). While these studies have provided useful information for researchers they have been of little practical use to classroom teachers.

A number of word frequency counts have been completed in the last fifty years. Some of these are based on tabulations of words in school materials (spelling programs and basal reading programs) and adult print materials, while others are based on word counts in student and adult writing. Dolch (1939) and Harris and Jacobson (1972) developed lists of high frequency words (basic sight vocabulary) taken from basal reading programs in an effort to determine which words students should recognize immediately upon exposure. Horn (1926) tabulated five million words in *adult* writing; Rinsland (1945) tabulated six million words in *children's* writing; and Thorndike-Lorge (1944) counted four and a half million words in *adult* printed matter. Most recently, Hillerich (1978) counted 379,694 words written by *students* in grades two to six over one school year.

Word frequency counts were not designed to be used as a guide to evaluating word choice in student writing, although when used with proper caution, they can be quite useful for this purpose. To some degree, these counts can give an indication of maturity or immaturity of word choice, since they identify high frequency (thus overused and common) nouns, verbs, and adjectives. Hypothetically, this sounds promising, but there are some cautions associated with this method of evaluating word choice.

Finn (1977) points out that *low* frequency words are used by immature writers when the topic is so specific that it demands the use of certain words. A baseball story, for instance, would probably include the words stadium, bleachers, umpire, foul, home run, strike, and innings. These words Finn labels "Topic Imposed Words." The choice of words is not based on maturity of vocabulary use, but on the necessity of their use in responding to the topic. The use of certain other low frequency words, such as slang, contractions, and proper nouns do not reflect maturity in word choice because they generally are not heavily used in print materials, even though they do appear more frequently in children's writing. On the other hand, invented words, which do not appear on word frequency lists at all, reflect high maturity because the student has consciously formed a new word for his or her own purpose.

The source of the words must be considered when using word frequency lists for evaluating writing. Horn's list (1926) reflected words used by *adults* and contained the words: letter, order, and received. These words are not listed in Hillerich's (1978) list of one hundred most frequently used words in children's writing. Even so, vocabulary lists of high frequency words (the first one hundred) are likely to remain fairly constant over time (Hillerich, 1978). Larger lists will change and reflect the prevailing vocabulary of the times. For example: Older lists do not contain some of the space and communications vocabulary that students use with ease today.

Most word frequency lists are arranged in alphabetical or frequency order. However, when these lists are rearranged by parts of speech, some interesting patterns emerge. In Hillerich's list, for example, the largest group of words are verbs and the same is true for the Dolch list (Table 2-2). Analysis of verb usage can indicate the level of vocabulary maturity of the student.

Hillerich's word counting method listed each word form (e.g., verb tense forms, plurals) separately. Therefore, certain verb families which are used frequently do not appear in the first one hundred. A review of the word frequencies of verb families as a whole provides a different listing (Table 2-3).

Table 2-2 The One Hundred Words Used Most Frequently by Children in Their Writing. . . . Arranged by Parts of Speech

Nouns	Verbs	
back*	am	got
day	are	had
home	be	have
house	came	is
man	can	know
mother	could	like
one	did	put
people	didn't	said
school	do	saw
things	done	see
time	don't	think
two	get	was
	go	were
		would

Adverbs	Adjectives	Conjunctions
just	all*	and
now	little	as
some		because
then		but
there		if
too		or
very		so

Pronouns	Possessive Pronouns	Objective Pronouns
he	her*	her*
I	his	him
it	my	me
she	our	us
them	your	
that		
they		
this		
we		
you		

Prepositions		Articles/Determines
about	in	a
after	into	an
around	of	the
at	on	
by	out	
down	over	
for	to	
from	up	

*Indicates that word may be a different part of speech depending on context in which it is used.
Adapted from Hillerich, R. L. A Writing Vocabulary of Elementary Children. Springfield, IL: Charles C Thomas, 1978. Used with permission of the author and publisher.

Since the lists of one hundred most frequently used words remains relatively constant, these can be used at least to compare maturity of word use. Students who rely very heavily on these words exhibit limited control over vocabulary use in writing. Three broad levels of vocabulary use are described below.

LIMITED LEVEL On the first level of vocabulary use, students tend to rely almost exclusively on high frequency nouns and verbs. Function words, such as prepositions, pronouns, articles, and conjunctions are also very heavily used. Any words that are not on the frequency list are nouns that are directly related to the stimulus.

> There are two menon a raft. One men is in the raft. the other
> is in the water. Thecolor of the water is green and white. The
> color of the raft is yellow They are on the ra pids It is in the
> summer The men arecold
>
> *Grade 5*

Occasionally, students write down the spoken version of a word, phonetically spelled, even though the word is a mispronunciation of the word they really need. This occurs as students fail to notice the separateness of words in oral language so they

Table 2-3 Most Frequently Used Verbs in Writing

ask	(asks, asked, asking)
be	(is, am, are, was, were)
come	(comes, coming, came)
call*	(calls, called, calling)
can*	(could)
do	(does, doing, done, don't, didn't)
eat	(eats, eating, ate)
get	(gets, getting)
go	(goes, going, gone)
have	(has, having, had)
know	(knows, knowing, knew)
like	(likes, liked, liking)
live	(lived, lives, living)
look	(looked, looking, looks)
make	(makes, making, made)
name*	(names, naming)
play*	(plays, played, playing)
put	(puts, putting)
run	(runs, running, ran)
say	(says, saying, said)
see	(sees, seeing, saw)
start	(starts, started, starting)
tell	(tells, telling, told)
think	(thinks, thinking, thought)
try	(tries, tried, trying)
walk*	(walks, walked, walking)
want	(wants, wanted, wanting)
will*	(would)
work*	(works, worked, working)

*Indicates that word may be a different part of speech depending on context in which it is used. Word frequency lists do not distinguish between parts of speech.

Adapted from Hillerich, R. L. A Writing Vocabulary of Elementary Children. *Springfield, IL: Charles C Thomas Publisher, 1978. Used with permission of the author and the publisher.*

either reduce words to abbreviated forms ('em for them); separate them incorrectly (e.g., a nother for another); combine them with other syllables (e.g., "hasta" for "has to," "sposto" for "supposed to," "wanna" for "want to"); or completely substitute them for more commonly known words ("The boy lives *next store*."). These errors are basically *language errors* rather than spelling errors because they relate directly to the way the student pronounces the words or uses them in oral language. Frequently they are spelled correctly phonetically.

GROWTH LEVEL The second level of vocabulary selection and usage represents the "growing stage" where students begin to experiment with new words in their writing and begin to substitute specific nouns, verbs, adjectives, and adverbs for vague or overused words of the Limited level. At first, writers include specific proper nouns and verbs directly related to their own experiences or to the writing topic. The following two examples are based on a story starter. The first student includes words that would be expected when discussing a canoe trip: swim, canoe, current, shore, and paddle. The writer overuses the verbs "got" and "tried" and uses no adjectives at all. "Current" is the most sophisticated word used in the sample, but even it can be considered a topic imposed word.

> "Jerry! I can't swim!" cried Frank. Then the canoe tipped over Frank kept on yelling "help!" "help!" Jerry tried to swim by him put the current kept on pulling him back. Jerry got to him after he tried a couple of times, Jerry tried to hold Frank up and then turn the canoe backover, then he did He got Frank back into the canoe then Jerry got in it and tried to paddle to shore. They got to shore and went home and told their parents all about what happened.
>
> *Grade 6*

By contrast, the next example based on the same story starter shows greater maturity in vocabulary use. The writer uses specific verbs (thrashing, drifting, clinging, grasped, gasping, oozing, grinding, ripping); specific adjectives (dazed, bruised); and specific nouns (flesh, bolt of lightening, downstream, splinters).

> "Jerry! I can't swim!" cried Frank. Just then, a bolt of lightening struck the canoe. The boys were thrown out of the canoe. Frank and Jerry were thrashing their arms and trying to get to the canoe which was drifting downstream. Then Jerry looked in horror as a huge tree came crashing down on Frank. For a moment, Jerry thought he might never see his friend again. But then Jerry saw Frank clinging to the log. Frank was dazed and bruised, but he was alive. Jerry fought the waters with every ounce of strength that he had left in him to get to the log and Frank. A few moments later, his bare hands grasped the log. His hands were bleeding from the splinters of the log and he was gasping for air. "Frank! Frank! You've got to help me! Wake up!" cried Jerry. It was no use. Then Jerry felt mud oozing up through his toes and rocks grinding and ripping at the flesh of his bare feet. He realized he was on the other shore! So he dragged the log up on the shore and he and Frank just layed their gasping for breath. Then help came and all would be well, but Frank and Jerry would never forget that day.
>
> The End
>
> *Grade 6*

As students strive to include more sophisticated words and word arrangements in their writing, they do begin to make additional kinds of errors. Students may inappropriately add or omit inflectional endings, prefixes, or suffixes. Occasionally they may invent new words by combining incorrect prefixes or suffixes, or they may choose a very similar sounding word to the one they really need. The National Assessment of Educational Progress (1972) stated that vocabulary errors were made when students tried to use words with specific meanings even though they did not have a clear understanding of the words' meanings. Thus they created new words by combining already existing words, using nouns as verbs, and verbs as nouns.

Greene (1969) informally analyzed errors that are due to misunderstanding of the word meaning and identified several error patterns. While this was a report based on observations and not a statistically controlled study, it still provides valuable information on different thinking approaches used by students when dealing with vocabulary. Generally, two groups of errors can be identified—those that relate to mispronunciation of the word and those that relate to misunderstanding of the meaning of the word. These errors are basically *language* errors rather than spelling errors.

1. Students mistake one word for another with similar sound or appearance. Sometimes this is caused by careless mispronunciation or by inadequate listening habits. Greene quoted one student who said, "You don't have to look up words, you can just take for *granite* what they mean from the way they are used."

2. Students recognize a segment of one word and use this to define the whole word.

   <u>sin</u>ister   one who breaks sacred laws
   <u>dog</u>matic   allergic to dogs

3. Students recall a word from a specific context, but do not completely understand the word, then use it inaccurately in different context.

   The *risque* little squirrel wasn't afraid of the dog.

   Here the student knows one meaning of the word but uses it inappropriately.

MASTERY LEVEL Vocabulary choice and use on the Mastery level is the most sophisticated. Students have learned to make subtle distinctions between closely related words and consistently choose words which most accurately convey their intended message. Finn (1977) suggests three categories of words that appear to reflect maturity of word choice:

Abstract Nouns	alternatives, efforts, evils, menace, reasons, suicide
Cognitive Verbs (as opposed to action verbs)	abuse, blame, complain, investigate, manage, support
Judgmental Adjectives	adequate, controversial, drastic, genuine, potential, unnatural

In addition to mature word *choice*, students at the Mastery level demonstrate mature word *use*. They select words which are appropriate for the style of writing, and also select words to create special effects (alliteration, rhyming, repetition) when appropriate. Overall, the student writing at the Mastery level has complete control over vocabulary choice and arrangement.

Sentence Structure

Sentence structure has been the focus of a number of research studies, primarily because sentences can be quantitatively analyzed by counting words and clauses. Strickland (1961), Loban (1963), Hunt (1965), and O'Donnell, Griffin, and Norris (1967) have identified sentence length and complexity as one indicator of syntactical maturity.

Hunt uses the T-unit as the research unit related to the sentence and defines it as "one main clause plus the subordinate clauses attached to it." Using Hunt's method, writing samples are divided up into the smallest possible T-units, regardless of punctuation. Compound sentences are treated as two T-units because both parts are equal main clauses. The average number of words per T-unit is then computed. Hunt found that main clauses in sentences increased in length as students increased in age and that more subordinate clauses were attached to the main clause. Thus, T-unit length is an indication of syntactical maturity. Lundsteen (1976a) suggests one caution regarding sentence length: "It is not 'how long you make them, but *how* you make them long.'" In other words, run-on sentences can be very long, but they are very immature. Sentences that have a lot of description can be awkward and phony because they are overloaded with unnecessary detail. Complex sentences in which dependent clauses are attached to the main clause are more mature than the previous two examples.

For practical purposes (i.e., reviewing student writing samples on a daily basis), it is *not* necessary to count words and clauses. However, it is important that teachers be able to quickly identify the basic sentence types found in student writing, since these will give an idea of the maturity of the writer and also will provide a starting place for instruction. Table 2-4 summarizes the basic sentence types. One sentence type, expanded sentences, is included on the chart even though it is generally not

Table 2-4 Sentence Types

Command/Request Sentences	Eat! Run! Help! Stop! Fire!
Kernel Sentences contain subject and verb	Dogs eat. Fish swim. Bears growl.
Simple Sentences contain subject (noun or pronoun), verb, and object or adjective and may use a form of the verb "to be"	The dogs eat <u>bones</u>. It <u>is</u> a boat. They <u>are</u> hungry.
Expanded Sentences are really simple sentences with additional descriptive details or phrases*	
1. descriptive words	(Large, slender, rusty-colored) Irish Setters munch (crispy, crunchy) dog bones.
2. when, where, how phrases	An enormous bear chased me (in the woods) (yesterday afternoon).
3. compound subject	A mother bear and chased me. her baby bear

4. compound predicate	An enormous bear growled at me
	                    and
	                    chased me.

Compound Sentences contain two independent clauses** joined by and, but, or, nor, for	(The students go outside for recess) (but) (the teachers go to the library.)
Complex Sentences contain one independent clause and one dependent clause*** joined by a subordinating conjunction	(The students go out for recess) (*when* the weather is good.)
Compound-Complex Sentences contain two or more independent clauses and at least one dependent clause	(The students go outside for recess) (when the weather is good) (but) (the teachers go to the library.)

*A *phrase* is a group of related words that does not contain a subject or verb. Generally a phrase adds when and where information.

**An *independent clause* contains a subject and predicate and can stand alone as a complete sentence.

***A *dependent clause* is *not* a complete sentence but depends on an independent clause to complete its meaning, even though it does have a subject and predicate. It is joined with an independent clause by a subordinating conjunction (if, when, since, that, who, where, etc.)

found in language texts. An expanded sentence is a version of a simple sentence, but it has descriptive words and/or phrases, and possibly a compound subject or verb. The presence of these items in a student's writing indicates a degree of growth, since beginning writers tend to rely on short, simple sentence constructions.

The level of complexity within a complex sentence varies according to the specific subordinating conjunction used and the number of clauses reduced and embedded in the sentence. However, since highly complex sentences are not generally found in the writing of the middle grade students, no attempt was made to differentiate between levels of complex sentences. Furthermore, those students who write highly complex sentences with embedded phrases and clauses generally do so only after specific training activities in sentence combining and not as a result of incidental learning. While this training is valuable for students at a high school or college level, it is of little value to younger writers who are not developmentally ready to learn to write highly complex sentences.

The discussion of sentence structure in this manual also includes capitalization of sentence beginnings and punctuation, since these are so closely related to sentence structure. This section will delineate sentence types at three levels: Limited, Growth, and Mastery.

LIMITED LEVEL   Poor writers do not have a well developed sentence sense and tend to rely on a few common patterns: short, choppy, simple sentences; run-on sentences; fragments; and inconsistent punctuation. Simple sentences generally fall into several patterns as demonstrated by the samples below (Lundsteen, 1976a).

1. subject-verb
   The dog barked.
   The boy cried.

2. subject-verb-object
   The boy eats candy.
   The dog bit me.
   I rowed a boat.

3. subject-verb-noun-noun
   She gave Mary a new coat.

4. subject-linking verb-noun
   The boat was a canoe.
   This is squad 51.
   It was a big fire.

5. subject-linking verb-adjective
   The camp was fun.
   The boy was safe.
   It is big.

The overall impression of writing at the Limited level is of short, choppy sentences as seen in the following two examples.

(My Dog Name is king) (he a German shepherd) (I take him out a lot of time) (he Bit My Brother) (he want to the hospital) (he was all right) (then I got Bit to and I wasall rigt to)
Grade 5

A Story about camp wing.
once I went to a camp. The camp was fun. I rowed a Boat. The Boat was a canoe. I rowed The canoe to The pond. and The pond had a Turtle named Big Mike. Big Mike tipped a row boat over. a Boy was in The Boat. The man came to Help The Boy. The Boy was safe. The Boy's name was Anthony.
Grade 4

The first student used primarily short, choppy sentences in his story (parentheses are added to show sentence units), but he completely omitted punctuation and used capitalization inappropriately. The second student wrote short, choppy, simple sentences, used capital letters inconsistently, but did use periods correctly.

An early type of writing found at the Limited level is repetition of simple sentences with slight changes of wording. Punctuation is used inappropriately.

> He will fall and hurt him Self?
> He will hit a rock.
> He will hit a willie and fall?
> He will have a soreleg.
>
> *Grade 4*

Run-on sentences are quite common and normal in the work of young writers (grades one and two). As they rush to tell their story, they link each sentence with "and," "and then," or "and so" following the pattern used in oral language. Gradually, with more exposure to reading and more practice in writing, the average writer learns to eliminate this pattern. Some writers, in the fourth grade and above, persist in writing run-on stories after it is developmentally normal. In the following example, the writer demonstrates awareness of punctuation but still essentially writes a run-on story.

> One day a big Dog come up <u>and</u> scared my cat the Dog.
> Chase The cat up the tree. <u>And</u> he started to cry. <u>And</u> when I
> came home I See a big Dog! <u>and</u> I scared him away of the tree.
> <u>and</u> my cat came down. I Love you cat somuch.
>
> *Grade 5*

Older writers occasionally write a run-on sentence within the body of their story, but this is frequently due to lack of punctuation or lack of proofreading rather than an inability to write other kinds of sentences.

In the next sample (typed in sentence format rather than typed as written), the writer has made numerous errors leaving the overall impression of very limited ability in sentence writing skills. However, if you look at the sentence in terms of thought units, it is easy to see that the writer is using some of the more difficult sentence structures used in oral language.

> When steve open the door he here a gromed
> he push the door
> there he say a man dead.
> Steve scream
> and no one was a round so steve got on
>   his horse and stated to ride
> he final got up to some one
> Steve say that a dead man is in norn house
> his name is mike.
> when the man get there uther people
>   alround him and these hold him and
>   take him to jail for the murder of
>   mike.
> and he was proven killed.
> he was hang.
> he was insent. [innocent]
> the person who Kill mike was one of the
>   heird hand and from that day one steve
>   was hang for nothing he commintee.
> and no one now the true.
> and he walking around free.
>
> *Grade 7*

GROWTH LEVEL At the second level, writers begin to use a variety of sentence types: expanded (when and where phrases added), compound, complex, and compound/complex sentences.

At first, they write expanded sentences with modifying phrases (when/where) as in the following examples.

The girl walks	to school.
There's a little white house	in the garden.
The man is walking	on the moon.
The man is riding	on a horse.
I was walking	in the woods.

Simple sentences with compound subjects or compound predicates are used.

Compound Subjects:

A boy and his father	went skiing.
Tina and Geraldine	were playing.

Compound Predicates:

The racoons	come out and eat the garbage.
The boy's mother	came and told the police.

Writers also use more of the complex sentence structures that they use in oral language. The subordinating conjunctions because, if, so, and when are most frequently used.

> When I stand up on the dirt road, I can see all the colors.
> We don't have a washer or dryer so my mother has to wash the clothes by hand.
> All the people are screaming and clapping because they want the fight to start.

As writers begin to write longer sentences with more complex structures, they occasionally write awkward or incorrect sentences, some of which are due to inadequate punctuation. They sometimes shift their line of thinking in the middle of the sentence and then fail to proofread to catch the errors. Even so, awkwardness appears primarily as an oversight or lack of proofreading, since the writer uses more complex constructions in the rest of the work. Words and punctuation are added or omitted inappropriately and more subject-verb and pronoun agreement errors creep in the writing. Non-parallel constructions may be found in compound and complex sentences and in sentences that contain a series of phrases separated by commas.

> He had the throne heired to him when he was young and evil toads had corrupted him.

> The young king's name was Paul and his evil advisor, Ivan (the terrible) who directed him to do dastardly deeds.

MASTERY LEVEL Longer sentences reflect the increased ability to handle more complex syntactical arrangements and to clearly represent thought through language structures. Sentence length is increased through the use of descriptive words, phrases, and clauses which describe the noun, and through the appropriate addition of clauses.

> The frog king, a tough old army sergeant from the ant-eater wars, was preparing to declare war on the toads.

Mature writers also use more stylistic features: deliberate sentence fragments, questions, dramatic punctuation, and the repetition of words and phrases for impact. Hunt (1965) points out that mature writers also use clauses, infinitives, and gerunds as subjects in place of the more common nouns and pronouns. These writers also eliminate wordiness by reducing clauses to phrases and embedding them in the sentence.

Complexity for its own sake is no mark of maturity (Moffett and Wagner, 1976). The writer at the Mastery level has a well developed sentence sense and consistently and deliberately uses sentence types that are appropriate for the writing purpose—whether they be fragment, simple, expanded, compound, complex, or compound/complex sentences.

Spelling

Spelling is a complex task which requires the simultaneous use of auditory, visual, or motor skills. Hodges (1966) defines spelling as the act of encoding the phonemes of speech into the graphemes of the writing system. Furthermore, spelling is a kind of information processing in which many cognitive processes are involved, including visual, auditory, and motor skills (Hanna and Hanna, 1966; Hodges, 1966; Rudorf, 1966). A model of the process is shown in Table 2-5. If a student has difficulty in any of these areas, he or she will have spelling problems (Boder, 1971; Hodges, 1966; Mann, Suiter, and McClung, 1979). A student who has difficulty with auditory skills will probably make more errors on phonetically regular words. On the other hand, if the student has poor visual skills, he or she will probably make more errors on basic sight words and phonetically irregular words. Students who have both auditory and visual weaknesses will have difficulty with spelling in general. Although people learn to spell in different ways, they all rely on the intactness of these basic abilities.

Table 2-5 Information Processing in Spelling

Spelling is a complex process which requires the use of the following skills:

1. Auditory Skill: The student must
   - analyze the distinct sounds within a given word or syllable
   - analyze the sequence of sounds, and/or
   - analyze the sequence of syllables within a multi-syllable word (including roots, prefixes, suffixes, superlative endings, inflectional endings)
2. Visual and Memory Skills: The student must
   - recall the shape and form of the letters that correspond to the sounds within a word or syllable
   - recall the sequence of letters and syllables
3. Motor Skill: The student must
   - execute the correct motor pattern for writing the letter, and
   - write the sequence of letters correctly.
4. Proofreading Skill: The student must
   - read to identify possible errors
   - correct errors

Three broad levels of spelling ability are described below.

LIMITED LEVEL

Students in fourth grade and above who make spelling errors on basic sight vocabulary and on one and two syllable phonetic words have limited ability in spelling. At times the student misspells so many words that comprehension of the written message is difficult.

Spelling errors should be analyzed to determine whether an error pattern exists and to identify learning styles so that specific spelling remediation strategies can be used. The following error patterns may be evident.

1. *Errors on basic sight words and other phonetically irregular words.* Students may have difficulty in recalling or "revisualizing" the correct letter for a given sound. They may also be unable to identify whether a word has been spelled correctly once it has been written. Words may be spelled differently several different ways within the same paper.

   Specific types of *visual* spelling errors are described below:

   - Short common words misspelled
   - Sight words spelled phonetically: "wun" for "one"

- Incorrect sequence of letters on "sight words": "becuase" for "because"
- Reversal tendencies: b/d p/q was/saw
- Inversions of letters: u/n m/w
- Part of word correctly spelled, but the rest forgotten
- Extra letters added

2. *Errors on phonetic words.* Students may have difficulty analyzing words into separate sounds and syllables. While poor auditory discrimination is a major cause of spelling problems, inaccurate pronunciation, poor articulation or other speech problem, or poor hearing acuity may also interfere with spelling ability. Students may spell words as they pronounce them. For example: "Enemy" may be pronounced as "emeny," and may also be spelled "emeny."

    Specific types of *auditory* spelling errors are described below.

- Substitution of letters on phonetically regular words
    confusion between voiced and unvoiced consonant sounds
    voiced sounds: b   v   th   d   g   z   j
    unvoiced sounds: p   f   th   t   k/c s/c ch
    confusion between similar sounds   p   t   k   b   d   g   sh/ch z/j m/n
    confusion on vowel sounds
- Omission of letters on phonetically regular words (e.g., omitting a letter from beginning or ending blends)
- Omission of syllables in words
- Omission of prefixes, inflectional endings/suffixes
- Mixed sequence of letters/syllables on phonetic words
- Substitution of whole words: home for house

3. *Errors on both phonetic and sight words.* When students have difficulty with both auditory and visual skills in their spelling, written production may be difficult to comprehend. The spelling may be totally unrelated to the sounds in the words, as if the student had just made a random guess.

> Thar having a wor and tha cachered wun nashinlspi and the maricins have 17 tanks and the murincis have 7 rmechuks and a mrinkis 1001 men. and the a merinkuns wun.

> (They are having a war and they captured one national spy and the Americans have 17 tanks and the Americans have 7 army trucks and Americans 1001 men. and the Americans won.)

In this sample, the student seems to have some ability with auditory skills as he was able to phonetically analyze the words American and National Spy; however, each time he came to the word he analyzed it a different way. He spells words as he pronounces them as in the words "cachered" for captured, and "chuks" for trucks. The pronunciation problem is directly related to his auditory discrimination of the word. On a spelling test this student was generally able to spell phonetically regular words at lower levels, but had difficulty on longer phonetic words and the majority of sight words.

    The next sample also exhibits both visual and auditory spelling errors.

> This is a chrishmas. Ween This little gril gets a book it is a big. Shy dig not open The book undey till last.
> At chrishmas she Had pooney Talles in Her Hear. Her Hear is blened. She had blue leys and a penk drass on. The book was wight. Shy open The book it was a kittin. The bowe was Red.

Grade 5

Bizarre spelling is generally found in the writing of students who have neither auditory or visual skills. Some of these students gradually learn basic sight words and short phonetic words, but their spelling of longer words is sometimes incomprehensible, such as in the following student sample taken from a spelling test using Morrison–McCall Spelling Scale.

arrange	awwathe
search	shuck
interest	enrtsen
celebration	clerbreick
career	cousered
acquaintance	oupites

Other kinds of spelling errors apart from auditory or visual skill weaknesses may occur.

4. *Vocabulary errors.*

- Homophones: Children may substitute the spelling of one homophone for another, e.g., "here" for "hear"; "there" for "their"; "to, too, and two."
- Unknown vocabulary: Students may have difficulty spelling words they have never seen in print and/or whose meaning is unclear. (See vocabulary section for more detail on this point.)

5. *Poor proofreading skills.*

- The student has not learned to monitor his or her own writing by proofreading to spot errors.

GROWTH LEVEL   Spelling of basic sight words and short phonetic words are generally correct, but misspelling does occur on multisyllable words and words with unusual spellings. Some misspelled words may be phonetically correct, while other words may have been misunderstood or mispronounced. Endings may be dropped on words with inflectional or superlative endings and syllables may be dropped or sequenced incorrectly on multisyllable words. When word endings are dropped, it is important to notice the student's oral language pattern to see whether endings are dropped in normal speech. Students whose native language is not English may also drop endings (especially verb tense endings) since their own native language may not indicate tense by verb form changes.
Homonym errors continue to be a problem.

MASTERY LEVEL   There are relatively few errors in the final written product. Errors may be made on difficult words (multisyllable words or words with unusual spellings) but not more than one or two errors per page on a draft copy. Errors are eliminated on all final copies.

Handwriting   Manuscript handwriting is generally taught in the first and second grades and the transition to cursive is made sometime during the second or third grade (Otto, McMenemy, and Smith, 1973). There has been considerable discussion of the merits of manuscript and cursive, and whether or not one system is better than the other. Proponents of *manuscript* writing feel that this style is most appropriate because it requires less sophistication in fine motor control and because of its similarity to letter formations in print materials. They also feel that considerable time is wasted in the transition from manuscript to cursive handwriting. Proponents of *cursive* handwriting suggest that cursive writing is also highly motivational. Furthermore, in a comparison of strokes in manuscript and cursive writing, cursive letter formations have more consistent letter formation patterns (i.e., initial strokes, final strokes, directions) than do manuscript (Kaufman and Biren, 1979).

Regardless of the controversy, the general practice is to begin teaching cursive writing at about the third-grade level. By and large, with proper instruction and adequate practice, most students are able to make the transition without major difficulty. For that reason, the emphasis in this section is on the evaluation of cursive writing.

Handwriting evaluation is most commonly accomplished using informal scales or checklists. Handwriting scales, such as the Zaner-Bloser Scale, generally show writing samples of varying qualities using the same sentence and require the user to match a student's writing as closely as possible to one of the samples provided. This kind of evaluation does not identify specific difficulties that a student may be experiencing, but only gives an idea of level of performance in comparison with other students. To identify specific weaknesses in handwriting ability, further informal diagnosis is necessary.

Three levels of performance in handwriting are described below.

LIMITED LEVEL Limited handwriting has many errors and may be difficult to read. This may be a result of visual perceptual and/or visual motor integration difficulties. The following specific problems may be found in handwriting samples.

1. *Poor or inaccurate letter formation.* Students who have experienced motor awkwardness in manuscript writing will probably have difficulty with cursive writing unless the motor patterns are carefully taught and sufficient supervised practice is provided.

   The most common error in cursive writing is the failure to close letters properly. The letter "a," for instance, may be formed like a "u," "i," "ci," or like an "o." Failure to dot "i's" and cross "t's" is responsible for another large group of errors. The letters "r" and "s" also cause considerable difficulty.

   Some students form letters incorrectly because they have not had enough practice with the specific motor patterns required to produce different letters, or because certain letters require several changes in direction while being written (g, h, z, j, q, p, y). Because they cannot remember letter formations, or the sequence of movements to use in writing the letters, they frequently look to writing wall charts for help. Students occasionally visually analyze letter formations and attempt to reproduce the letter in segments rather than in a continuous motor pattern.

2. *Letter substitution.* Substitution of rounded strokes for straight strokes (m for w, n for u, and vice versa) and substituting a short loop for a short straight stroke (e or i) adds to illegibility of handwriting. Lower case letters may be substituted for capital letters when students have not had enough practice on capital letter formations. Some students may continue to substitute b and d.

3. *Spacing problems.* Words may be jammed together and difficult to read. Spaces may be placed inappropriately within words or between words.

4. *Spatial organization.* Words may not be written on lines, and writing may go uphill or downhill regardless of lines and spaces. Letter size may be inconsistent.

5. *Slant.* Letters may be written in varying mixed slants: leaning backwards, forwards, and up straight.

6. *Illegibility.* Carelessness or rushed words with many erasures or writeovers produce a messy looking paper. Occasionally the student writes one letter over another hoping the teacher will choose the correct spelling.

7. *Speed.* Some students may write very slowly and may produce very little because of their speed. When rushed, they become frustrated and make more errors. As students move into upper grades, they must write faster to complete assignments and tests in alloted time periods. The Zaner-Bloser scales provide the following handwriting rate scale to determine whether students are writing at an appropriate speed for their grade level.

Grade	4	5	6	7
Rate (letters per minute)	45	50	67	74

GROWTH LEVEL Overall handwriting is adequate and readable, although there may be a few awkward letter formations and/or inconsistent letter slant, especially if the student is just learning cursive writing. Students may use margins inconsistently and may present papers that are not always totally neat in overall appearance.

MASTERY LEVEL   Completed assignments exhibit carefully produced, readable writing and an overall neat appearance. All letters, both upper and lower case, are written accurately.

INFORMAL
EVALUATION
PROCEDURES

One purpose of this manual is to provide guidelines for the systematic review of student strengths and weaknesses in writing ability. Before beginning, it is best to carefully read the previous sections, giving special attention to the charts that summarize the three levels of performance in the six skill areas.

Next schedule specific sessions for collecting the writing samples. Do not attempt to collect all writing samples in one day since student writing varies according to a number of factors such as type of assignment, time of day, interest, and motivation (Braddock, Lloyd-Jones, and Schoer, 1963).

The following samples would be useful:

1. Story written from a picture stimulus
2. Story written from a "story-starter" stimulus
3. Oral language sample (optional—see below)
4. Paragraph summary
5. Paragraph written from dictation
6. Handwriting sample (optional)

It may also be useful and/or necessary to collect oral samples from students who exhibit moderate or severe writing problems. To collect the oral samples, repeat items 1, 2, and 3, but let the student dictate responses. Tape record and/or write out the student's reponse. Use these oral stories and paragraphs to compare with the student's written sample. If the oral language samples show weakness in level of thinking, organization of ideas, vocabulary usage, and sentence structure, the student will probably need a great deal of work at an *oral* level. Progress in oral expression must precede progress in written expression.

Quickly review a random sampling of papers (at least one-third) from a particular evaluation activity before you begin to evaluate them. This will help you get an idea of the range of possible responses. Sorting papers in rough piles of high, middle, and low performance will also help to classify the features that are most prevalent at each level. Follow the guide questions as you first begin to evaluate the papers. Gradually, as you practice, you will internalize the questions and you will then be able to judge the papers more quickly using general impression responses.

If possible, have a second teacher go through this process and judge papers of your students in return for judging a series of his or her papers. Follow this by a short discussion on those papers where disagreement exists. This will definitely take more time, but the results should yield more accurate information which can then be used to develop a valuable learning plan for students. Ideally this self-training process will help you to internalize the features of good writing and will emphasize the need to consider all aspects of writing. Most important, it will emphasize the need for looking at strengths in student writing ability and will, therefore, de-emphasize identification of errors, or at least put error identification in proper perspective.

The ideas section of the informal evaluation will be most useful with narrative-type writing, although a few features listed at the Growth and Mastery levels, such as making generalizations, drawing conclusions, and making judgments, may be appropriate for other kinds of writing. For assignments other than those suggested, it will be necessary to judge how well the students meet the primary goal of the assignment.

The remaining five sections of the informal evaluation (organization, vocabulary, sentence structure, spelling, and handwriting) should be appropriate to most kinds of writing, even though the primary purpose of each writing activity will affect style, level of formality, and originality.

It is best to make complete notes on this first evaluation since comparisons can be made at midyear and end of year.

Informal Evaluation Activity 1: Writing Sample Using Picture Stimulus

PURPOSE   To determine level of performance in idea generation, organization, vocabulary use, sentence structure, spelling, and handwriting using a picture stimulus.

MATERIALS   A large (at least 9" x 12") color or black and white picture that shows evidence of problem situation, several characters, and setting. It should be obvious that the illustration has a past, present, and future aspect. In other words, the student should be able to surmise what happened before the picture was taken and draw some conclusions about what might happen next. Avoid cluttered pictures with too many irrelevant details.

PROCEDURE   1. Say to the student(s): "Look carefully at this picture. What is it all about? Think about it for a few minutes, then write a story about it. You may take up to thirty minutes to complete your story."
2. Do *not* prompt the student(s) in any other way since it is important to establish an unaided level of response. (If desired, for comparison's sake, the activity can be repeated on another day and specific leading questions can be asked to help the student in forming a response.)
3. Allow the students a reasonable amount of time to complete the task (usually twenty to thirty minutes). When time period is up, encourage the students to read over what has been written. Allow them to make any changes they wish.
4. Collect papers.

EVALUATION   Evaluate the idea generation, organization, vocabulary use, sentence structure, spelling, and handwriting using the Skill Level Charts, the following guide questions, and the Results/Interpretation Charts.

Content Evaluation

The main concerns will be to determine how well the student is able to develop a storyline, elaborate on given stimulus, and make relevant generalizations.

- Did writer develop and continue a storyline or topic?
- Did writer make any generalizations? What were they?
- Did writer include information (descriptive details, facts, examples) that were not evident in picture or story starter?
- Did story have continuous movement from beginning to end? Or did it start or stop abruptly?
- Were characters named and described? Did characters interact?
- Did the writer give evidence of original ideas? (imagination, fantasy, humor, etc.)
- Did writer show indications of a personal style?
- Did writer include dialogue?
- Did writer keep consistent point of view?
- Did writer make a judgment or suggest a moral?
- Did writer appeal to reader's emotions?
- Did writer use any special literary devices? (flashbacks, anecdotes)

Student Result	Interpretation
1. The student only identified separate items in the picture and made no attempt to link them into a story. The student wrote a story using only observable details with no originality of thought or personal involvement.	The students may need help in generating ideas. Complete Informal Evaluation Activity 3: Oral Language Sample and compare the results. It is important to determine whether the student cannot generate ideas at all, or whether he or she can generate them at the oral level but not at the written level. Use activities in "Get Them Writing!"
2. The student wrote a story which identified the problem or identified the characters and setting or told a sequence of events (what happened before or how the situation was resolved), but did not include all three elements.	The student may need help in planning a story sequence which includes all three elements. Try the Scene I, Scene II, Scene III Activity and activities dealing with characters and settings.

The student identified the characters, setting, situation, and explained how the situation came to be and how it was resolved. The story was generally okay—but lacked imagination or personality.

The student may benefit from brainstorming activities which will help generate other ideas. Encourage student to plan story ahead of time and consider possible options.

3. The student used the picture as a springboard for thinking and developed an original story which included information not readily evident in the picture. Characters and settings were named and described and dialogue was used when appropriate. A moral or some other judgment was stated or implied. The writer's personality was evident as was the writer's involvement in the story. Literary techniques were used when appropriate.

This student has good writing skills. Be sure he or she has experience with many different kinds of writing.

Organization Evaluation

The focus in this section is to determine the way the student arranges the information in his or her story.

- Did student include a title?
- Did student have clear introduction to story (i.e., a statement of the problem or beginning of storyline)?
- Did student add relevant supportive information? (facts, details, examples)
- Did student avoid gaps in organization of storyline? (Or did student assume the reader knew something about the topic?)
- Did student write more than one paragraph?
- Did student indent at beginning of paragraphs?
- Did student sequence information appropriately?
- Did student attempt any other form of sequencing of ideas other than narrative? (such as spatial or logical)
- Did student include only relevant information (or did student include irrelevant information)?

Student Result	*Interpretation*
1. The writing sample was totally inadequate. It lacked a title, proper paragraph structure, logical sequencing, and included possible irrelevant details. There were gaps in the line of thinking.	The student needs activities which will help him or her organize information. Try all sequencing acitvities—Scene I, Scene II, Scene III; Storyboards.
2. The writing sample adhered to paragraphing conventions (indentation, topic sentence, details, conclusion), but paragraphs were not sufficiently developed.	Try activities in Organization Section of this manual, especially "What's the Big Idea?" "Prove It."
3. The writing sample was clear, coherent, and well developed with good topic sentences, appropriate and sufficient supportive detail, and concluding statement.	The student has mastered basic organization skills. Provide additional activities to maintain these skills.

Vocabulary Use Evaluation

In evaluating vocabulary use, notice how students use words and what kinds of words they use. Ask the following questions after you read the writing samples:

- Did the student use only limited vocabulary?
- Did the student use topic related words? List them. It is important to note whether writers use specific words spontaneously (without any stimulus) or whether students use some specific words because the subject requires their use.
- Did the student use specific nouns? List them. Did the student identify persons, places, or things by specific word choice? Mr. Barnabus Quimley, instead of the man? Lincoln Elementary School, instead of the school? The automatic ice dispenser, instead of the thing?
- Did the student use specific descriptive words? List them. Did the student use common adjectives such as big, little, brown; or more specific adjectives such as monstrous, miniature, cocoa-brown?
- Did the student use specific verbs? Or did the student overuse is, are, have, make?
- Did the student invent any words for names of people, places, or sounds?
- Did the student create any original comparisons?
- Did the student use any literary device? Onomatopoeia (such as buzz, whack, swish), alliteration, repetition?

Student Result	Interpretation
1. The student used only limited vocabulary.	Compare oral language vocabulary with written language. If the student uses limited vocabulary when speaking, then the student needs many vocabulary building activities at an oral level. If student uses more mature vocabulary when speaking, he or she may choose simpler words because of a spelling problem.
2. The student used: topic related words, specific nouns, specific verbs, specific adjectives, invented words, original comparisons, onomatopoeia, alliteration, repetition.	If the student uses one or more of these items, there is evidence of growth in vocabulary use. Provide activities that encourage more of these features.
3. The student used a variety of elements described directly above.	Use these students to be tutors in vocabulary game-playing sessions.

Sentence Structure Evaluation

The following questions will focus on the types and variety of sentences used, syntax, and punctuation.

Sentence Types
- Did the student use:
  simple sentences exclusively?
  when and/or where phrases in simple sentences?
  descriptive phrases?
  any compound sentences?
  any complex sentences?
  a variety of sentence types and lengths?

Syntax
- Did the student use:
  correct word order in all sentences?
  consistent verb tense throughout story or report? (For example: Is past tense used consistently throughout story or report?)
  correct subject-verb agreement?

Punctuation
- What forms of punctuation were used correctly?
- What forms were not used correctly or omitted?

Student Result	Interpretation
1. The student used short, choppy, simple sentences exclusively.	Spend a lot of time on some of the sentence building activities: building kernel sentences, adding phrases and descriptive detail, and combining simple sentences. Do not try complicated sentence combining activities until the student begins to show progress in his or her daily writing.
The student omitted words or confused word order in sentences.	Make a word finder (a small piece of cardboard with a rectangular hole in it). Move it slowly across the student's writing. This forces student to read only one word at a time. Tape record as the student reads, then play back the tape. Ask the student to listen and to try to identify the places where word order is confused or words are omitted. If this does not help, rewrite the story using a cloze procedure (i.e., leave blanks where

Table 2-6   Spelling Checklist

Name_____ School _____ Date _____
Grade _____Date of Birth _____ Age_____Examiner _____

Errors Noted on Phonetically Regular Words	*(Check)*

1. Substitutes consonants.   (circle)
    b v th d g   z j   (voiced)
    p f th t k/c s ch (unvoiced)
	_____

2. Substitutes similar sounds. (circle) p t k b d g sh/ch z/j m/n	_____
3. Substitutes vowel sounds. (circle) a e i o u	_____
4. Omits letters such as on beginning or ending blends.	_____
5. Adds unnecessary letters.	_____
6. Mixes sequence of letters: (fast/fats) syllables: (enemy/emeny)	_____
7. Omits endings: s ed ing	_____
8. Omits syllables.	_____
9. Unusual spelling (has no relationship to actual sounds in word).	_____

Errors Noted on Basic Sight Words

1. Spells sight words phonetically. (one/wun)	_____
2. Mixes sequence of letters. (girl/gril)	_____
3. Writes part of word correctly, forgets the rest. (wrk/work)	_____
4. Reverses letters or words. (b/d dog/god saw/was)	_____
5. Inverts letters. (ton/tou)	_____

Vocabulary Errors

1. Substitutes spelling of homonyms.	_____
2. Misspells words whose meaning is unclear.	_____

a word should be filled in). Ask students to read the story and fill in the blanks. Use familiar stories, such as The Three Bears.

2. The student used a mix of sentences: simple sentences, expanded sentences, compound and complex sentences. Some sentences may have some awkward constructions and an occasional fragment may be present. Excess wordiness may also be a problem.	Emphasize the need to have a variety of sentences in writing. Continue with sentence building and combining sentences.
3. The student consciously used a variety of sentence patterns. Awkward and fragmented sentences are totally eliminated.	Let this student serve as a tutor for those who are having difficulty with sentence structure.

Spelling Evaluation

List any:

basic sight words that are misspelled,

topic related words that are misspelled,

mature words that are misspelled.

Complete the Informal Spelling Checklist (Table 2–6) to identify whether the student has more difficulty with phonetically regular words or with irregular sight words.

Informal Evaluation Activity 2: Writing Sample Using Story Starter

PURPOSE — To determine level of performance in idea generation, organization, vocabulary, sentence structure, spelling, and handwriting using a story starter stimulus. This second writing sample is suggested in an effort to see whether different levels of performance are given when a more specific stimulus is used.

MATERIALS — A story starter which provides specific characters, setting, and a problem situation. Short one- or two-line story starters are not acceptable for the activity because not enough specific information is given.

PROCEDURE —
1. Say to the student(s): "I am going to read an unfinished story to you two times. When I am finished, I want you to stop and think for a few minutes, then write an ending to the story. You may take up to thirty minutes to complete your story."
2. Do not prompt the student(s) in any other way since it is important to establish an unaided level of response. If desired, for comparison's sake, the activity may be repeated on another day using a different story starter and perhaps some prewriting discussion or guide questions.
3. Allow the student(s) a reasonable amount of time to complete the task (usually twenty or thirty minutes). When time period is up, encourage the student(s) to read over what has been written. Allow them to make any changes they wish to make.
4. Collect papers.

EVALUATION — Use the guide questions and evaluation charts for Informal Evaluation Activity 1. Compare the results of both stories. Note whether one stimulus resulted in a better writing sample than the other.

Informal Evaluation Activity 3: Oral Language Sample (Optional)

PURPOSE — To determine level of performance in idea generation, organization, vocabulary, and sentence structure in oral language sample.

To elicit oral language sample which can be compared with written language sample.

MATERIALS The picture from Informal Evaluation Activity 1 or another that fits the same requirements.

PROCEDURE
1. Say to the student: "Look carefully at this picture. What is it all about? Think about it for a minute, then tell me a story about it."
2. Do not prompt the student in any other way since it is important to establish an unaided level of response. (If desired, for comparison's sake, the activity can be repeated on another day and specific guide questions can be asked before the student responds.)
3. Tape record the story (if possible) then transcribe for easier analysis. Otherwise, write the story down verbatim as the student responds.
4. Repeat the procedure on another day and use a story starter as a stimulus.

EVALUATION Evaluate the idea content, organization, vocabulary, and sentence structure using the guide questions from Informal Evaluation Activity 1.

Informal Evaluation Activity 4: Paragraph Organization

PURPOSE To determine level of performance in paragraph organization when topic information is provided. (Do this activity only if the student performed Activity 1 and 2 with some degree of success.)

MATERIALS Sample paragraphs.

PROCEDURE
1. Choose a sequence of three or four related paragraphs on a reading range appropriate for your grade level. Generally, a paragraph one grade level below the students' reading is best. Choose a paragraph for your lowest readers, one for your average readers, and one for your best readers. Good sources of paragraphs are the *Be a Better Reader* series (Prentice-Hall), *New Practice Readers* and *Reading for Concepts* (Webster Division-McGraw Hill), Reader's Digest *Skill Builders*, or materials from Barnell–Loft.
2. Divide class into groups. Choose appropriate paragraphs for each group.
3. Say to students: "Listen to these paragraphs as I read them to you. Listen for the main idea and details. When I finish reading the paragraphs, write down as much as you can remember. I will read the paragraphs twice."
4. Read the paragraphs to students twice.
5. Ask students to write as much of the paragraphs as they can remember.

EVALUATION This activity requires the student to listen, identify, remember, and sequence main ideas and details.

Student Result	*Suggestions for Teaching*
1. The student could not handle this task. He or she missed the main ideas and forgot the details. The writing sample was completely irrelevant and totally unorganized.	Repeat the same activity (using a different paragraph sequence) at an oral level. Read paragraph to student twice, then ask him or her to tell the sequence orally. If student still has difficulty, then much more practice is needed at an oral level. If student is successful at an oral level, repeat this evaluation activity on a weekly basis, but ask student to restate the main ideas and details orally before writing the information down. Or, use incomplete outlines for students to fill

	in as they listen. Then have them write the paragraphs using their own completed outline. Try other activities from Organization Section of this Manual.
2. The student made a general statement about the topic but forgot some or all of the details. The student listed all the details but did not make any topic statements. The student remembered the details but could not put them in meaningful order.	Repeat this kind of activity on a regular basis. Emphasize either details or topic sentences by giving students partially completed outlines which they can fill in as they listen. After students improve at this level, try Evaluation Activity 4 again. Use activities in Organization Section of this Manual.
3. The student was able to remember the main ideas and details and organized the paragraph appropriately using proper indentation.	Use these students as tutors for others who had difficulty. Use activities suggested above and others in the Organization Skills Section of this Manual.

Informal Evaluation Activity 5: Paragraph Dictation

PURPOSE To determine level of performance in use of capitalization, punctuation, and spelling when paragraph is written from dictation.

MATERIALS Sample paragraphs.

PROCEDURE
1. Choose several paragraphs on a reading range appropriate for your class in which a variety of basic capitalization and punctuation, periods, commas, question marks, quotation marks, is needed. Choose a paragraph for your lowest readers, one for your average readers, and one for your best readers. Use a paragraph below the students' reading level for best results so students are not required to spell too many unknown words.
2. Say to students: "Listen to this paragraph as I read it through. When I am finished, I will dictate it in short phrases. I want you to write down what I say. Remember to put in capital letters where necessary and all punctuation."
3. Read the paragraph through once so that students will get a complete idea of the content.
4. Proceed to dictate the paragraph *in short phrases* so that students can write down what you dictate. Repeat each phrase at least twice before going on to the next phrase.
5. Reread the whole paragraph to students when dictation by phrases is finished. Encourage students to check over their use of capital letters and punctuation symbols as you read the selection.

EVALUATION Compare the original selection with the students' copies. Note the following kinds of problems. Review other samples of writing gathered in previous evaluation activities.

Capitalization

Student Result	*Suggestions for Teaching*

1. Capital letters used totally inaccurately:
  a. omitted or used inconsistently at beginning of sentences _____
  b. omitted or used inconsistently on proper nouns _____
  c. interspersed randomly throughout writing _____
	Student does not have adequate knowledge of when to use capital letters. Try Visual Dictation Activity (see Tackle the Troublespots) focusing on one type of capital letter situation (e.g., names of students).

2. Capital letters used inconsistently:
   a. on beginning of sentences   _____
   b. on proper nouns   _____
	Student has some knowledge of capitalization skills but needs review. Try Capital Contest Activity at least once a week until student improves. Also try Visual Dictation Activity from Tackle the Troublespots.
	    Complete the Student Writing Checklist (Table 2-8) with student. Review Capitalization Chart (found in Tackle the Troublespots) with student. Have student tape a copy to the desk or put in a notebook.

3. Capital letters used correctly:
   a. at beginning of sentences   _____
   b. on proper nouns   _____
	Let these students tutor other students who have difficulty with capitalization.

Punctuation

1. Punctuation symbols omitted or used totally incorrectly:
   periods   _____
   commas   _____
   question marks   _____
   quotation marks   _____
   others   _____
	Begin with simple proofreading activity sheets in which one type of punctuation is featured. Use only single sentences with one new sentence per line. Try the Visual Dictation Activity described in Tackle the Troublespots.

2. Punctuation symbols used inconsistently (sometimes correct, sometimes not):
   periods   _____
   commas   _____
   question marks   _____
   quotation marks   _____
   others   _____
	Use proofreading activities in which one type of punctuation error is made consistently throughout a paragraph or story. Have students proofread and correct errors. At first, tell students how many errors are included. Later, as students improve, do not specify the number of errors on the selection. Gradually, add a second kind of error and repeat the process until the student masters the symbols in question. Continue providing visual dictation as well as regular dictation on a weekly basis.
	    Use the Student Writing Checklist to help the student focus on the specific punctuation symbols that cause difficulty. Give the student a copy of the Punctuation Chart found in Tackle the Troublespots.

3. Punctuation symbols used correctly:
   periods   _____
   commas   _____
   question marks   _____
   quotation marks   _____
   others   _____
	Use these students as tutors for other students who have difficulty with punctuation. Perhaps they can monitor dictation practice for those students who need it.

Informal Evaluation Activity 6: Handwriting Samples

PURPOSE   To gather three samples of student handwriting: fastest, best, and normal.

MATERIALS   Sample sentences which contain all letters of the alphabet.

> The quick brown fox jumps over the lazy brown dog.
> Pack my box with five dozen jugs of liquid.
> The five boxing wizards jump quickly.

1. Explain to students that you want to collect some samples of their usual, best, and fastest handwriting. (This procedure was suggested by Otto, McMenemy, and Smith, 1973.)
2. Write one of the suggested sentences on the board and have students read it out loud.
3. Ask students to write the sample in their *usual* writing five times.
4. After a few minutes relaxation, ask the students to write the sentence three times in their *best* writing. Do not put a time limit on this.
5. After another short period of relaxation, ask the students to write the sample *as many times as they can* in three minutes.
6. Have students look over their three samples and make any comments about differences between the three samples.

EVALUATION Use the Handwriting Checklist (Table 2-7) to identify specific handwriting difficulties. This checklist is concerned with overall legibility as well as with the following specific features in handwriting: letter formation (including reversals, inversions, or substitutions of letters); size of letters and writing in general; use of guidelines; slant; and speed.

Table 2-7 Handwriting Evaluation

Student_____Date_____Grade_____Age____

Handedness: left ___   right ___   Manuscript___   or Cursive___

Overall legibility: poor___adequate___excellent___

Position of paper accurate?   Yes No

Pencil grip accurate?   Yes No

Position of body appropriate?   Yes No

Letter Formation: (circle incorrectly formed letters)

i u w t j p s r	P R B K H F Q X Y Z
e l b h k f	T G S L
m n	M N W V U
c o a d g q	C O A E
v x y z	I J D

List any reversals, inversions or substitutions of letters: _____

Refers to charts for letter formation? Yes No

Writes letters in segments rather than one continuous motion? Yes No

Size of letters:	Tall letters: too short___adequate___
	Short letters: too tall___adequate_____
	Lower loops: too small__ closed___adequate____
Size of writing:	too small__ too large___inconsistent___ adequate___
Spacing between words:	none___adequate___inconsistent ___
Use of guidelines:	inconsistent___adequate____
Slant:	consistent__ inconsistent__
Speed:	slow___average___excellent___

A second feature of the Handwriting Checklist is that it requires that the user *observe* the student during the sample. Obviously, this is not possible to do for all students, but it should be done with those individuals whose writing has limited legibility. The following questions need to be considered:

1. Does the student refer to handwriting charts frequently? (This indicates that the student cannot remember the shape or formation of letter.)
2. Does the student write each letter in one continuous movement, or does he or she write the letter in unusual segments? (This indicates that the student cannot remember the shape or formation of the letters, but tries to visually analyze their formation.)

Table 2-8   Student Writing Checklist

Name: _____Grade_____
Student Writing Checklist

	Yes	I need practice
1. Do I use complete sentences?	_____	_____
with capital letters?	_____	_____
and punctuation?		
periods	_____	_____
question marks	_____	_____
exclamation marks	_____	_____
quotation marks	_____	_____
commas	_____	_____
2. Do I avoid "run-on sentences? (Or do I use "and", "and then", "and so" a lot?)	_____	_____
3. Do I avoid sentence fragments? (Or do I sometimes forget to finish my sentences?)	_____	_____
4. Do I avoid using the same old words *over and over*? (like is, are, am, was, were, have, said, make)	_____	_____
5. Do I try to make my writing more interesting?	_____	_____
by using specific words?	_____	_____
adding descriptive details?	_____	_____
adding facts and examples?	_____	_____
adding conversation?	_____	_____
using different kinds of sentences?	_____	_____
using clear time sequences?	_____	_____
using my imagination?	_____	_____
6. Do I proofread my work to find my errors?	_____	_____
7. Do I re-write some of my stories or reports after I have made corrections, changes, or additions?	_____	_____
8. Do I have another special problem in writing? What is it?	_____	_____

9. I will work on the following problem in the next few weeks.

_____

_____

_____

_____

_____

signed by _____

date   _____

3. Does the student stop and start before each new letter, or are letters joined in
   continuous motion? (Some students have difficulty with connections between
   letters, or have difficulty with letters that require several changes in direction.
   The Handwriting Checklist groups letters together according to similar sequences
   of movements and as presented in the teaching sequence recommended in this
   manual.)

4. Are the student's body position, posture, pencil grasp, and paper position appropriate? Does the student bend his or her head close over the paper? Is posture poor or adequate? Is paper aligned correctly? Left-handed writers require different arrangement of paper on the desk. (See the Handwriting Section in Tackle the Troublespots for specific teaching suggestions for handwriting problems.)

Student Writing Checklist

One way to encourage student involvement in the evaluation process is to use a student writing checklist, such as Table 2–8. Checklists can be varied according to the reading and ability levels of students by adding or deleting items. Use the following procedures with the student checklist.

1. Review a small collection of the student's writing with the individual student to identify specific strengths and weaknesses. (You may want to share your evaluation notes made previously using the evaluation guidelines presented in this chapter.) If there are a great many errors in the student's writing choose just one skill area to work on. Remember, the first important goal is to increase writing fluency (i.e., the quantity of writing a student does).

2. Review the items on the checklist and have the student mark the column that is most appropriate (Yes or I Need Practice!). Occasionally a student will check "yes" when in fact he or she has not mastered the particular skill in question. A quick scan through some writing will help the student recognize the areas where help is needed.

3. Decide with the student which problem will be the focus of writing for the next week or two. Agree on a specific time period in which this goal is to be mastered. Often the student masters the goal very quickly since his or her attention is focused on that particular item.

4. Point out positive signs of growth whenever you see them.

Get Them Writing!

It is impossible for the teacher and student to keep all facets of writing in mind during the actual writing session. However, some general suggestions should help to smooth out the process.

1. *Build a positive atmosphere.* A positive atmosphere provides encouragement, praise, and motivation, and numerous opportunities to write. Students should feel free and safe enough to risk making mistakes—to express their thoughts without being criticized for making structural and mechanical errors. Hillerich (1979, p. 770) supports this view and states that "the most outstanding and consistent finding in research literature is that children learn to write better when praised than when criticized." In a more relaxed atmosphere, with less emphasis on absolute correctness of mechanics usage, students will develop a more positive attitude toward writing (Beaven, 1977), and they will also exhibit increased sophistication in language and style (Hillerich, 1979). Students should not have to concentrate on absolute mechanical correctness as they write; rather, they should focus on idea generation, vocabulary choice, and, perhaps, sentence variety.

    Teachers should look for and point out indications of strength in writing ability—the choice of a specific word, an original comparison, an interesting sentence, or an unusual idea. This kind of acknowledgment of student ability provides encouragement and increased pride and interest in writing. This does not mean that mechanical errors should be totally ignored. The next few points will elaborate on this idea. Too often we try to encourage students by giving general responses such as, "Your writing is improving." This kind of statement is useless unless the factors that indicate improvement are stated. Use specific statements such as, "You're using very specific verbs instead of the most commonly used ones" or, "You're using a variety of sentence patterns." Try to offer at least one positive statement for every paper you read.

2. *Recognize that progress in writing is often slow and irregular.* Developmentally, it is not until the fourth or fifth grade that students have sufficiently mastered the lower level skills (handwriting, spelling, mechanics) and thus are ready to use writing as a tool (Burrows, 1966). Before this time, students are more involved in the actual formation of the letters, or in sounding out

the words, and in combining letters into words. Students are caught up in the performance of lower level tasks and are unable to write their ideas fluently. While it is true that there are students who exhibit unusual writing ability as early as the first grade (Graves, 1979), this is not the case for the majority of students.

Thus it is important to keep the age and ability of students in mind when planning. Ignoring this principle leads to instruction that is ineffective and possibly detrimental to the student's achievement. (Lundsteen, 1976a; Myklebust, 1965; Braddock, Lloyd-Jones, and Schoer, 1963). It is also important to recognize that students do not improve in writing simply by writing. It is the preparation for writing and feedback they receive that enables them to improve.

3. *Alert students to specific items that will help improve their writing.* Use the students' writing to identify instructional needs. Avoid teaching unnecessary rules or using prepared textbook exercises which have no relationship to students' actual needs. Research clearly shows that the teaching of grammar, especially, is totally unrelated to student progress in writing, and, in fact, can be detrimental because it uses up class time needlessly (Braddock, Lloyd-Jones, and Schoer, 1963).

To be able to participate fully students need to be aware of objectives chosen and the reasons for their selection. A list of objectives can be posted in the classroom to alert students to the qualities and factors that improve written expression. Some students may choose to work on several objectives at a time, while others may need to focus on only one easily mastered objective before moving on to another.

An informal Student Writing Checklist may be useful in helping students to begin to evaluate their own writing. (See Table 2–8 in Evaluation Section.) One student stated confidently after going over the checklist, "I can do that! Now I know what to do!" Another stated that he could tell he was getting better in his writing because "I always reach my goal."

Different groups of students within the classroom may have different objectives depending on individual needs. It is very helpful to have students write their personal objective at the top of every paper (including science, social studies, and even math, when appropriate) so that student and teacher review may focus on the selected objective. State the objective in positive terms. (Some students seem to understand the word "goal" better than the word "objective.") At the bottom of the paper have the student write the word "Goal" again, then draw a line.

When students have completed their assignment, ask them to proofread for their target objective and write *Yes* or *No* on the Goal Line to indicate whether they feel they have met the objective. Most students like to write *Yes*, so they quickly proofread and make corrections, when necessary,

Figure 3–1
Goal Setting

GOAL: Remember capital letters at the beginning of every sentence.

GOAL: Yes

before asking for assistance from the teacher or another student. A few students will fill in *Yes* without proofreading for their goal. These students may need additional practice in proofreading skills.

Petty (1978) cites a research study conducted by Sawkins which pointed out that even the children who wrote the poorest compositions were quite aware of many of their problems, were willing to discuss them, and seemed eager to improve.

4. *Provide motivating prewriting experiences.* Brainstorming, role playing, reading, listening, speaking, drawing. . . all of these help students to develop, expand, then organize their thoughts before writing.

Brainstorming is a popular technique for generating a large number of ideas on a given topic in a short period of time. The process encourages divergent thinking and provides for random or unusual associations rather than just linear or sequential relationships. This process encourages students to stretch their imagination and play with ideas before writing, instead of writing in the same old way.

Several important factors should be considered when using this procedure.

a. Anything goes! Any idea expressed should be accepted without judgment of right or wrong, good or bad. Frequently, one person's idea can be expanded, developed, and refined into a totally new concept by another person. Each new idea then becomes a potential stimulus for further ideas.

One way to introduce brainstorming techniques is to use a nonserious topic as a stimulator so that all answers will be equally acceptable. One such topic could be, "What can you do with an alligator (or any other living or nonliving thing)?" See Alligator Antics in the Creative Writing Activities section.

b. Collect as many ideas as possible in a given period of time. Limit the brainstorming session to a specific period of time, depending on the interests and attention span of students, but allow enough time to generate a variety of ideas. Five to ten minutes should be enough time. Too short a period of time will not permit the expression of enough ideas. Too long a time period will produce boredom.

Appoint one or two students to be notetakers to write down all ideas. Restate ideas after they have been given. Record each idea or statement where all participants can see it. (Use a chalkboard, overhead transparency, or large chart.)

c. Encourage students to elaborate, combine, or expand ideas as they are mentioned. Very often the idea, suggestion, or word from one student triggers another idea, suggestion, or word from another student. This multiplies the number of ideas that an individual can draw upon for his or her own writing. Thus, instead of having only one idea (his or her own), a student can now combine and choose the best parts of many ideas.

5. *Get them writing!* Require that students write something, regardless of length, after each brainstorming or role playing session, whether they invent new material, elaborate on previously discussed material, or simply summarize what was presented in the prewriting sessions.

Reluctant writers frequently write the minimum amount to complete the assignment—often using the shortest and simplest sentences and the most limited vocabulary. For these students a minimum word count may be used to increase writing production. To begin, establish a base by counting the number of words a student uses in his or her writing assignments. Then determine a reasonable number of words that should be written. For example: A minimum for third grade might be thirty words; for fourth grade, forty words; and so on. When a student's amount of writing (fluency) is charted over a few weeks, writing production will be seen to increase gradually. Students will begin to write more fluently when they realize they will not be penalized for spelling or other mechanical errors. Gradually, they become more involved in their writing rather than in counting words.

Once writing productivity has increased, it becomes possible to determine students' strengths and weaknesses, and an instructional plan can be developed.

6. *Call each paper a "first draft."* Have students write on alternate lines of their paper to allow room for words to be inserted, notes to be added, or lines to be crossed out and rewritten. Calling each piece of writing a "first draft" acknowledges that the paper is not absolutely perfect and that it *may* be revised and rewritten. Point out, however, that not every piece needs (or deserves) to be rewritten. Keep *all* first drafts together in a writing folder until a later time when one or more may be expanded, revised, and rewritten. Emphasize that all writing is important even if it is never revised and rewritten.

7. *Schedule a weekly or biweekly period for proofreading, editing, and revising.* Ask students to choose one story or report from their writing folder for review and revision. Preferably this should be done several days after the first draft has been written since students tend to read what they intended to write rather than what they actually did write when they read it immediately after it has been written.

    Students may read papers silently, out loud to a partner or small group, or on to a tape which can be played back. Frequently, oral reading of written work helps students identify their own errors more easily. Group members can offer suggestions for additions and revisions. In addition, oral reading of the story will help students to identify their own mistakes in logic or organization or places where more explanatory material is necessary.

    Prepare for revising and rewriting by suggesting a second objective relevant to students' papers.

    Examples: Add more descriptive detail.
               Add some character interaction.
               Add some character dialogue.

    After students revise for the suggested objective, have them share their results with a small group. Encourage students to respond with positive comments on the style and content of the writing by asking questions such as "What was the most specific name or place? The most descriptive word?" or, "How do you think the characters are feeling? What could be added to the story? What was the most interesting event? The funniest?"

    Collect a number of before and after versions of stories, display them on a bulletin board, and ask students to note the changes. Ask students to identify the better story, and the qualities that make it better.

    Younger students do not like to rewrite stories. They consider a story to be finished as soon as they put their pencil down. Since they often develop their story as they write, it may meander or change directions abruptly as the student becomes involved in a new train of thought. The younger student writes in verbal shorthand as if he or she assumes the reader will understand and fill in the information that is missing. Two approaches may be used to correct this problem. First, it is often best to ask these students to write something related to the story they have already written *instead* of revising their original story. For example: A student might be asked to tell more about one of the characters in the story, or to tell more about the setting, or more about the emotional climate of the story. How do the characters feel? What might happen next? In this way students can be encouraged to explore a topic without feeling they are being asked to revise the original story.

    If students have difficulty with proofreading, help them focus on one error type at a time by providing activities that isolate that error *pattern* only. (See Tackle the Troublespots for specific suggestions and activities for developing proofreading and editing skills.)

8. *Provide many opportunities for students to share their writing efforts.* (Some writing, such as a diary, is personal, and not meant to be shared.)

Establish regular sharing periods when students pair up and read the results of their efforts to each other, or to a small group, or even to the whole class. When stories or reports are read aloud, encourage students to respond with positive comments.

Additional goals for writing should be to establish an individual or class writing collection, a bulletin board display, or a school newspaper.

9. *Keep an abundant supply of reading and writing materials in the classroom at all times.* Every writing program should be based on large doses of reading. This should be a combination of oral reading sessions in which the teacher, an older student from another grade, or a student from the classroom reads to the class; and individual reading done by students in regularly scheduled silent reading periods in which students read material of their own choosing.

Identify series of books that are especially popular with students. You can do this in two ways: (1) talk to the school or community librarian and find out which books are most frequently read by students of different age and grade levels; or, (2) have students interview students in other classrooms to determine both the general reading interests of students and specific titles and series that students particularly like. Post a list of the most popular books on the bulletin board. Keep the names of various students who have recommended books and arrange an occasional cross grade book discussion period where students can share viewpoints on selected books. Some books that seem to be popular are listed in Appendix A.

Try to identify the special interests of individuals by asking students to fill out a reading interest questionnaire (Table 3–1). Avoid asking yes–no questions (e.g., Do you like to read?). Instead, ask questions that will encourage students to make a choice (e.g., Which are more interesting to you, true stories or imaginary stories?).

Collect examples of published student writing so that students may see what their peers elsewhere around the country are writing. Use these to stimulate writing sessions.

Provide read-along or other audio-visual materials for those students who are reluctant to read or whose reading skills are below grade level.

10. *Correlate writing instruction with other curriculum areas.* One useful technique is asking the students to summarize a discussion in science or social studies classes. This often helps teachers to identify those students who have not grasped the concepts discussed and who may need additional review. Students often have difficulty putting concepts they think they understand in written form.

When giving homework assignments, have students first write down the instructions that you give, then read the instructions back to the class. Clarify any directions that are not restated clearly.

Notetaking and outlining during class discussions should be encouraged. At the end of each discussion period, leave enough time to review and compare notes or outlines. At first, you may want to have students fill in partially completed outlines.

Remember that any good teaching, speaking, or writing experience works best when you follow this simple sequence.

1. *Tell them what you are going to tell them.*
   (introduction, topic sentence, topic paragraph)
2. *Tell them.*
   (give your main points, supporting facts, details, examples, etc.)
3. *Tell them what you told them.*
   (summary and conclusion)

The activities in the Organization Section may also be helpful in curriculum content areas.

CREATIVE WRITING ACTIVITIES

The activities in the Get Them Writing! section are divided in two categories: Creative Writing Activities and Practical Writing Activities. The creative activities encourage students to use their imagination and memory as sources for writing topics. For those

Table 3-1 Questionnaire About Reading

1. Circle the kinds of reading materials that you like. You may circle as many kinds as you like.

about boys	cowboy stories
about girls	Indian stories
about family	pioneer stories
about friends	outdoor life
about growing up	racing (cars, motorcycles)
about school	sports
adventure	hobbies
sea adventure	how-to-make-it books
exploration	historical stories
space exploration	biography
science fiction	war stories
mystery	science
detective	inventions
animals	nature
cats	fantasy
dinosaurs	fairy tales
dogs	myths and legends
horses	humor
wild animals	jokes and riddles
others?_____	careers
_____	
_____	

   plays
   poetry

2. How many books did you read last year?

3. What are the names of the books that you have enjoyed the most? (You may look up authors' names if you have forgotten them.)

Title	*Author*
_____	_____
_____	_____
_____	_____
_____	_____

4. How many books do you think you will read this year?

5. What kind of book would you like to start reading? (Choose one kind from the list.)

students who have trouble getting started the Picture File, Storybooks, Story Starters, and Titles, Topics, and Twisters activities should be successful. The activities dealing with characters, settings, and points of view will be useful for students who have developed writing fluency, but who need to develop skill in adding descriptive detail and developing storylines. Suggestions for models from age-appropriate literature are included when appropriate.

The activities in each section of this manual start out at an easy level and gradually become more difficult. Most activities have extensions that suggest variations which may be used when students need more practice on a certain skill or topic. All activities can be made easier or more difficult by the selection of vocabulary.

Remember to use goal-setting procedures to encourage students to become more responsible for their own writing progress.

Picture File

OBJECTIVE   To make a picture file for use in writing activities.

MATERIALS   Magazines; old calendars; scissors; posterboard, oaktag (9″ x 12″), or manila folders; stapler, or scotch tape.

PROCEDURE

1. Ask students to bring old magazines and calendars from home. Have them look through the magazines for pictures of interesting characters, settings, and situations to put in the picture file.
2. Have students cut pictures out. (You may want to straighten edges using a paper cutter.) Staple or tape pictures to posterboard or oaktag. Keep the size of posterboard or oaktag consistent so the pictures can be filed easily.
3. Put the mounted pictures in a brightly decorated box in the classroom. Use larger pieces of oaktag as dividers, or use manila folders.
4. Sort the pictures as the collection grows. Ask the students to help you categorize the pictures. They can suggest the labels for the manila folder. Some labels might be: Undersea Pictures, Cowboys, Vacations, Hobbies, Animals, Adventures, Dangerous Situations, Interesting Characters, Settings.
5. Use the pictures in the following brainstorming, and writing sessions.

EXTENSION   Continue to collect pictures throughout the year. Bring lots of magazines into the classroom. Students can look for pictures (and *read* the magazines) during free time.

RESOURCES

Pen-Ups: The Picture Writing Set
Perfection Form Company
    Twenty different black and white photographs form the basis of this packet which is designed to stimulate writing activities.

Write Away
Joy Littell
McDougal, Littell and Co.
    Writing assignments in different forms (paragraph, story, list, tall tale, etc.) are suggested for each of forty-eight photographs in this kit.

Write to Spell
Judith M. Schifferle
Curriculum Associates
    Write to Spell presents eighty picture/activity cards which act as a stimulus for a writing assignment with the stated purpose of identifying and correcting a student's spelling and writing needs.

Storytelling Posters
Developmental Learning Materials
    Twelve full-color or black and white posters depict various settings and situations that students can use as a springboard to oral and written expression.
    Ask students: "What happened before this picture was taken?" or "What will happen Next?" or "How do the people in this picture feel about what is happening?" Ask lots of questions, and talk about all possibilities *before* you ask students to write a story.

Got to be Me!
Developmental Learning Materials
    Forty-eight colorfully illustrated cards feature thought-provoking unfinished sentences (ninety-six unfinished sentences in all) to encourage students to express themselves orally and in writing. The accompanying teacher's guide suggests ideas for playing games, writing, drawing, role playing, and going on interviews.

    "If I were very tiny, I would . . ."

Pathways to Value
Doubleday Multimedia
    Six color and sound filmstrips present moral dilemmas for students to discuss and write about. Recommended for Grades 4–6 ($93.50).
    "Loyalty or Truth?"
    "Truth or Trouble?"
    "For Self or Others?"
    "What Honesty Costs."
    "When Friendships Change."
    "Is it Fair to Cheat?"

OBJECTIVE   To write original children's storybooks.

MATERIALS   Many samples of children's storybooks, drawing papers, crayons, or magic markers.

PROCEDURE
1. Tell students that they are going to write original storybooks for younger children. Have them look over a number of storybooks to see what they contain (many pictures, a few sentences on each page, easy words to read, an interesting story).
2. Ask students to think of a story that might interest younger children. It could be a personal experience that happened to a student at a younger age; or it might be a "how to" book which tells children how to make something; or it might be a poetry book.
3. Have students draw the illustrations and write the first draft of the story.
4. Go over the first draft and have the student make necessary corrections. Copy the first draft neatly by writing a few sentences under each picture, or on a separate sheet of paper.
5. Bind all the pages of the book together.
6. Go to lower grade classrooms and read the books to children.

EXTENSION 1   Look in the library for picture books without words. Have students write the narrative for each picture. Write the final draft on slips of paper which can be clipped to the pages; or have students draw pictures to go with the narrative.

EXTENSION 2   Have students choose a picture, or a book with words, and take it to a lower grade classroom. There they can have a younger student dictate a story about the picture or book. The older student can write the story down as the child dictates it. The younger child can then draw pictures to go with his or her story. The story and pictures can be bound in a booklet. Read completed stories to both classes.

RESOURCES
Bubble, Bubble
Mercer Mayer
Parent's Magazine Press, 1973
      A young boy buys a magic bubble maker and discovers that he can blow bubbles in the shapes of everything from mice to elephants. When an animal gets too dangerous, the boy simply blows another bubble animal to control the dangerous one. Delightful pictures.

Mine
Mercer Mayer
Simon and Schuster, 1970
      A young boy claims most anything in sight as his own. Unfortunately, the real owners appear and claim rightful ownership.

The Great Cat Chase
Mercer Mayer
Scholastic Book Co., 1977
      A clever cat escapes from his young owner and leads everyone on a merry chase.

Two More Moral Tales
Mercer Mayer
Four Winds Press, 1974

      "Just A Pig At Heart" is the first picture story in this flip book. A male and female pig primp and dress in their finery, only to go out to play in mud puddles.
      "Sly Fox's Folly," the second story, shows the sly fox outwitted by two animal characters.

What Do You Do With a Kangaroo?
Mercer Mayer
Scholastic Book Co., 1975
      A little girl faces all kinds of problems when many different animals enter her life.

You're the Scaredy-Cat
Mercer Mayer
Parent's Magazine Press, 1974
      Two adventurous boys decide to camp out in the back yard one night. One boy decides to tell a very spooky story which then causes him to have nightmares. The story is told almost completely in pictures.

A Boy, a Dog, and a Frog
Mercer Mayer
Dial Press, 1979

Frog, Where are You?
Mercer Mayer
Dial Press, 1969
A Boy, a Dog, a Frog, and a Friend
Mercer Mayer
Dial Press, 1978

Creepy Castle
John S. Goodall
Atheneum, 1975
    A brave mouse and his lady friend discover a deserted castle and run into lots of problems.

Jacko
John S. Goodall
Harcourt Brace Jovanovich, 1972
    Jacko, an organ grinder's monkey, escapes and embarks on an adventure that takes him to his original island home.

Naughty Nancy
John S. Goodall
Atheneum, 1975
    Naughty Nancy causes lots of problems at a wedding.

Paddy's Evening Out
John S. Goodall
Atheneum, 1973
    Paddy's friend drops her fan from the theater box just as the performance begins. Paddy, being the perfect gentleman, tries to catch it, but instead falls and lands in the tuba in the orchestra. And that's only the beginning!

Paddy Pork's Holiday
John S. Goodall
Atheneum, 1976
    Paddy starts on a short camping trip and, of course, it doesn't take long for problems to develop!

The Ballooning Adventures of Paddy Pork
John S. Goodall
Harcourt Brace & World, 1969

The Midnight Adventures of Kelly, Dot, and Esmeralda
John S. Goodall
Atheneum, 1973
    A koala bear, a doll, and a mouse encounter adventures and danger when they climb into the picture on the wall.

A Flying Saucer Full of Spaghetti
Fernando Krahn
Dutton, 1970
    Elves help out a starving boy.

April Fools
Fernando Krahn
Dutton, 1974
    Two boys create a monster that mysteriously appears and disappears all over town. They reveal their prank only when they are caught in a jam.

The Self-Made Snowman
Fernando Krahn
J. B. Lippincott Co., 1974
    A snowman grows from a clump of snow knocked from a mountain peak by a mountain goat. Eventually he becomes the hero in town.

Drip Drop
Donald Carrick
Macmillan, 1973
    The rain begins and causes lots of problems in this house.

The Dirt Road
Carol and Donald Carrick
Macmillan, 1970
    A boy takes a long walk to a neighbor's house and stops to look at many exciting things along the way—
    a stack of logs,
    some bumps and holes in the road,
    footprints of a deer.

I See a Song
Carle Eric
Crowell, 1973
    Brightly colored designs represent music played by the violin. This would be a good example to show students before drawing designs to music.

Animals Should Definitely Not Wear Clothing
Judi Barrett
Atheneum, 1974

Storyboard Sequence

OBJECTIVE   To recall a sequence of events.

MATERIALS   Blank storyboard, crayons, colored pencils, short story or play.

PROCEDURE
1. Read a play or short story to a group of students. Have students retell the story orally, emphasizing the sequence of events.
2. Give each student a blank storyboard. Ask students to first draw the main events of the story in the separate boxes, then write a description of the action for each picture.
3. Have students read story sequences out loud to class members. Read the story a second time so students can check their storyboard sequence.
4. Give students an extra blank storyboard and ask them to write and draw their own sequence story. (You may want to use some of the suggested sequence resource material listed after this activity if students cannot think of their own ideas.)
5. Have students cut each segment of their storyboards and pictures apart. Then switch stories between pairs of students. See whether the second student can match the picture with the matching sentences, then arrange pictures and sentences in correct sequence.

RESOURCES

Sequential Picture Cards
Sets I, II, III, IV
Developmental Learning Materials
Students who have difficulty sequencing their ideas in writing may benefit from using these cards.
Set I contains ten series of three cards each. Each set shows a familiar scene that can be readily put into order.
Set II is a bit harder. The student must arrange a six-card series to show such activities as riding a sled, helping in the house, getting dressed, and going to school.
Set III features six-card series on topics of growth, seasonal and twenty-four hour changes, and food production.
Set IV cards are geared to a higher level of interest and feature space travel, teen-age activities, and ecology topics.

Open Sequence Cards
Developmental Learning Materials
Eighteen different sequencing situations are presented in incomplete form in this set. The student must insert the missing part in the correct space and tell (or write) about the sequence.

Photo Sequential Cards
Developmental Learning Materials
These full-color photographs show a series of sequential activities which students can arrange in order. Students can use them as a stimulus for "What will happen next?" stories, or "What happened before this picture was taken?" or "Why is this happening?"

Multi-Ethnic Sequential Cards and Tape
Developmental Learning Materials
The themes of these five-card stories are holidays or festivals of different cultures.

Sequential Strips
Developmental Learning Materials
Four different picture sequences show a story without words. Students can explain the sequence both in oral and written expression. The four sequences are "Eating Out," "My Special Friend," "Making Pizza," and "Fish for Breakfast."

Photo Sequence Cards
Modern Education Corporation
The *Photo Sequence Cards* come in three sets: Occupations, Recreation, and Daily Living. There are ten different sequences in each set, with four pictures in each sequence. Picture size is 8-½" x 11".

Picture Sequence Cards
Modern Education Corporation
The *Picture Sequence Cards* show indoor and outdoor events in a sequence of four pictures. One set shows a masked robber holding up a banker, running away from the scene, being arrested by a police officer, and finally sitting in a jail cell. Students sequence the pictures and then write a description of each scene. They can also draw the scenes on storyboards, then write their description next to the picture.

Photo Stories
Houghton Mifflin
Levels 1, 2, and 3 contain five sets of photographs which can be arranged in order by the student. The student can then tell or write a story about the pictured event.

Figure 3–2
Storyboard

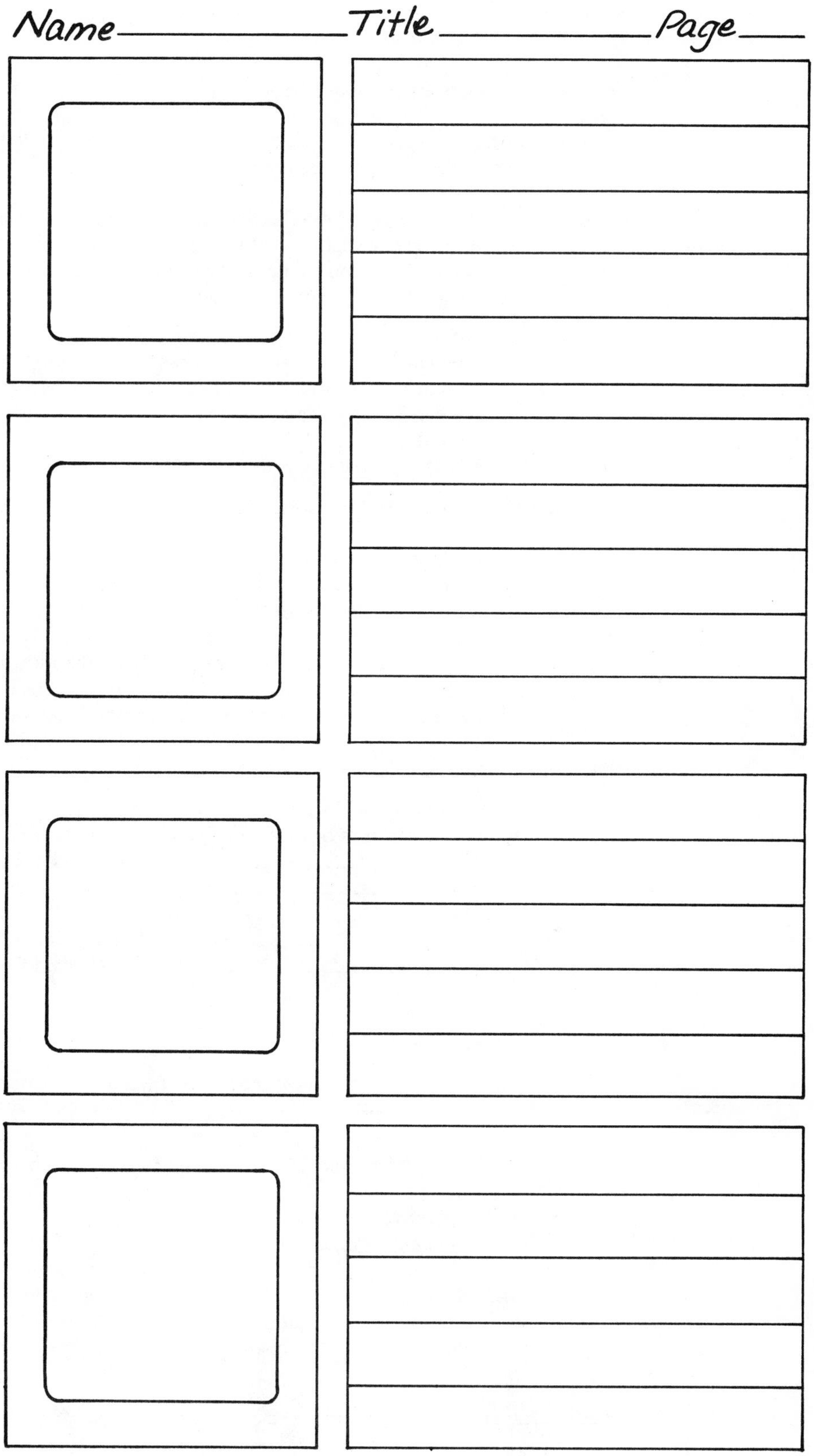

Name—————————*Title*—————————*Page*———

Creatures, Monsters, and Dragons

OBJECTIVE   To create an imaginary creature or monster.

MATERIALS   List of creatures identified in *Kickle Snifters and Other Fearsome Creatures,* or *Professor Wormbog in Search for the Zipperump A Zoo.*

PROCEDURE

1. Give a copy of the list to each student. Read over the names of the creatures. Have each student pick his or her favorite creature and tell what it might be like. Read a few sample descriptions from the suggested books.
2. Ask questions as students describe a creature.

   - What unusual features does this creature have?
   - Where does it live, and what does its home look like?
   - What kind of disposition does this creature have? (friendly, angry, moody, dangerous, etc.)
   - What does it eat?
   - What unusual habits does it have?

3. Have students choose one creature and write a newspaper report that provides information about the creature, where and when it was first identified, and what the local government plans to do about it.
4. Have students share their reports with class members, If students have used a creature name from one of the suggested resources, compare their description with the original description written by the authors. Which student came closest to the original description? How were student descriptions different? Explain that all writers think differently so all descriptions will be different.
5. Make a creature and monster book complete with illustrations.

EXTENSION 1   *Follow-up Installments*

Extend the lesson in following days by having students write follow-up installments about their creature or monster. Try some of these titles:

The _____ is Captured
The _____ Escapes
The _____ Meets the President
The _____ Finds a Mate
The _____ Goes to School
The _____ Joins the Swim Team

EXTENSION 2   *Creature Point of View*

Have students write a newspaper report from the creature's point of view.

RESOURCES

Kickle Snifters and Other Fearsome Creatures
Alvin Schwartz
J. B. Lippincott Co., 1976
    Here's a sampling of Schwartz's fantastic creatures:

Snawfus	Glytodont
Squonk	Tripodero

Goofus Bird	Squidigicum-Squee
Rubberado	Hoopajuba
Lufferland	Kickle Snifters

Professor Wormbog in Search for the Zipperump-a-Zoo
Mercer Mayer
Golden Press, 1976

Comic Strips

OBJECTIVE   To sequence and write about a comic strip.

MATERIALS   A collection of comic strips taken from newspapers or from comic books, writing paper, index cards or construction paper.

1. Cut comic strips apart into individual frames and place each strip in an envelope.
2. Have each student choose an envelope, read the separate frames, then arrange the frames in the correct order. Paste, tape, or staple each frame to a separate sheet of paper.
3. Have students write a narration of the action in each frame of the comic strip underneath the individual frame.
4. Bind pages together in booklet form.
5. Or, put each frame on a separate 4" x 6" index card. Have the student write the narration of each frame underneath the comic frame.
6. Mix up cards and give to another student to read and arrange in correct order.

EXTENSION   Remove "speech" part of cartoon. Have students write in new discussion between the characters in the comic strip.

RESOURCES

Comics Reading Library
King Features
    Eight different full-color comics are included in this kit. Puzzle and game pages emphasize important reading skills, including using context clues, predicting outcomes, making inferences, and others. Beetle Bailey, The Phantom, Blondie, and Popeye are some of the characters included in the series. Specially designed with reluctant readers in mind.

Super A and **Super B**
Science Research Associates
    Batman, Wonder Woman, Super-man are some of the heroes in *Super A* and *B*. Reluctant readers, as well as avid readers, enjoy the stories in the four different readers in each kit. Vocabulary is carefully controlled for reading levels which range from grade two to grade four. Spirit master activity sheets and task cards accompany the kits.

Comics
Houghton Mifflin
    Three separate books, entitled *Comics*, are written at three different reading levels.

Slide-Tape Show

OBJECTIVE   To develop a slide-tape show.

MATERIALS   A selection of library books, storyboards (slide size frames), Kodak write-on slides, projection marking pens.

PROCEDURE
1. Explain that students are going to make their own slide-tape show based on a children's storybook. (Later, students may want to use this format to do a book report on their own reading.) Plan to take several weeks to a month for this project depending on class size. Emphasize the need to have a clear plan and script completed before the slides and tapes are produced.
2. Let students choose a book for making a slide-tape show. The book may be a picture storybook on an easier reading level in which there is a clear sequence of events, or it may be grade-level reading material.
3. Ask students to read books and note sequence of events. For each main event, have the student draw one picture on the storyboard, then write the narration beside it. Have them read sequence out loud to another person to see whether it makes sense and enough information is presented.
4. Give blank slides to students and let them trace or draw the sequence of events following the storyboard plan.
5. Make the audio portion of the program. Include sound effects when appropriate. Sound effects records are generally available in the school or local library. Play some introductory music, then turn the music down as the student reads the narrative. Use a clicker to indicate when the slide should be changed. You may have to do the taping session two or three times to get the music and reading in the best form.

6. Show the completed production to the whole class. Invite other classes in to see the shows.

EXTENSION 1   *Slide Tape—How To*

Ask several students to do a slide-tape sequence on how to make a slide-tape show. Use it as an introductory lesson for other students.

EXTENSION 2   *Transparency-Tape Show*

Use overhead transparencies for students who have difficulty drawing on the small space of the write-on slides. Follow the same procedures as above, but let students use 8" x 10" blank drawing paper to plan their scenes.

RESOURCES

Animating Films Without a Camera
Jacques Bourgeois
Sterling Publishing Co., 1974
  Simple techniques for making animated films are described in detail in this book. Designs, characters, and sequences of events are drawn directly on ordinary movie film. Photographs and line drawings clearly illustrate the process.

Film Animation as a Hobby
Andrew and Mark Hobson
Sterling Publishing Co., 1975
  This book takes you step by step through the planning and shooting of a complete animated film. Lots of helpful hints are provided along the way. Photographs throughout the book illustrate the process clearly. Andrew and Mark Hobson started making animated films while they were doing a geometry project in high school.

Moviemaking Illustrated: The Comicbook Filmbook
James Morrow and Murray Suid
Hayden Book Co., 1973
  This is a book about how films work. Comicbook style is used to explain different film techniques such as speed changes, and picture size enlargement or reduction. This book would be interesting for older students who might be interested in special effects and other filming techniques.

Classroom Projects Using Photography
Vol. I, Vol. II
Eastman Kodak Company, 1975
  Many of the activities in these two manuals involve writing in some form: making notes on a problem, writing captions, writing out directions, writing dialogues, and others. Each activity is illustrated with color photographs.

Scene I, Scene II, Scene III

OBJECTIVE   To write about a sequence of events.

MATERIALS   Newspaper or magazine pictures that show characters involved in an activity or problem situation.

PROCEDURE
1. Choose one picture to show to the students. Ask students to identify the main characters and the setting. Write this information on the board. Decide what must have happened *before* the picture was taken. Write students' comments on the board under the title "Scene I."
2. Discuss what was happening at the time the picture was taken. Write comments on the board under "Scene II."
3. Discuss what the *outcome* of the situation might be. Write comments under "Scene III."
4. Ask students to write a story based on the information discussed using the "Scene I," "Scene II," and "Scene III" format.
5. Or, have students choose a new picture and write a story using the "Scene I," "Scene II," and "Scene III" format.
6. Have students read their stories out loud.
7. Allow students to illustrate their stories.

Figure 3-3
Scene I, Scene II, Scene III

Characters: _____

Character Description
_____
_____
_____   _____
_____
_____   _____
_____
_____   _____
_____

Setting Description

Setting: _____   _____
_____

Scene I: _____
_____
_____
_____
_____
_____

Scene II: _____
_____
_____
_____
_____

Scene III: _____
_____
_____
_____
_____
_____

Story Starters

OBJECTIVE   To write original story starters.

MATERIALS   Several samples of story starters.

PROCEDURE
1. Read a number of story starters to the students. (There are a number of different kinds of story starters. Some consist of only a sentence or two, others provide more detailed beginnings which include character and setting detail, as well as a problem. For this activity, use the longer variety.)
2. Ask students to note the common elements in the story starters.
   a. characters
   b. setting
   c. problem
3. Ask students to explain why the story starters ended where they did.
4. Ask students to make up a story starter on their own. Remind them to include a character, setting detail and a problem situation in which the character or characters must make a decision. Do not have them complete the story.
5. Have students read their original story starters to the class. Have class members listen to see whether required elements are included.
6. Have students copy story starters on large index cards. Suggest that they illustrate the card, too. Put these in a class story starter box. On another day, let students choose a story starter from the box and write an ending.

EXTENSION 1   *Stop the Action*

Read an exciting short story to the class. Stop at the point the character or characters must make a decision that will affect the rest of the story. Have students write an ending to the story. Read students' endings and compare with original ending.

Have students choose a picture from the picture file and write a story starter based on characters and action in the picture. Have students stop writing at the decision point in the story. Put these story starters on cards and clip them to the picture. Let other students choose the picture that interests them and finish the story.

Figure 3-4
Sample Story Starter:
From *Stories*
You Can Finish

THE LOST RIVERBOAT

Cast of Characters:

Jerry Todd	— a wiry bayou boy
Edith Todd	— his younger sister
Tate Magoun	— engineer of the *S.S. General Jackson* who was burned about the face horribly in a boiler explosion
Gail Magoun	— his deaf-mute sister, who lives with him on the boat
Caliban	— the Magouns' blood-eyed, pet alligator

* * * * * * * * * * * *

"Shhhhhhhhhh."

Jerry pushed the Spanish moss aside with his boat pole. Edith, his sister, stopped trailing her hand in the water and leaned forward.

"It's there," whispered Jerry. "Look at that huge paddle. It's two stories high."

The big riverboat lay in a lake of moonlight. Vines crawled over its crumbling decks. Its thin iron stacks were lifeless.

"Look!"

A light winked in the pilot house, then vanished. High in the cypress trees, an owl said whooooooooooo. Then a cloud scrubbed out the stars. Jerry pushed on the pole. The dingy slid alongside the rotted hulk, leaving a glitter of phosphorus.

"Throw the rope, Edith."

They pulled themselves onto a mossy deck. Here the ruin was total—broken deck chairs, smashed doors. Jerry took an old life preserver from its cradle and read the dim words printed on it.

"*S.S. General Jackson*," he said. "Say! That's the showboat that vanished on the Mississippi in 1928!"

"Wasn't it carrying the payroll for Fort Perkins—in gold?" said Edith.

They stepped inside. At that moment, a voice—ragged as a rusty razor—shouted, "You there!"... Edith screamed.

Special permission granted by "Stories You Can Finish," published by Xerox Education Publications © 1962, Xerox Corp.

RESOURCES

Reasons for Writing
Connie Markey
Curriculum Associates

Reasons for Writing is a collection of fifty different activities (stories, poetry, and grammar ideas) for students in the intermediate grades. One activity is to write a story about a 24-hour mission to catch the largest alligator possible without any equipment!

Story Starters—Primary
Story Starters—Intermediate
George Moore and G. Woodruff

Curriculum Associates

Each set of thirty-two cards consists of a beginning sentence and four sequenced questions. The questions help students organize their writing.

A Child-Centered Language Arts Program
P. Hewitt-Buell
Curriculum Associates

The eighty-seven cards in this program present activities for oral language, written language, and role playing.

"We interrupt this broadcast to bring you. . ."

Recipes for Creative Writing
Springboards to Creative Writing
Storystarters, Set I and Set II
Creative Teaching Press

Four different kits which provide quick suggestions for story starters, plot ideas, adventures, and make-believe situations for intermediate grades. Students may use cards from these kits independently or in small groups.

Stories You Can Finish
Xerox Education Publications

This small collection of story beginnings encourages students to deal with character, setting, and plot development. Students will like the stories!

Expressions
Harcourt Brace Jovanovich

Seventy self-motivating activity cards encourage students to express themselves in words as well as actions. Art, music, dance, drama, creative writing, photography, film making, and architectural and industrial design are all covered on various cards within the set. The illustrations and photography are very well done.

Animal Box
Special Days Box
Monster Box
Serpent Box
Detective Box
Resources for the Gifted

The Coal Bin has developed a number of activity boxes useful for motivating students to write. Two primary level boxes (*Animal Box* and *Special Days Box*) include one hundred teacher cards on twenty different themes.

Three intermediate level boxes include sixty activity cards for student use, twenty "how to" cards for teacher use, and a large color poster. Titles of these boxes are *Monster Box, Serpent Box,* and *Detective Box.*

Open-Ended Stories
Milton Velder and Edwin Cohen
Globe Book Co.

Twenty unfinished stories that appeal to adolescent readers and writers. Subjects include modern social problems, the search for identity, values, friendships, generation gaps, and running from reality. The reading level is about grades four/ five, but the interest level is much higher.

Open-Ended Plays
Milton Velder, Edwin Cohen, and Elaine Mazzarelli
Globe Book Co.

Twenty short plays which present young people with problems and conflicts—but no solutions! Students must supply endings for the scripts.

What Happens Next? Stories to Finish for Intermediate Writers
Andrew D. Washton
Teachers College Press, 1978

This book uses the unfinished story technique to encourage creative writing. Forty different story starters feature characters and the beginning of a plot.

Titles, Topics, and Twisters

OBJECTIVE   To write a story using a "title," "topic," or "twister" for young children.

MATERIALS   Collection of children's storybooks, list of topics, "Title Twisters."

PROCEDURE
1. Write the titles of a number of children's picturebooks or short storybooks on the board. Try to find unusual and interesting titles that will spark students' imaginations. (Or, have students go to picturebook section of the library and each find three titles that are interesting.)
2. Choose one title and ask students what they think the book might be about. Let a number of students volunteer about a title Read the book to students and have them compare their own ideas with the author's ideas. Repeat this procedure with a number of books.
3. Let students choose a title and write a story or small book. Encourage them to draw pictures to illustrate their story. Bind the pages of the final draft together to make a storybook.
4. Have students find the original book in the library or classroom and compare the author's story to their own. Have students read stories aloud to class, then take

their books to younger grades to read out loud.

5. Place the new books in the school or classroom library. Have students prepare a library file card and a sign-out card for their books.

RESOURCES   A number of *title twisters* are available from Resources for the Gifted. Title wheels are 16" x 20".

Monster Wheel (256 possible titles)
Serpent Wheel (256 possible titles)
Detective Wheel (256 possible titles)

Primary Wheels
   Once Upon a Time (100 possible titles)
   Let's Pretend (100 possible titles)

Intermediate Wheels

Secondary Wheels
   Time Machine Wheel (256 possible titles)
   Wild Wheels Wheel (256 possible titles)
   Insights

Alligator Antics

OBJECTIVE   To brainstorm uses of unlikely subjects or items.

MATERIALS   A selection from *100 Ways to Have Fun With an Alligator.*

PROCEDURE
1. Ask students what they would do with an alligator if they had one. Encourage them to think of different or unusual responses. Read several examples to them from *100 Ways to Have Fun With an Alligator.*

   Examples:
   let him play first base on the Little League team,
   tickle him with a long stick,
   take him sky diving,
   use him as a surfboard,
   teach him to juggle in a circus.

2. Write student suggestions on the board as they mention them. Accept all ideas. (Review brainstorming procedures suggested in the introduction to this chapter.)
3. Let students draw pictures of an alligator activity. Put them up on the bulletin board with short description of what is happening.
4. Or, bind the pictures and the written descriptions in a book titled *100 Ways to Have Fun With an Alligator.*

EXTENSION 1   Try to find other books on alligators or crocodiles. Many have interesting titles, and students might like to invent their own story for a title. Put several different titles on the board and let students choose one that interests them. They may choose to do a series of alligator or crocodile stories.

EXTENSION 2   Have an "Alligator and Crocodile Week." Read lots of alligator and crocodile books, and have students write and illustrate stories about alligators and crocodiles.

RESOURCES   100 Ways to Have Fun With an Alligator & 100 Other Involving Arts Projects   *Norman Laliberte and Richey Kehl*
Art Education, 1969

Telephone Conversations

OBJECTIVE   To write dialogues of telephone conversations.

MATERIALS   Sample telephone conversation, tape recorder.

PROCEDURE

1. Give students a copy of the sample telephone conversation. Ask two students to choose parts and read it to the class.
2. Discuss the various kinds of telephone conversations that students have. Make a list of their suggestions on the board. Add some suggestions provided below.
3. Have students work in pairs and choose a topic for a telephone conversation, then role play the conversation. Tape record the conversation.
4. Play back the tape and have students write down the dialogue that they have just acted out.
5. Have student pairs read their telephone conversations to the whole class.

SAMPLE TELEPHONE CONVERSATION

Tommy: Hello, is Ralph there?

Woman: Who is this please?

Tommy: I'm Tommy, Ralph's friend from school.

Woman: Just a minute. Ralph is upstairs in his room doing his school work.

Ralph: Hi Tommy. What are you doing?

Tommy: Nothing right now. Let's go swimming.

Ralph: OK. Where shall we go?

Tommy: Let's go to the pool at the high school.

Ralph: Do we have to take a bus or a train to get there?

Tommy: We have to take a bus to the high school. It stops at the corner near my house.

Ralph: OK. What time do we meet and where?

Tommy: Let's meet at my house at 4:00 sharp. Don't be late. The session starts at 4:30 and I don't want to miss any time.

Ralph: OK. I'll get my bathing suit and leave in a few minutes. I'll see you at 4:00 on the nose.

Tommy: See you later. Good-bye.

Ralph: Bye.

TOPICS FOR TELEPHONE CONVERSATIONS

Let's Go to the Movies

Did You See the Fight Today?

I'm Being Punished

What was the Final Score?

Let's Go Hiking (or other sport)

Why was She Crying?

I'm Not Feeling Well Today

Do You Like Your New School?

My Tooth Fell Out Today

It's a Surprise Party

I Just Got a Good Job

I Found Some Money

I Just Won a Prize

Do You Like Our New Teacher?

Help Me with My Homework

Emergency Calls

House on Fire

Car Accident

Robbery

Child Lost

EXTENSION 1 *Telephones*

Borrow telephone training units from the telephone company. This set includes two real telephones and a small control box for making the phones ring or give the busy signal. Practice making emergency calls on them.

EXTENSION 2 *Play Dialogue*

Use simple dialogues to lead into play reading and writing. Start out with the two-character "Echo Plays" and then move on to other plays which have more characters.

When People Talk on the Telephone,
Books A and B
R. Turner
Teachers College Press
    This book presents a collection of sample telephone conversations.

Plays for Echo Reading
D. Durrell, L. DeMilia
Harcourt Brace Jovanovich
    A good collection of two-character plays with controlled reading vocabulary. Good for use in primary grades or with older remedial readers and writers. Records are also available so students can listen, then echo the lines for practice.

Read and Act
C. Unsworth
Xerox Education Publications
    This booklet has several short plays for oral reading. Although the plays are written at a high second grade level, they can be used for remedial readers in the intermediate grades (4–5).

The Story Plays: Self-Directing Materials
for Oral Reading
D. Rector and M. Rector
Harcourt Brace Jovanovich
    A series of short four-character plays with each part written at a different reading level. For elementary grade readers.

Plays for Reading Progress I, II, III
Educational Progress Corporation

Three separate kits provide multiple copies of plays for students with varying reading levels. The reading level of each character is charted so the teacher may easily match reading levels and roles.

Stage Door
J. Williams
Xerox Education Publications
    A series of ten short plays written at a fourth grade reading level. Older students enjoy them, too.

Raise the Curtain
C. Herrman, W. Lefkowitz, and
J. Mongillo
Xerox Education Publications
    Several short plays written at approximately a third grade reading level. Good to use with remedial readers in grades four and five.

Plays for Laughs and
More Plays for Laughs
J. Matus
Xerox Education Publications
    Two booklets which contain a collection of two-page comical plays. Themes are based on everyday experiences. Appropriate for grades five through eight.

Short Plays I and II
Scripts I, II, and III
Houghton Mifflin
    Each booklet contains several plays or scripts for acting out. For grades four and above.

Journals

OBJECTIVE   To encourage personal writing through the use of a journal.

MATERIALS   Looseleaf notebook, notebook dividers, notebook filler paper, copies of categories and guide questions.

PROCEDURE
1. Ask students to purchase a looseleaf notebook, dividers, and paper. Explain that each student will start a journal that will be used *at least* twice a week for writing on different topics of personal importance. Each topic will have its own section in the notebook.
2. Have students label each divider with a topic category (see following list). Use fewer categories with younger writers, then add categories as needed. For older writers, use all categories. Have students keep all blank filler paper in back of notebook. Paper can be added to category sections when needed.
3. Give students a list of the categories and related questions. Ask them to complete the personal identification information for the front of the journal. Explain that writing in notebooks will not be graded but that it may be reviewed occasionally to be sure students are writing.
4. Have students decide on a category to write on for the first journal session. (At first, schedule specific journal writing sessions. Later, as students become more

familiar with the process, let them schedule their own writing time. Encourage students to write in journals as often as possible.)

5. Provide some time for students to share their writing with small groups.
6. Have students keep a log of entries (like a table of contents) in which they record the date and kind of entry. Keep this in the front of the journal.

EXTENSION   Some library books are written from the first person point of view. Have students identify some of these books and notice how the main character talks about his feelings and attitudes. Fill out a character grid for the main character. (See Characters I activity.)

SUGGESTED CATEGORIES

Too often student journal writing falls into a tedious accounting of "what I did today." While this is occasionally acceptable, it is more important to have students think, review, and compare broader ranges of experience. As they remember and sort ideas, reactions, and feelings about these suggested categories, they will uncover raw material for journal writing and for later writing activities. Duplicate this list of categories so students may refer to it when ever they write. Have them choose only *one* question per writing session. Encourage students to add other topics or questions to the list.

About Myself

Who Am I?

What do I look like?
What do I like? Why?
What do I dislike? Why?
What do I like best about myself?
What do I like least about myself?
What things do I do well?
What things are difficult for me?

My Feelings: What causes this feeling? What do I do when I have this feeling?

Fear
Anger
Sadness
Happiness
Jealousy
Pride
Worry
Hate

Memories: What is the memory? How did I feel then? How do I feel about it now?

My Earliest Memory
My Happiest Memory
My Saddest Memory
My Angriest Memory
My Biggest Decision
My Biggest Mistake
My First Punishment at Home
My First Punishment at School

Important Events

First Day of School
Birthdays
Christmases
Holidays
Vacations
Others?

Leisure Time Activities

My Hobbies
My Favorite Activity
My Favorite TV Program, Movie, Book
My Favorite Sport
What Do I Do When I Am Alone?

Dreams: What dreams do you remember?

My Future

What I Will Be Like in the Future
My Hopes for the Future
My Education Plans
My Career Plans

About My Family

Who Are My Family Members?
What do they look like?
What kind of persons are they? Give examples of things they do
that show what kind of persons they are.
Who is my best friend?
Who is my enemy? Why?
About Others
Who are the other important people in my life?

Autobiography

OBJECTIVE   To write an illustrated autobiography.

MATERIALS   Writing paper and drawing paper, colored pencils, crayons, magic markers.

PROCEDURE   1. Plan to do this activity after students have written a number of entries in their journals.
2. Discuss important factors in the lives of the students.

Past: birth, first day at school, first birthday party

Present: life at school, life at home, friends

Future: graduation, occupation choice, marriage, children, future plans

3. Ask students to suggest other factors that affect their personal lives. Add these to the list.
4. Ask students to illustrate these events and write a narration for each event. (Each event can be a separate chapter in the autobiography and can be done on a different day.) Some students may choose to use the storyboard format. Students may choose to revise something already in their journals or they may write totally new pieces.
5. Have students put the events in order according to their life span and make a table of contents to go along with the sequence.
6. This activity will take several weeks to complete. Encourage children to make corrections as they go along so that the task does not become overwhelming at the end.
7. After revising and editing their autobiography, have students make a cover for the autobiography, then bind it.

EXTENSION   Make up a fictitious character and write a biography for him or her. Include past events, present circumstances, and future hopes. These biographies can be realistic or they can be imaginary and humorous. The title of the book can be a reflection of the character's name.

Suggestions: "My Life as a Chimney Sweep"
by Charlie Broom

"My Life as a Star of Stage and Screen"
by Miss Star Let
"The Life and Times of a Female Detective"
by Ima Spy

Other possible characters:

Ima June Bug	Cal Q. Lator
Tillie Tightwad	Cal Lifornia
Mr. G. Whizz	Luke Warm
Lala Palooza	Ben E. Fit
Ima Phoney	Tom Ato
Sam Sonite	Rose Bud
Miss Ann Thrope	Neb Raska
Ella Fant	Ida Ho
Leo Pard	Carol Lina
Ana Mul	Connie Tecut
Brock Alie	Ari Zona
Lillie Tiger	Mary Land
Ann Teak	Minnie Apolis
Cora Apple	Fran Cisco
Ella Vator	Prince Apal
May O. Naise	

Zany Stories

OBJECTIVE To write a story when character, setting, time, situation, and style are given.

MATERIALS Three inch by five inch index cards of different colors, lists of characters, settings, time, events, and style.

PROCEDURE
1. Choose five colors of index cards or construction paper. Write the suggested phrases for each category on a different color card. Do not mix the sets of cards. Include the style category when working with more sophisticated writers.
2. Place cards on the table in the different groups. Ask each student to draw one card from each pile, read the card, then try to develop a Zany Story with the given character, setting, time, situation. All information on the selected cards must be included in the story. Develop several stories orally with the group so that students get the idea.
3. Next have students select one card from each category for their own written story. Provide any spelling words that students think they might need *before* they start writing.
4. Allow students to choose an additional character to make the story even crazier.
5. Have students share completed stories by reading to a small group of classmates.
6. Continue working on the stories on another day. Ask students to proofread stories and make necessary corrections, then copy stories in preparation for making a class collection of Zany Stories. You may want to put these stories on duplicating masters so that each student can have his or her own collection of stories. Have students illustrate their Zany Stories, then bind stories and illustrations in a book form. Present a copy of the book to the school library.

EXTENSION Ask students to add other characters, settings, times, and situations to the card sets.

characters	*settings*
a humanized robot	a musty attic
an old man	a haunted house

a timid muscleman
a lion tamer
Superman
Mighty Mouse
a man of super-human strength
a frightened ghost
a greedy goblin
an early pioneer
a microscopic person
an astronaut
an old maid school teacher
a grumpy principal
a mischievous child
a mad scientist
a chemistry genius
a whiz kid
a nosy reporter
an army sergeant
a hobo
a sheriff
a pirate

a mucky swamp
a deserted island
an abandoned graveyard
on another planet
in another galaxy
in outer space
in a rocket ship
in a stage coach
in a movie theater
on a safari
on a movie set
in a hayloft on a farm
in a space capsule
in a playroom
on a hang glider
in a skyscraper
on a mule caravan
in a football stadium
in a crowded department store
on a sinking ship
in an imaginary world
in a foreign country

time

in the far future
in the year 2000
in the year 1000
in the present
in pioneer days
at midnight
at high noon
New Year's Eve
Halloween
April Fool's Day
Christmas
dawn
at sunset
at dinner time
during prehistoric times
at the Boston Tea Party
on Election day
on your birthday

event

being chased by a shark
losing something valuable
winning a prize
having a fight
finding a million dollars
flying an airplane
being arrested
falling in love
being robbed
hunting a lion
having an accident
getting lost
being trapped in a time machine
getting married
first day at school
first day at work
a birthday party
joining a parade
going on a camping trip
discovering gold

style (optional)

drama
comedy
soap opera
narrative
play
newspaper report

poem
dialogue
interview
children's storybook
T.V. guide article

Fables

OBJECTIVE   To write a fable.

MATERIALS   Several published fables.

PROCEDURE
1. Write several morals from fables on the board. Ask students whether they know where these sayings have come from. If no one knows, tell them about Aesop and how he told stories that were intended to teach a lesson. Point out that Aesop did not write his fables down, but told them to many people. Eventually someone wrote them down.
2. Read several fables to the students. For each one ask the following questions. List answers on the board.
   Who are the characters?
   What problem developed?
   How was the main character fooled?
   What lesson did the characters learn? (moral)
3. Ask students to suggest other fables that they are familiar with. List these on the board and read the known fables and their morals to the class. Make a list of morals on the board. Ask students to explain what the morals mean.
4. Ask students to choose one saying and make up a story to go with it. Students who have difficulty writing may choose to write about one of the fables outlined on the board.
5. Have students illustrate their stories, then share them by reading out loud to the class. Use Untermeyer's version as a model for illustration of fables.
6. Display fables and drawings on bulletin board, or collect and bind in book form.

EXTENSION 1   Have pairs of students choose a fable and act it out for the class members. Some may choose to pantomime the fable. Have students guess the moral and the fable.

EXTENSION 2   Compare several different versions of the same fable and have students notice differences in style and wording.

RESOURCES

Aesop's Fables
adapted by Louis Untermeyer
Golden Press, 1966
   This collection of forty fables features full-page color illustrations of the sequence of entire fables. Students may use some of these as a model to illustrate their own fables.

Aesop's Fables
(Large Type Edition)
Franklin Watts, Inc.
   This extensive collection of fables is illustrated with black and white line drawings.

Three Aesop Fox Fables
Paul Galdone
The Seabury Press, 1971
   Paul Galdone cleverly illustrates "The Fox and the Grapes," "The Fox and the Stork," and "The Fox and the Crow."

Fables of Aesop
More Fables of Aesop, *1974*
Jack Kent
Parent's Magazine Press
   Lovely art work adds to the retelling of these fables. Younger students will enjoy reading these fables and looking at the amusing pictures.

Fables and Folktales
Webster Division
McGraw Hill, 1972
   Students will enjoy listening to or reading these fables. Vocabulary building activities are included.

Old Tales 1&2
Folktales 1&2
Fables
Legends
Myths
Houghton Mifflin
   These booklets are written at different reading levels, so you can choose the most appropriate ones for your students' reading abilities.

OBJECTIVE   To listen for character detail as a descriptive selection is read.

MATERIALS   Selections from reading material with good descriptive character detail (see suggested books with good character description); "Character Grid" on overhead transparency.

PROCEDURE   1. Review the items on the "Character Grid" so students will know what to listen for.
2. Read a character description and have students listen for character details.
3. Ask students to recall details after the selection has been read. Write details on the grid as students suggest them.
4. Read the selection again if students missed some of the details. Have students listen specifically for the information needed.
5. Have students try to visualize the character and make suggestions about information that was not included in the reading selection.
6. Have students write a short descriptive paragraph about the character using information provided on the grid. Share paragraphs by reading aloud. The students may draw a picture of the character if they wish.

EXTENSION   Have students look for descriptive detail as they read their library books. Encourage them to use the character grid to collect information as it appears in different places in the book. Then have them write a descriptive paragraph about the main characters. Illustrate. Keep completed character grids with the character descriptive paragraph. Display final draft of description on bulletin board to show how details can be incorporated into descriptive paragraph.

RESOURCES   **Who's Who in Children's Books:**
A Treasury of Familiar Characters
of Childhood
Margery Fisher
Holt, Rinehart and Winston, 1975
    Margery Fisher presents some characters from children's literature that have become favorites with young readers (primary and elementary grades). In *Who's Who* she depicts both real and imaginary characters, providing details of their appearance and the settings in which they live, as well as the particular circumstances of the story in which they appear. This book is useful to the teacher and the elementary student, as both can peruse the volume to read capsulized information about a character or to discover new characters to read about.

Figure 3–4
Character Description Grid

1. Name of character_____Age _____
                                                (young, old, teen-age, etc.)
2. Size (height, weight, shape) _____
3. Hairstyle and color_____
4. Eyes (color, size, shape) _____
5. Style of dress _____
   (clothing)

   _____
6. Speech characteristics _____
   (accent, stutter, loud voice, etc.)
7. Manner of movement _____
   (graceful, clumsy, awkward, etc.)

   _____
8. Personality clues _____
   (friendly, mean, kind, etc.)

   _____
9. Hopes, desires, dreams _____
10. Occupation and work habits_____
    (always on time, hard worker, etc.)

    _____
11. Anything else? _____

The Mysterious Disappearance of Leon (I mean Noel)
Ellen Raskin
Dutton, 1971

Lots of interesting (peculiar?) people appear in this book. Have the students track down all the information about the following characters: Mrs. Corillon (at age five, twelve, nineteen, and thirty-nine), Mrs. Baker, Mr. Banks, and Augie Kunkel.

The Tatooed Potato and Other Clues
Ellen Raskin
Dutton, 1975

Dickory does not know what she is in for when she responds to the ad: "Wanted: Assistant to well-known portrait painters. Observant! Quiet!" She lands the job because of her precise observation ability. Through the course of the book, she meets a number of notorious or honorable characters—all of whom have unique personalities.

Harriet the Spy
Louise Fitzhugh
Harper and Row, 1964

Harriet, as the spy, maintains a list of interesting characters that she regularly spies on: Mrs. Plumber, the Del Santes at the grocery, Harrison Withers and his twenty-five cats, snobbish Mr. and Mrs. Robinson, and many others. Unfortunately, Harriet's friends manage to read her very honest, sometimes cruel notes, and Harriet's life suddenly changes—for the *worse*.

Sounder
William H. Armstrong
Harper and Row, 1969

The poor, black sharecropper's boy learns to handle sorrow, humiliation, and anger as his father is taken by the indignant sheriff and his deputies for stealing food for his hungry family. Sounder, the loyal coon dog, is shot when he chases the sheriff's wagon.

The Witch of Blackbird Pond
Elizabeth George Speare
Houghton Mifflin, 1958

Kit Tyler causes quite a stir after she arrives in puritan New England, in 1687. Raised on the island of Barbados, Kit's lifestyle is markedly different from her cousin's with whom she must now live. This story tells how Kit maintains her spirit and independence, yet learns to compromise on the day-to-day necessities of life.

Speare's characters and settings are superb in this Newbery Award winning book.

The House of Sixty Fathers
Meindert de Jong
Harper and Row, 1956

Tien Pao, a young Chinese boy, is separated from his family during the Japanese occupation of China when the family's sampan breaks loose from its moorings and is caught in the current of the rushing river. Tien Pao and his pig, Glory of the Republic, bravely set out to find his family, along the way encountering and aiding a wounded American pilot. Eventually, the pilot and his sixty fellow pilots help Tien Pao find his family.

Tuck Everlasting
Natalie Babbitt
Farrar, Straus & Giroux, 1975

Winnie is kidnapped after she discovers the secret of the Tuck family: a magic spring that provides everlasting life. Both character and setting are superb in this book.

The Man Who Was Magic
Paul Gallico
Doubleday, 1966

Adam leaves home and travels to the magical city of Mageia to seek fame and fortune as a magician. The story is told with a wealth of character and setting description.

My Side of the Mountain
Jean George
Dutton, 1959

Sam Gribley leaves his home and family in New York to search for his great-grandfather's farm in the Catskills, determined to live there by himself. During his year in the mountains, Sam records his observations about plant and animal life, changes in the seasons, his daily struggles to find food, and he also adds his thoughts and feelings—which range from fear to complete self-satisfaction.

Characters II

OBJECTIVE   To write a character description.

MATERIALS   A collection of character pictures gathered from magazines; "Character Grid."

PROCEDURE
1. Ask students to cut out pictures of different people from magazines. Encourage students to look for a wide variety of facial expressions. News magazines (*Time*, *Newsweek*) and newspapers are a good source of candid photographs. *National Geographic* magazine and *Psychology Today* also have good character pictures. This could be done as a homework assignment or an in-class activity.
2. Review the information required on the character grid after a large number of pictures have been collected.
3. Choose one picture and talk about the prominent features of the pictured character. Write students' comments on the grid (on chalkboard or overhead transparency).
4. Discuss other characteristics of the character that cannot be seen in the picture (for example, personality clues, mannerisms, speech patterns). Have students suggest additional information about the character (for example, family structure, home, location of home, occupation).
5. Ask students to write a short descriptive paragraph about the character using some of the information listed on the character grid.
6. Have students read their descriptions to the rest of the class. Compare the ways different students wrote their descriptions.
7. Do this activity with different pictures on other days. Continue to have students write a short paragraph after each brainstorming session.

EXTENSION   After many brainstorming sessions, let each student choose a picture and do a character description on his or her own. Perhaps the students could involve the character in a sequence of events or a problem. Share descriptions with classmates.

Character Moods

OBJECTIVE   To make a collage showing character moods.

MATERIALS   Magazines, scissors, paste, construction paper.

PROCEDURE
1. Have students collect old magazines at home and bring them into school. Again, encourage them to look for a wide variety of emotional response.
2. Ask students to look through the magazines for pictures of characters showing different facial expressions and cut them out.
3. Categorize these pictures according to the expression: Happy, Sad, Angry, Worried, Surprised, Fearful, etc. Make a collage for each expression.
4. Take one completed collage at a time and ask students to suggest words that describe this mood. List clues that helped determine the mood of each picture.

      Worried: eyebrows knit, frown, thoughtful look; intent
      Surprised: eyes open wide, mouth open wide

    Encourage the use of a thesaurus. Ask students to use suggested words in complete sentences.
5. Display the collages and word charts on the bulletin board.

EXTENSION 1   Have students choose one character and mood, fill out a character grid, then write a few paragraphs that describe the character and the reason for the mood. Display final drafts of the paragraphs with their corresponding pictures.

EXTENSION 2   Have students role play an emotion. Have observers note what actions, mannerisms, and facial expressions aid in identifying the emotion portrayed.

RESOURCES   **The Many Faces of Children Posters**
Developmental Learning Materials
    Twelve posters, some color and some black and white, depict various adults and children in different situations—some happy, some lonely, some

watchful, and some sad. Students may use these as the basis for a discussion on feelings, facial and bodily expression, and familiar experiences.

The Many Faces of Youth Posters
Developmental Learning Materials
Twelve color and black and white poster photographs of teen-agers showing various emotions and situations are included in this set.

Understanding Our Feelings: Classroom Role Playing
William LaRue and Sydney LaRue
Century Communications
Stimulating photographs of children in different situations form the basis for class discussion and role playing sessions. The teacher's guide provides many suggestions for leading role playing sessions, and also provides many suggestions for follow-up writing activities (story starters and title suggestions).

Cartoon Characters

OBJECTIVE To identify exaggerated details in political cartoons.

MATERIALS Cartoons of political figures collected from editorial pages of newspapers, photographs of the same political figures.

PROCEDURE
1. Have students collect cartoons of different political figures from newspapers and news magazines. Also have them look for photographs of the characterized political figures.
2. Make a bulletin board display of the political cartoons. Arrange cartoons and photographs of each politician in a different group. Have students note the similarities and differences between the cartoons and photographs.
3. Choose one group of cartoons and photographs to discuss with the class. Ask students to note exaggerated features. Ask how the exaggeration helps in identifying the character. (Note that political cartoons rarely identify the characters but rely on the characterization to carry the message.)
4. Have students suggest descriptive words for the exaggerated features. List these on the board.
5. Have students write a short description of the character including some of the exaggerated details.
6. Share descriptions with class members by reading aloud. Post final drafts on the bulletin board next to the corresponding cartoons and photographs.

EXTENSION Ask interested students to try drawing some political cartoons.

Points of View

OBJECTIVE To identify and evaluate different points of view in a given situation.

MATERIALS Jones vs. boys situation.

PROCEDURE
1. Put the first situation (Jones vs. boys) on a ditto or overhead transparency. Have one student read the facts to the rest of the class.
2. Present Mr. Jones's point of view on ditto or transparency. Ask the following guide questions:
   What facts does Mr. Jones emphasize?
   What facts does he ignore?
   What emotionally charged words does he use?
3. Present the boys' point of view. Ask the same guide questions.
4. Ask students to write the story from the point of view of another neighbor (friendly or unfriendly), of the invalid mother, or of the boy who hit the ball through the window.

5. Have students write a report for the Chief of Police from the policeman's point of view. (Remind them that the policeman can only state the facts so his report must be very objective.)
6. Have students read final results to rest of class.

EXAMPLE: *JONES* vs. *BOYS: THE FACTS*

1. The boys play ball every afternoon and on Saturdays in the empty city-owned lot on Maple Street.
2. Mr. Jones lives with his invalid mother in the mansion next to the empty lot.
3. On Saturday the boys started a new baseball game. The score was 1 to 1. The boys were cheering, shouting, and yelling.
4. Bobby hit a foul ball that rolled over into Mr. Jones's flower garden. John went and picked up the ball.
5. Eddie hit a ball that went through Mr. Jones's window and broke a lamp. The boys did not run away.
6. Mr. Jones came out and yelled at the boys. Eddie apologized for breaking the window and the boys offered to pay for it.
7. Mr. Jones went back into the house yelling, "I'm going to call the police!"
8. A few minutes later the police arrived. Here are the stories that the policemen heard:

Mr. Jones's story:

That wretched, noisy gang of hooligans and troublemakers deliberately destroyed the prize-winning rose bushes that I have been cultivating for a long time. Then they shattered my plate glass window and their ball smashed my priceless antique lamp. Glass is all over the place. Besides that, they have been yelling and screaming all day and they know that my mother is an invalid and needs absolute quiet all the time. I want the police to make them get away from my property. They cause nothing but trouble.

Boys' story:

We don't know what he's so mad about. The ball only rolled into his flower garden and we didn't damage any of his plants when we got the ball. We did break the window, but we offered to pay for it. Mr. Jones is just a mean, old, selfish man. He always calls us names and blames us for everything that happens around here. He just wants to cause trouble for us because he doesn't want us to play here. But where else can we play?

EXTENSION 1 Bring several news articles into class and read them to the students. Ask them to choose a person in the story and write the story again from that person's point of view. Have them include emotional reactions and opinions. Encourage the deliberate use of emotionally charged words. Have students read their different versions aloud. Have class members identify differences of opinions, emotionally charged words, and emotional reactions. Compare student papers with the original newspaper story.

RESOURCES Points of View
Ann Elwood and John Raht
Globe Book Co.
This book provides excellent stories for use with this activity. Each selection is of interest to the adolescent and is told from two different view points. Suggestions for additional follow-up activities are given.

First Person Point of View

OBJECTIVE To identify tone and style of books that use the first person point of view.

MATERIALS A collection of library books written with first person point of view. (See list of titles at end of this activity.)

PROCEDURE

1. Collect the suggested library books and place them in one spot in the classroom.
2. Read some beginning paragraphs of the suggested books to students. Ask them to identify the main character. (Most often the name of the character will not be given right away—so students will only be able to say, "I.") Point out that this kind of story is told from the first person point of view as if the main character is telling the story him or herself. To point out the difference from other stories, read a few beginning paragraphs from several books that use the third person point of view.
3. Ask students to browse through the collection of first person books and select one for a book report.
4. Ask students to pay particular attention to the teller of the story. Have students complete a character grid (from Characters I Activity) as they read the story so they can get a complete picture of the main character.
5. Place all completed character grids on the bulletin board.
6. Focus on first person stories for at least a month. Ask students to identify the ages of the main characters. (They may make the observation that the majority of the stories deal with preteen-agers and teen-agers. Ask students to speculate on why that might be.) Ask students to identify any themes that might be common to the majority of the stories. Do these stories seem any more realistic than third person stories?
7. Ask the students to comment on their reactions to first person stories.

RESOURCES

The following books are all written from the first person point of view. Reading levels range from fourth to seventh grade levels while interest level range is fourth through eighth.

The Great Brain, *1967*
More Adventures of the Great Brain, *1969*
The Great Brain Does it Again, *1975*
Me and My Little Brain, *1971*
The Great Brain Reforms, *1973*
The Great Brain at the Academy, *1972*
Jack D. Fitzgerald
Dial Press

Tom Fitzgerald, self-proclaimed "Great Brain," outwits many people with his devilishly clever financial schemes, and most often he comes out of each adventure with money in his pocket. John Fitzgerald tells of his admiration for and annoyance with his brother's antics.

Are You There God? It's Me Margaret, *1970*
Deenie, *1973*
It's Not the End of the World, *1972*
Otherwise Known as Sheila the Great, *1976*
Tales of a Fourth Grade Nothing, *1976*
Judy Blume
Bradbury Press

Judy Blume writes first person stories which reflect the everyday concerns of fourth, fifth, and sixth grade girls.

And Now Miguel
Joseph Krumgold
Crowell, 1953

Miguel has reached the age where he desperately wants to take a role in the sheepherder's life. He tells of the many disappointments and hopes of the summer when he finally gets his wish.

No Applause Please
Marilyn Singer
Dutton, 1971

Ruthie and Laurie are best friends, that is until they win a contest and Laurie decides to become a professional singer.

A Girl Called Al
Constance C. Greene
Viking Press, 1969

This is a first person story about friends, growing up, and coping with loss.

Summer of My German Soldier
Bette Greene
Dial Press, 1973

Patty Bergen tells the story of the summer she met and aided an escaped prisoner of war, how this compounded her already unhappy family life, and how she manages to cope with the whole situation.

The King's Fifth
Scott O'Dell
Houghton Mifflin, 1966

The greed for gold led explorers on long journeys into unknown country. Esteban, a young map-maker, travels with some Spaniards in their dangerous quest for gold. He tells his story while he is imprisoned and gives flashbacks of scenes of his adventures.

Will the Real Monday Please Stand Up?
Pamela Reynolds
Lothrop, Lee & Shepard Co., 1975

Monday describes her attempts to sort out her conflicting feelings toward her family after she reports her brother for marijuana possession.

Island of the Blue Dolphins
Scott O'Dell
Houghton Mifflin, 1960

A young Indian girl is accidentally left on an island and spends eighteen years alone coping with the necessities of finding food and shelter and the wild dogs.

Onion John
Joseph Krumgold
Crowell, 1959

Andy tells about his friendship with Onion John, the local hobo, and the way his relationship with his father changes as they begin to disagree on how to help John.

It's Like This, Cat
Emily Neville
Harper and Row, 1963

Fourteen-year-old Dave Mitchell adopts a stray tomcat named Cat and gets caught up in many new adventures.

My Brother Sam is Dead
James Lincoln Collier and
Christopher Collier
Four Winds Press, 1974

A story of revolutionary times, in which Sam is shot for supposedly stealing the family cows.

The Truth About Mary Rose
Marilyn Sachs
Doubleday, 1973

Mary Rose finally succeeds in learning the sad truth about her Aunt Mary Rose whom she had idolized for so long.

Dorrie's Book
Marilyn Sachs
Doubleday, 1975

Dorrie's teacher allows her students to write a book instead of doing the usual unit on King Arthur. Her book tells about how her life changes when her mother gives birth to triplets.

Freaky Friday
Mary Rodgers
Harper and Row, 1972

Annabel Andrews, age thirteen, disorganized, sloppy, and behind in her homework, suddenly reforms after a one-day body switch with her mother. Annabel provides amusing descriptions of her experiences.

Dorp Dead
Julia Cunningham
Pantheon Books, 1965

Gilly Ground has a secret that nobody knows—not his dear grandmother, who has just died; not any of his various unfortunate teachers; and not the big, overstuffed Mrs. Heister at the orphanage. Gilly's secret is that he is ferociously intelligent, even though he's a very poor speller. Gilly tells of his survival both at the orphanage, and later in his foster home with the eccentric Mr. Kobalt.

Berries Goodman
Emily Neville
Harper and Row, 1965

Berries experiences his first taste of anti-Semitism in a suburb fifty miles out of New York City.

My Side of the Mountain
Jean George
Dutton, 1959

Sam Gribley records his adventures in the Catskills during the year he lived by himself.

Settings I

OBJECTIVE To listen for descriptive words and phrases in setting paragraphs.

MATERIALS Selections from books or magazines that have good setting description.

PROCEDURE
1. Review the items on the "Setting Grid" so students will know what to listen for.
2. Read a setting description and have students listen for details.
3. Ask students to recall details after the selection has been read. Write details on the grid as students suggest them.
4. Read the selection again if students missed some of the details. Have students listen specifically for the information needed.
5. Have students try to visualize the setting and make suggestions about information that was not included in the reading selection.
6. Have students write a short descriptive paragraph about the character using information provided on the grid. Share paragraphs by reading aloud.

Figure 3–5
Setting Grid

1. General Location: _____

2. Prominent features in the *foreground* (man-made or natural) size, shape, color, texture, composition, function, unusual detail, etc.:

    a. _____: _____
       _____
       _____

    b. _____: _____
       _____
       _____
       _____

    c. _____: _____
       _____
       _____

3. Prominent features in the background:

    a. _____: _____
       _____
       _____

    b. _____. _____
       _____
       _____

4. Weather conditions, lighting, time of day, season, year: _____
   _____

5. Sound effects: _____
   _____

6. Smells: _____
   _____
   _____

7. Textures: _____
   _____

EXTENSION 1
Have students use the setting grid to collect details as they read on their own. Have them write descriptive paragraphs about the settings that they have found. Ask them to illustrate their setting paragraphs.

EXTENSION 2
Collect a group of setting pictures from magazines or calendars. Choose one picture and try to fill in the setting grid, taking suggestions from everyone in the class. When the setting grid is complete, ask students to write a short paragraph about the setting using the information provided on the grid.

After a number of brainstorming sessions, let each student select his or her own picture and write a descriptive paragraph. Share all paragraphs by reading aloud.

EXTENSION 3
Have students take photographs of different settings, then spend about ten minutes at the spot observing and jotting down descriptive details of the area. When this is complete, have students write a descriptive paragraph without naming the spot. Display the photographs without identifying the settings. Have each student read his or her description to the class without naming the setting. See whether students can identify the place from the descriptive detail given by the student. Have other students try to guess the spot from the description. Later, match descriptions with photographs and display on bulletin board.

Owls in the Family
Farley Mowat
Little, Brown, 1961

This fast-paced book relates how Billy and Bruce discover two baby owls, Wols and Weeps: Wols in a storm-wrecked tree and Weeps in an old oil barrel where he is being teased by two neighborhood boys. Wols and Weeps become members of the Mowat family and manage to bring numerous humorous complications to the family and neighborhood. The story includes a wealth of descriptive detail about the natural environment of Saskatoon, Saskatchewan.

Julie of the Wolves
Jean Craighead George
Harper and Row, 1972

Julie, whose Eskimo name is Miyax, suddenly leaves her unhappy living situation and wanders in the North Slope of Alaska.

She is befriended by a pack of Arctic wolves after she learns to communicate with them. They provide her with companionship and sometimes food as she courageously begins her search for her long lost father.

Many beautiful detailed descriptions of the Arctic are provided throughout the book.

Call it Courage
Armstrong Sperry
Macmillan, 1961

Mafatu, The Boy Who Was Afraid, decides to overcome his fear after he becomes tired of the taunts and jibes of the people in his tribe in the South Seas. Quickly leaving his village, he shoves off in a native canoe with his faithful dog, Uri, and his pet albatross, Kivi. Mafatu is immediately caught in his first challenge: a storm at sea. Gradually, Mafatu meets and conquers other challenges before he eventually returns home in his own hand-made canoe, wearing a necklace of boar's teeth, and carrying an impressive spear.

Mountain Born
Elizabeth Yates
Coward-McCann, Inc., 1943

Biddie, the little black cosset sheep who was practically raised with Peter and his family, becomes leader of the flock of sheep and saves the sheep from a hungry wolf and bad weather with her natural intelligence. The author traces the growing years of Peter and his relationship with Biddie in a story that has vivid setting descriptive detail.

The Wheel on the School
Meindert De Jong
Harper and Row, 1954

After Lina writes a composition about storks the class decides to launch an investigation into the reasons why the storks do not nest in Shora. Since storks supposedly bring good luck, the children are anxious to have the storks come back. Eventually, after much hard work, their wish comes true.

The Good Master
Kate Seredy
Viking Press, 1935

This book describes the adventures of Jancsi and Kate as they grow up on a large horse farm in Hungary.

Blue Willow
Doris Gates
Viking Press, 1940

Janey Larkin, whose big wish is to have a permanent home, is the ten-year-old child of migrant workers. The Blue Willow plate is a symbol of that home.

Master Simon's Garden
Cornelia Lynde Meigs
Macmillan, 1929

This book reviews the life of a New England colony from the time of the puritans through the revolutionary days.

Other books which have setting description. Blurbs for these titles have appeared in earlier activities. In addition, other titles from the authors listed in this section have abundant descriptive detail.

The Witch of Blackbird Pond
Elizabeth George Speare
Houghton Mifflin, 1958

Tuck Everlasting
Natalie Babbitt
Farrar, Straus & Giroux, 1975

The Man Who Was Magic
Paul Gallico
Doubleday, 1966

My Side of the Mountain
Jean George
Dutton, 1959

OBJECTIVE To identify sounds and smells in the environment.

MATERIALS Paper and pencils.

PROCEDURE
1. Tell the class that you are going out into the neighborhood to make a list of sounds and smells in the environment.
2. Divide the class into small groups. Assign some groups to listen and write down all sounds that they hear. Ask other groups to notice different smells and write them down.
3. Return to the classroom after about fifteen minutes. List the different sounds and smells that students listed on their papers.
4. Take one sound or smell at a time and ask students to suggest and/or write sentences with more descriptive detail. Read results to class.
   Example: The sound of a truck going by.
   > The huge moving van, with the red tractor and trailer, roared down the street.
   > The muffler sound rumbled and echoed through the neighborhood.

EXTENSION Try some of the synonym activities in the vocabulary section to increase the use of specific nouns, verbs, and adjectives.

How Do Stories Begin?

OBJECTIVE To identify various ways to begin stories.

MATERIALS A small collection of reading books from the library, or an anthology of stories (see suggested list of titles).

PROCEDURE
1. Explain to the class that you want them to notice how different stories begin. Read the beginning few paragraphs from the suggested books. Read at least one from each category. After each selection, ask the students to identify the way the author began his or her story.
2. List suggestions on the board. Suggestions might be:
   a description of setting
   a description of a character
   a description of the weather
   an action by a character
   a question to be answered
   a conversation
   a time
3. Continue reading the opening paragraphs of stories, and let the students identify the type of beginning.
4. Ask the class to evaluate which beginnings were most interesting. Which beginnings tempted them to read the book?
5. Ask various students to read the beginning of their own library books out loud. Count the number of beginnings that fall into each category. Were any additional categories added? Which categories were most common?
6. Have students look over their own file of stories. Ask students to notice what kinds of beginnings they used in their own stories. Do students use a variety of story beginnings? Or do they generally use the same pattern over and over?

EXTENSION 1 Ask students to choose one of their previous stories, then write two or three alternate beginnings for the story using the list of story beginning types developed in the previous lesson. Ask students to share their different story beginnings with other students, and ask for comments regarding which beginning is most effective.

EXTENSION 2 Ask students to write a different beginning to one of the stories read in the first activity.

Eye Witness News

OBJECTIVE   To write objective news reports.

MATERIALS   Pictures that have characters and action (e.g., sports pictures, accident, fire, graduations, etc.) from newspapers or magazines.

PROCEDURE
1. Choose one picture and have students identify "who," "did what," "when," and "where" information. Write their comments on the board.
2. Encourage students to be very specific and objective in their comments. Remind them that news reporters cannot add their own emotional reactions and opinions in their reports.
3. Have the students choose a title for the picture and article. Then have them write an objective news report using the information provided on the board.
4. Let some students choose a different picture and do this assignment by themselves.
5. Have students read their news reports out loud. Have class members listen to see whether any statements that show emotional response or opinions were used.
6. Save these reports for use in the Points of View Activities.

EXTENSION   Give some students interesting headlines from newspaper stories, and some a list of facts from the stories. Ask them to write news reports to go with the headlines. Then let them compare their report with the original report.

New News

OBJECTIVE   To write sports news articles.

MATERIALS   Sports pictures from newspapers or magazines.

PROCEDURE
1. Collect interesting action pictures from the sports section of newspapers or magazines. Ask students to help you collect them.
2. Let students choose a picture and write an "on the spot" news report using an announcer point of view. (Read sample to class.)
3. Encourage students to use short sentences loaded with action verbs and exclamations of excitement.
4. Read results to class.

Example:

> The score is ten to nine. First out. Second out. He's up at bat. Man on third. Strike. Holy Cow! What a hit! Looks like a home run! Oh, just missed first base. Man on third going home. He slides safe. What a game. Ten to ten.

5. Have each student rewrite their "on the spot" report as a report for the daily news. Remind students that newspaper reporting is more objective than "on the spot" type reporting and generally does not include the exclamations of excitement or statements of opinion. Remind them to include information on who, what, when, and where.
6. Read results to the class.

EXTENSION 1   Present some articles or pictures without headlines. Let students write some catchy captions.

EXTENSION 2   Present some catchy titles found in the sports section of the newspaper. Also present an outline of information which provides who, did what, when, and where. Let students write an article to match the title and information. Encourage them to describe an interesting scene in the game.

EXTENSION 3   Have a student follow one team or sports hero through a period of time by collecting pictures from the newspaper and writing short reports on each picture. Bind all of the articles and pictures in book format. Newspaper pictures xerox very well, so many students can use the same pictures.

EXTENSION 4   Have students listen to televised sports news programs. These programs generally use quite precise verbs in their descriptions of games. Ask students to jot down some of the descriptions and bring them into class.

RESOURCES

Eyewitness: The TV Newscast
Perfection Form Company
    This filmstrip/casette program features the production procedures and problems of a television newscast.

In Print: Getting Out a Newspaper
Perfection Form Company
    A visit to a modern news plant shows how news gets into the paper and ends up on our porches. A news story is following from beginning to end. Filmstrip/cassette program.

News In Print
Homer A. Post and Harold Snodgrass
Allyn and Bacon
    Designed for grades nine through twelve, this book is a help for students who want to produce a school newspaper. Discusses the different types of articles and features in a newspaper. Describes the printing process from beginning to end.

Pro and Con

OBJECTIVE   To identify pro and con arguments.

MATERIALS   A controversial topic and a list of pro and con statements.

PROCEDURE
1. Put topic and pro/con statements on ditto or overhead transparency. Have one student read the arguments.
2. Make a chart on the board—one side pro arguments, one side con arguments. Also decide whether arguments are fact or opinion. List facts at top and opinions at bottom.

pro	con
facts	facts
opinions	opinions

3. Have students choose a side and write a paragraph giving the factual arguments. Next have them rewrite the paragraph giving opinions. Encourage students to use lots of emotionally charged words when giving opinions.
4. Share both paragraphs with class members.

EXTENSION   Have students write paragraphs from the opposite point of view that they chose in 3 above. Have them write both factual and opinion paragraphs.

Ads

OBJECTIVE   To prepare for a unit on advertising.

MATERIALS   Advertisements from all sources: magazines, newspapers, brochures, circulars, cereal boxes, etc.

PROCEDURE
1. Tell students that you are going to begin a unit on advertising. Ask them to look

around them for several days and make a list of the places they see or hear advertisements. For example: billboards, posters, bumper stickers, back of telephone book, on trucks, television, radio.

2. Make a class composite list of places that ads are seen or heard.

3. Have students collect magazines, newspapers, brochures, pamphlets, and other sources of advertisements and bring them into class. Collect materials for about a week.

4. Encourage students to look for unusual kinds of ads: bumper stickers, buttons, cereal boxes, posters, etc.

5. Make a bulletin board display of all the different sources and kinds of ads that students find.

RESOURCES

Advertising Posters
Perfection Form Company

"In-cola, the new soft drink" is featured in these twelve different posters based on common advertising techniques. Students will enjoy identifying the techniques used, and then developing and advertising their own products using some of these techniques.

The Advertisement Book
Stanley Skinner
McDougal, Littell and Co.

This book reviews the basic advertising appeals and how advertisers use them. Numerous real advertisements are used to illustrate each type of appeal.

1897 Sears, Roebuck Catalog
F. Israel, editor
Chelsea House Publishers

The introduction, written by S. J. Perelman and Richard Revere, provides background information on this catalog venture, and gives an idea of the trends of the time (urbanization, etc.).

Six thousand items are shown in 700 pages of the 1897 catalog. Here are a few examples: 57 cent Tonic Hair Restorer; 26 pages of elixirs, capsules, chemicals, tinctures, pills, and granules to meet any illness; nerve and brain pills to cure you of 1001 indescribable bad feelings, both mental and physical; cloth-

ing styles of the day; furniture; surreys, harnesses and flynets for horse; and, finally, many testimonies of satisfied customers.

Wonderful World of American Advertisements
1865–1900
Leonard DeVries and Ilonka Van Amstel
Follett, 1972

During 1865, a new type printing press was perfected and cheaper paper (newsprint) became available. Both of these changes aided the advertising business. This book is a collection of ads for items of the day, such as bicycles, "talking machines," telephones, cameras, carpet stretchers, tents, and many other interesting things.

Those Were the Good Old Days:
A Happy Look at American Advertising
Rev. Ed.
1880–1930
Edgar R. Jones
Simon & Schuster, 1979

Another collection of old ads. Students will find it humorous to try to identify the different advertising types.

They Laughed When I Sat Down:
An Informal History of Advertising
Frank Rowsome, Jr.
McGraw Hill

Targets

OBJECTIVE   To make collages of products made for particular target groups.

MATERIALS   Magazines, scissors, paste, poster paper.

PROCEDURE
1. Have students go through different magazines and cut out advertisements. Try to have a wide variety of magazines available.

2. Have students sort the advertisements according to target groups, i.e., which ads would appeal to new young mothers? to teen-agers? to young children? to housewives? to men? to women? to retired people? etc.

3. Have individual students, or small groups of students, choose one target group and design a collage using ads that appeal to that particular target group.
4. Have students make a list of the products that are directed to their target group. Encourage them to think of others that might not be on their collage.
5. Have one group make a collage of products that might be used by anyone.
6. Display collages and lists of products in the classroom.

EXTENSION 1   Make a collage of one kind of product: desserts, cleaning products, cosmetics, etc. Compare how different manufactureres advertise their products.

EXTENSION 2   Have students make up a product and write an advertisement that describes the product and its benefits. This can be serious or humorous. Students may want to have one of the celebrities from the Autobiography Activity, Extension 1, give an endorsement of the product.

PRACTICAL WRITING ACTIVITIES

Telephone Messages

OBJECTIVE   To write down telephone messages.

MATERIALS   Telephone message form.

PROCEDURE
1. Ask students to develop a telephone conversation in which the person answering the phone has to take a message for someone else. Discuss what some possible messages might be.
   Examples: Father called to say he would be home late.
              Dentist called to cancel an appointment.
              Mother's friend called to talk to mother.
              Brother's friend called to plan a meeting time.
2. Review the items that a person taking a message should always write down. Give students a copy of the message form on page 86.
   who the message is for
   time
   who called
   expected response: return call or wait for another call?
   telephone number to call
   message
3. Have pairs of students choose a sample topic or make up one of their own to use in writing a sample telephone dialogue which requires that a message be taken down. Remind them that messages and telephone numbers should be repeated back by the message taker in order to check the information.
4. After students have finished writing the message dialogue, have them tape record it and play it back for other students. Ask students to fill in message form as they listen to tape. Compare results. Play tape a second time for those students who missed some information.

Writing Letters for a Purpose

OBJECTIVE   To develop letter writing skills by writing for free materials.

MATERIALS   *Free Stuff for Kids, The Whole Kids Catalog, 100 Valuable Free Things,* writing paper, stamps, envelopes.

PROCEDURE
1. Place several copies of each book in the classroom. Let students look through the books to find items that interest them. (Many of the items are free, however, some require stamped, self-addressed envelopes; other items cost less than a dollar.)
2. Have each student compose a basic letter requesting the item. Or, compose a sample letter with the whole group together. Write the sample letter on the board.

Figure 3-6
Telephone Messages

TO: _____

DATE: _____ TIME: _____

WHILE YOU WERE OUT

MR.

MS. _____

OF _____

AREA CODE _____ PHONE _____

TELEPHONED		PLEASE PHONE	
CAME BY TO SEE YOU		WILL CALL AGAIN	
WANTS TO SEE YOU		RETURNED YOUR CALL	

MESSAGE: _____

_____

_____

_____

_____

MESSAGE TAKEN BY: _____

3. Emphasize the parts and placements of a letter: the heading, the salutation, the body, the closing, and the signature. Place a sample letter on the bulletin board.
4. Have students complete their own letters.
5. Explain correct envelope addressing procedures. Post a model on the board. If students have difficulty with placement of address, draw pencil guide lines for them.
6. Mail the letters. Keep a record of responses.

EXTENSION 1   Have students locate the cities and states that their letters went to on a map. Pinpoint the cities with markers. Keep track of responses. Warn students that sometimes companies run out of the material offered, but that they usually answer the letter anyway.

EXTENSION 2   Here are other letters that students can write. Collect coupons from magazines which offer free material (e.g., travel information, recipes). Have students write for some of this material. Use post cards instead of letters when money or self-addressed envelopes are not required.

EXTENSION 3   Collect a few humorous "Dear Abby" letters from the newspaper and read them to students. Have students make up a "Dear Abby" letter. Trade letters with students in another class. Ask them to respond with advice.

EXTENSION 4   Write a letter to Guinness *Book of World Records* describing the new world's record that you have set. Make it outrageous.

EXTENSION 5   Tell the students that they are away at camp for the summer. Have them write letters home to their parents about their activities, accommodations, likes and dislikes, friends and enemies, counselors, food, etc.
   Read some samples from *Hip Kids' Letters From Camp* (Bill Adler, New American Library, 1973).

RESOURCES   **Free Stuff for Kids**
Pat Blakely, Barbara Haislet, and
Judith Hentges
Meadowbrook Press, 1979
   Approximately 250 items are listed in this book. Specific directions are given to students in the front of the book as well as a sample letter and an addressed envelope. The book has a very easy-to-read format with type large enough for primary and intermediate students.

Figure 3–7
Letter Format

```
Jane Doe
95 Wood Lane
Woodside, CA  94062

                                    ┌──────────┐
                                    │          │
                                    └──────────┘


                    American Humane Education Society
                    350 S. Huntington Avenue
                    Boston, MA  02130
```

```
                                    95 Wood Lane
                                    Woodside, CA  94062
                                    July 25, 1979


Dear Sir or Madam:
     Please send one copy of the Dog Care Booklet. I have enclosed
20 cents for postage and handling.
     Thank you.


                                    Sincerely,
```

1001 Valuable Things You Can Get Free
Mort Weisinger
Bantam, 1979

This book lists 1001 items available free from business, industry, nonprofit organizations, and government. Some require only a postcard request, while others require a stamped, self-addressed envelope (SSAE). Get the most current edition available since some items become unavailable after a time. The small type used in this book makes it most suitable for intermediate or secondary students.

The Second Whole Kids Catalog
Peter Cardoza
Bantam, 1977

This book presents a combination of things to do (grow plants, build things, collect things) and things to send for (posters, booklets, pictures, samples). It also lists a variety of activity books that are available in local bookstores.

Teen Jobs Ads

OBJECTIVE To write a job wanted ad for Teen Jobs Wanted section of classified ads.

MATERIALS Sample teen job ads, ads from local newspaper (if available), classified ad cost schedule from local newspaper, sample blank ad form and ad rates (Figure 3-8).

PROCEDURE 1. Read some of the following ads that were taken from a "Teen Jobs" column of a local newspaper. Compare them with teen jobs in your local newspaper. How are they the same? Different? What was mentioned first in these ads? Identify words that give you clues to the teenager's personality. Notice that the first word or two is all caps.

2. Have students list some of the skills or jobs they have had or would like to have and plan an ad. Check with the local newspaper to figure costs for placing each ad. (Sometimes local newspapers run teen ads for free just before the summer season. Check to see whether your local paper does this.)

   Some rules to remember when writing a Teen Job Ad or other classified ad:

   a. *Get right to the point! Be specific!* Either state the job you want or who you are that qualifies you for a particular job.

   b. *Include all relevant information.* You may use standard abbreviations.

      First name

      Telephone number

      Your age or age range (e.g., teen-ager, high school student)

      Special facts: time available, own transportation, special tools owned (lawn-mower, pick-up truck, etc.)

      Adjectives: responsible, experienced, hard working, fast, prompt service, reliable

   c. *Avoid excess words.*

3. Fill out blank ad form, then figure out the cost of the ad based on local rates or use rates given on ad worksheet.

EXTENSION 1 Ask students to look for an ad that describes a job they could hold now. List features that job must have (e.g., part-time, requires no experience or specific skills). Make a list of abbreviations found in employment ads. (See HELP WANTED ads.)

EXTENSION 2 Ask students to write down the kind of job they would like to have in five or ten years. Next, have students read through the Classified Ads to find a job listing that comes closest to their desired job type.

TEEN JOBS

HIGH SCHOOL student available for stable work, gardening, etc. $2.50 hour. 3 years experience. References. 354-7150 Jim.

EXPERIENCED IN hauling, painting, land clearing, field mowing, chainsaw work. Joe, 354-0307. Free estimates.

GOING AWAY this summer? College student will care for home and animals. References. Debbie 854-3416, eves.

WINDOW WASHING and odd jobs. Reliable and experienced. Call Ross, 854-7720.

MAGICIANS—Looking for a way to make your child's birthday party something special? Call the Wise Wizards. Magic for all occasions. Reasonable, experienced and references. Matt, 854-2425, Tom, 854-2298.

ODD JOBS: Teen-ager will do: minor repairs, pool service, deliveries, babysitting. Own transportation. Steve. 854-0915.

RESPONSIBLE 18 year old will clean house. References. Call Sarah at 851-7202.

ENTERTAINING? SISTERS (one college age, one high school age) will help prepare, serve and clean up. Call Anne or Suzy, 854-2806.

NEED A housesitter? Animal sitter? Garden sitter: I'm a very responsible, reliable, college bound student willing to take care of your home, garden & pets anytime throughout the summer. If interested, call Lisa, 854-1054.

HORSE CARE: College student will clean, feed, etc. Experienced and reliable. Liz, 854-0725.

RESPONSIBLE 17-year-old will feed and care for horses, dogs, cats, plants in Westridge area for $2.50 day. Excellent references available. Call Janice, 854-0162.

HIGH SCHOOL honor student will baby-sit and-or tutor child. Very experienced. References. Lael, 854-1848.

TWO experienced 18-year-olds avail. for odd jobs. Call Erik, 854-0693, Craig, 854-0655.

SOCCER lessons. 2 High School varsity players will teach your children the basic skills of soccer. For more information, call Tom, 851-8351, or Rich, 854-9045.

EXPERIENCED and responsible girl will clean, groom and do other barn work. Call Stephanie, 854-0993.

DIRTY stalls? Call Bryan at 854-4208. 8 years experience with horses, sheep, poultry. Responsible and fast.

SUZI is your answer to housecleaning, animal care, babysitting. Help cook and serve at parties, watering and care of pets and plants while you're away. Excellent references. 854-1192.

HAULING. "Honest John." Extra large loads. Prompt and efficient service, $30 load. 854-0552.

HELP WANTED

CASHIERS wanted, part and full time. No experience needed. Thrift Village, 875 Main St., 364-5545.

Childcare. Assist mother with infant & toddler. Afternoons. Refs. req. 326-4675 aft. 5

Housekpr. Cleaning, ironing, 1 day week or 2½ days. Recent refs. Own trans. English speaking. 325-2739.

RECEPTIONIST NEEDED

Part-time person with excellent typing skills, cordial telephone manner. Small Office. Pleasant working conditions. 851-0730.

Salesperson-drug & variety store. Part and full time positions. 326-1930. Ask for Willis.

Sandwich shop help needed. Full or part time. Call after 2:00. Ask for Ida or Michelle. 323-4473

Service Stn. Attendant. Full & part time. AM & PM shifts avail. Up to $4hr. + comm. to start. Exper. or will train. Apply: Automotive Center btw. 9–4, Mon–Fri.

Service station attendant. Days. Gd. pay & benefits. 856-6388

SERVICE STA. ATTNDNT. The Bubble Machine, is now hiring P/&F time. Apply 1520 El Camino, R.C.

Service station, part time, 25 hrs/wk, day shift. Exp. pref. 948-0776.

TYPIST. Part time. Office in downtown. Flexible hours. EOE. 321-7911

Waiter/waitress, full or part time. Call Peggy, 948-1024

WAITRESS/WAITER
Now interviewing.
Family Restaurant
*No Experience Necessary
*Day & Night Shifts
W. El Camino, Mt. View, 2-4 p.m.

Want Ads

OBJECTIVE   To read and write ads of various kinds.

MATERIALS   Classified ad section from local newspaper.

PROCEDURE
1. Have students bring newspapers from home or contact a local newspaper office and try to get some complimentary copies for classroom use.
2. Have students look through the classified ad section and name the various kinds of ads that appear there. (Employment, automotive, used cars, real estate, rentals, service announcements.) Since papers handle ads differently, it may be useful to have classified sections from two or three papers.
3. Divide the class into small groups. Ask each group to find abbreviations and list all the abbreviations used in a particular section of the classified ads (e.g., employment, real estate, rentals, automotive). Ask students to list these abbreviations and their meanings on a ditto sheet or an overhead transparency. Duplicate the list of abbreviations for future activities in writing ads.
4. Compare ads in each newspaper with the same type ads in other newspapers. Do all newspapers use abbreviations? Are the same abbreviations used?

EXTENSION 1   *Car Sales*

1. Ask students to name the year and model of a car they would like to own. Have them read through the car sales section of the classified ads to see if they can find the car they have preselected.
2. Have students make a list of the kinds of descriptive information that owners or

car dealers provide in their ads.
3. Review list of abbreviations used in car ads.
4. Then ask students to write an ad to sell a car (real or imaginary). Include appropriate descriptive detail.

EXTENSION 2   *House/Apartment*

1. Have students look through real estate ads and locate an apartment or house that might be suitable for them after they leave high school.
2. Have students write an ad that describes their dream house.

EXTENSION 3   *Garage Sale Ads*

1. Have students ask parents if they have some items in the house or garage that they would like to sell. (An old vacuum cleaner, an old lawnmower, a chest of drawers, a piano, an old swing set, a baby stroller, golf clubs, etc.)
Example: BEAT inflation. Shop for Christmas. Stereo set
with case. Sterling, silverplate flatware, baskets.
Christmas pinecone candleholders, leather books,
egg collection, prints. Much more! 854-6321
for appointment and information.

Figure 3–8
How to Place Your
Classified Ad

1. Fill out form provided below.
2. Figure cost of ad using rate chart. (Minimum ad is 2 lines.)
3. Bring or mail ads to newspaper office. Be sure to include check or money order if you mail ad. Ads must be paid for in advance.

Name				
Address	Lines	# Of Weeks		Ad Cost
City, State, Zip	Exp. Date	Issue Date		By
Phone	Remarks Enclose Check Or Money Order With Ad			

AD RATES:

	1 Week	2 Weeks	3 Weeks	4 Weeks
2 lines	$1.30	$2.60	$ 3.90	$ 5.20
3 lines	$1.95	$3.90	$ 5.85	$ 7.80
4 lines	$2.60	$5.20	$ 7.80	$10.40
5 lines	$3.25	$6.50	$ 9.75	$13.00
6 lines	$3.90	$7.80	$11.70	$15.60

EXTENSION 4 *Lost and Found Ads*

1. Have students write an ad for something they might have found (keys, puppy, bike, bookbag). Check the local newspaper to see how much it costs to run a "found" ad.
2. Have students write an ad for something they might have lost.

It's My Opinion!

OBJECTIVE To write a letter to an editor of a newspaper.

MATERIALS Sample letters taken from "letters to editor" section of the local newspaper and magazines.

PROCEDURE
1. Have students collect letters to the editor from newspapers and magazines for at least a week. Make a bulletin board display of these letters. Review collected letters with students and answer the following questions. (You may want to put selected letters on a ditto.)

   - What kinds of letters are written to editors?
     (letters expressing pro or con opinions on different problems, letters expressing appreciation for certain articles, letters pointing out a problem in the community, letters complaining about editorial position on a problem, letters responding to another letter to editor)
   - What kinds of wording choices were made?
     (emotionally charged words? angry words?)
   - What approaches were used?
     (humorous? serious? hostile?)
   - How many stated their main point in the first sentence?
   - How many made a positive comment first, then stated their point of disagreement?
   - What kinds of transition words or phrases were used between paragraphs?

2. Develop a set of guidelines with students for use in writing letters to an editor. Suggestions:

   - Get to your point quickly.
   - State the facts as you see them.
   - Do not go into long drawn-out explanations or excuses.
   - Avoid the use of emotionally charged words.
   - State what kind of action, change, or response you would like to see.

3. Ask students to suggest a situation around the school or neighborhood that they have an opinion on and that they could use as a topic for a letter to the editor of the school or local newspaper. Examples:

   - School lunch periods are too short.
   - School starts too early in the morning.
   - Too much (not enough) homework is given.
   - Detention should be abolished.
   - Grades should be abolished.

EXTENSION Have students choose a letter to the editor from the group on the bulletin board and rewrite it from the opposite point of view.

Complain, Complain, Complain

OBJECTIVE To write a complaint letter.

MATERIALS Sample complaint letters, suggested problems for complaint letter.

PROCEDURE
1. Look in newspapers for columns that print complaint letter from readers.
   Example: I ordered seat covers for my car from Sharsky and Company in Chicago. They cashed my check but they haven't sent the seat covers.
2. Read the sample complaint with students and decide on what course of action should be followed by this reader.
3. Review some basic rules for writing complaint letters:
   a. *Make your letter look professional.* Write or print the letter neatly. Or better yet, type the letter.
   b. *Be polite. State the facts clearly and without anger.* Avoid accusations and name-calling.
   c. *State your problem as clearly as possible.* Include important information. If your letter is about a product you have purchased, state the name of the product, the date and place you purchased it, and the price you paid.
   d. *State how you want the problem resolved.* (e.g., "I would like my money back, please," "I would like the product replaced, please," or "I would like a replacement part, please.")
   e. Include your name, address, and telephone number.
   f. *Send your letter to the consumer service department of the company.* Send a copy of your letter to the Better Business Bureau and the State Consumer Protection Department.
4. Decide on a sample problem and have students write a complaint letter. Students may suggest different problems for practice letters.
5. Have students read and compare finished letters. Did all letters follow the rules? Modify those letters that do not follow the rules.

How Do I Get There?

OBJECTIVE   To write clear directions.

MATERIALS   Sample directions.

PROCEDURE
1. Ask students what they do when they want to go to a new place that they don't know how to get to.
   Suggestions: look at a map
   call the place and ask directions
   ask parents for directions
   ask friends
2. Tell students that giving careful directions is very important. (They may remember a few occasions when they or their parents got lost because they did not have good directions or did not write the directions down.) Give students copies of the sample directions and ask them to decide which one is better and to explain what features make it better. (The first gives names of streets, exact numbers of blocks, landmarks, specific house numbers. Ask students to guess why the student who wrote the direction went that way. The second one is too vague.)
3. Ask students to write a different set of directions using the given map.
4. Ask students (*in* class) to write down directions to their house from school from memory. Allow five minutes or so to do this. Have them draw a sample map to go with the directions. Next ask students to list the items they should have noted but could not remember (e.g., how many blocks from one place to another, what landmarks were along the way, names of all important streets).
5. For homework, ask students to again write directions from school to home. This time, ask them to write them down on the way home and include all specific information (street names, landmarks, number of miles or blocks, etc.).

EXTENSION 1   Giving oral directions is also a very important skill. Have several volunteers slowly dictate their directions two times to the class while the class takes written notes. Have several writers read back the directions to see if all information was written down.

Figure 3-9
Map

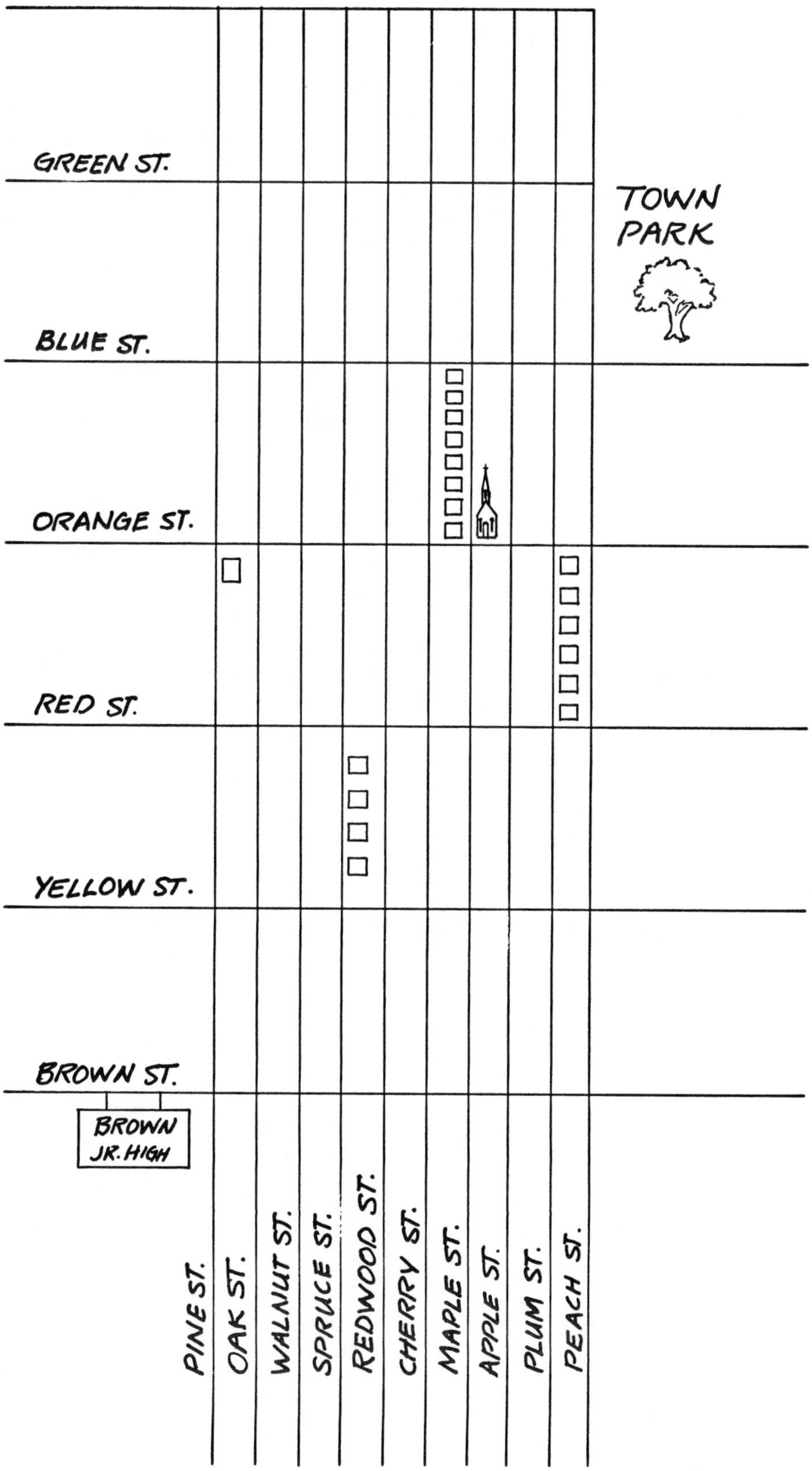

GREEN ST.

TOWN
PARK

BLUE ST.

ORANGE ST.

RED ST.

YELLOW ST.

BROWN ST.

BROWN
JR. HIGH

PINE ST.

OAK ST.

WALNUT ST.

SPRUCE ST.

REDWOOD ST.

CHERRY ST.

MAPLE ST.

APPLE ST.

PLUM ST.

PEACH ST.

Point out that people frequently get lost because they think they can remember directions and do not write them down, or they write down only parts of directions.

EXTENSION 2 Locate a local map of your city (town, district) and put it on the bulletin board. Have students trade written directions to their home (the homework assignment), then read and track the directions on the map. Ask students to note where they had difficulty.

EXTENSION 3 Use a road map or road atlas of the United States and plan a trip to a national park. Have students write sequence of directions that includes names of cities and states and specific highway numbers.

SAMPLE DIRECTIONS

1. From Brown Junior High School to 1039 Maple Street.

   Go out the main entrance of Brown Junior High School. Walk to the corner of Brown and Pine Streets. Turn left on Pine Street. Walk three blocks to Orange Street. A candy store will be on the corner. Turn right on Orange Street. Walk six blocks on Orange Street to Maple Street. A big church is on the corner. Turn left on Maple Street and walk to 1039 Maple. It is a big white house with green shutters. It is the fifth house from the corner on the left-hand side of the street.

2. From Brown Junior High School to 1039 Maple Street.

   Go down to the corner and turn left. Go a few blocks until you see the candy store. Then you have to go down that street for a ways. You'll see a big church. I live near the church.

Build Their Skills

"Build Their Skills" is divided into three sections: Organization Skills, Vocabulary Skills, and Sentence Structure. The activities in the Sentence Structure and Organization Skills sections are arranged in sequential order with each activity building on the skills developed in the preceding activity. Instruction at each particular level may continue as long as is necessary for students to grasp the basic concepts and use them in their writing. Obviously some students may move very quickly through the sequence, while others may need repeated practice at each stage. Some students may only need to review and/or practice activities near the end of the skill sequence.

Activities in the vocabulary section are not sequential and may be used in any order depending on the instructional purposes.

ORGANIZATION   Intermediate and secondary educational programs require that students have sufficient writing skills to answer test questions, write basic reports, and complete homework assignments. Poor writers have difficulty planning their writing. As a result, they do not always write clear topic sentences followed by appropriate, properly sequenced, supportive details, and relevant summaries or conclusions. Main ideas and details are improperly handled and are frequently unbalanced—either a generalization is given without supportive detail, or an overabundance of detail is provided with no generalization. Because poor writers lack planning skills, they have difficulty identifying a good starting point, keeping to their topic (they change line of thinking as new thoughts occur to them), and covering their topic completely.

Other students, who have mastered the basic paragraph structure (topic sentence, supportive details, conclusion), produce reports that are adequate, but not interesting or well developed.

Poor writers need activities that focus on these problems. The emphasis of the activities in this section is on building organizational skills through thinking, listening, and reading activities before actual writing assignments are given. The purpose is to teach students how to organize information *before* they begin to write.

The following specific organization skills are developed in this section.

Categorizing

Categorizing activities help students identify relationships between words and sentences and enable them to identify and eliminate irrelevant details and sentences from stories and paragraphs. These activities also develop basic outlining skills.

Sequencing

Sequencing in creative writing is relatively natural as students tell stories the way they happen. Expository writing, however, requires that students identify clear relationships (such as cause and effect, and comparison and contrast) and sequence them appropriately.

Stating the Main Idea

Writing topic sentences is a critical skill in expository writing. It involves the ability to make generalizations about a related group of facts or details. Students learn to restate questions in the form of topic sentences—a necessary skill for test taking.

Providing Details

In order for paragraphs to be well developed, sufficient appropriate details must be included. Students develop this skill by sorting and matching topic sentences and details and by selecting facts and details which *prove* basic generalizations.

Details can be arranged in a variety of ways in paragraphs. Practice in arranging details in different ways is also included in this section.

Notetaking

Students learn to take notes by listening to paragraphs that are read aloud and pinpointing the main ideas and details.

Outlining

Filling in a partially completed outline helps students understand broader and narrower relationships between topics and details. Partially completed outlines will be useful as guides in writing book reports or larger papers.

Eliminating Hasty Generalizations

Students must learn to avoid making unsupported or emotionally based generalizations. Activities designed to help students identify and correct these unsupported generalizations are included in this section.

Grocery List

OBJECTIVE   To categorize words and develop a simple outline.

MATERIALS   None.

PROCEDURE
1. Write a category name (e.g., Groceries) on the board and ask students to suggest as many items as possible that belong in the category (e.g., carrots, cheese, hamburger, milk, apples). Write words on the board or overhead transparency as students suggest them—do not attempt to organize the words as they are suggested.
2. Ask students to look over list to see whether any groups can be formed. Ask for group labels (e.g., fruit, vegetables, frozen foods, meat). Have students identify all foods that belong to each group.
3. Write suggested labels down in outline form. List all words that go with label.

      I. Groceries
        A. Vegetables

1. string beans	7. carrots
2. lima beans	8. peas
3. peppers	9. celery
4. cauliflower	10. lettuce
5. broccoli	11. cabbage
6. onions	12. cucumbers

13. squash
14. spinach
15. brussel sprouts
16. potatoes
17. sweet potatoes
18. leeks

B. Fruits
1. apples
2. bananas
3. pears
4. pineapple
5. peaches
6. plums
7. oranges
8. cherries
9. grapes
10. figs
11. nectarines
12. apricots

C. Meats
1. hamburger
2. steak
3. pork chops
4. ham
5. bacon
6. hot dogs
7. roast beef

D. Poultry
1. chicken
2. duck
3. pheasant
4. cornish hen
5. turkey

E. Dairy Products
1. milk
2. cheese
3. butter
4. yogurt
5. cottage cheese
6. cream
7. sour cream
8. margarine

F. Desserts
1. cake
2. cookies
3. pie
4. pudding
5. ice cream

G. Dry Foods
1. macaroni
2. spaghetti
3. dried beans
4. dried peas

H. Snacks
1. potato chips
2. pretzels
3. peanuts
4. popcorn

I. Herbs and Spices
1. paprika
2. chili powder
3. garlic powder
4. oregano
5. bay leaves
6. pepper
7. salt

EXTENSION 1 Give students a list which includes both topic and detail words. Have students identify the topic word.

Group 1 Identifying category label

1. dogs cats bears animals foxes
2. green color violet yellow orange
3. beets radishes corn vegetables stringbeans
4. buzzes snores ticks sounds mumbles
5. tools hammers axes saws screwdrivers
6. banana orange apple fruit fig
7. clothing hat coat dress sock
8. mother father family sister brother
9. hour time minute second day
10. balls toys bats dolls wagons

Group 2 Identifying category label

1. robins canaries birds sparrows eagles
2. tree oak maple pine dogwood
3. earring necklace jewelry bracelet ring

4. cotton velvet corduroy nylon material
5. Florida Massachusetts Virginia states California
6. Ford automobiles Chevrolet Cadillac Volkswagen
7. occupations farmers teachers writers doctors
8. singers dancers entertainers actors actresses
9. thunder weather wind rain fog
10. Chinese nationalities American Spanish Canadian

Group 3 Identifying category label

1. juice milk liquid lemonade water
2. diamonds opals jade pearls gems
3. insects flies mosquito fruitflies
4. tulips roses flowers gardenias buttercups
5. Science Math Social Studies subject History
6. Africa Australia Europe continents Asia
7. baseball game basketball hockey soccer
8. custard dessert pudding gingerbread cake
9. chocolate vanilla strawberry cherry flavors
10. school building hospital apartment store

EXTENSION 2   Give students a list of detail words. Ask them to fill in topic word. Do exercises orally first.

_____ robin sparrow eagle wren
_____ carrots peas corn beans beets
_____ Texas New York Maine California
_____ house garage barn church
_____ milk juice coffee tea
_____ rivers streams lakes ponds
_____ ten twelve nine six
_____ nose leg ear arm
_____ diamond ruby emerald garnet
_____ trout bass flounder salmon

EXTENSION 3   Give students a topic word and let them supply the detail words.

buildings _____ _____ _____ _____ _____
countries _____ _____ _____ _____ _____
cities _____ _____ _____ _____ _____
colors _____ _____ _____ _____ _____
animals _____ _____ _____ _____ _____
fruits _____ _____ _____ _____ _____
flowers _____ _____ _____ _____ _____
vegetables _____ _____ _____ _____ _____
toys _____ _____ _____ _____ _____
clothing _____ _____ _____ _____ _____
occupations _____ _____ _____ _____ _____

EXTENSION 4   Give students a list of detail words and have them identify the irrelevant word. Make differences gross at first—then gradually require the student to make finer and finer distinctions.

1. turkey chicken turtle pheasant goose
2. seven eight nine blue five
3. Christmas Easter Friday Halloween Labor Day
4. Africa ocean Asia Europe Australia

5. Monday   Friday   March   Sunday   Tuesday
6. uncle   farmer   fireman   teacher   policeman
7. aunt   cousin   uncle   grandfather   fireman
8. April   December   May   Friday   July
9. apple   bears   figs   bananas   oranges
10. trees   bushes   flowers   plants   garden

EXTENSION 5   Ask students to complete partially completed outlines.

Example:

I. Living Things in Nature
A. Plant Life   B. Animal Life
  1. Trees   1. Domestic Animals
    a._____   a._____
    b._____   b. _____
    c. _____   c. _____
    d. _____   d. _____
    e. _____   e. _____
  2. Flowers   2. Wild Animals
    a. _____   a. _____
    b. _____   b. _____
    c. _____   c. _____
    d. _____   d. _____
    e. _____   e. _____
    f. _____   f. _____

Jumbled Jokes

OBJECTIVE   To sequence sentences in correct order.

MATERIALS   Joke book.

PROCEDURE
1. Select five or six jokes from the joke book. Choose shorter jokes (three or four sentences) at first, then gradually include longer jokes.
2. Copy each sentence of each joke on a separate strip of paper. Put strips of each joke in a separate envelope. Do not mix jokes together. Or, write sentences in mixed up order on a ditto. Students can then cut ditto apart in strips.
3. Give one envelope (or ditto) to each student. Have each student read the mixed up sentences and arrange them in logical order.
4. When finished, have students read jokes out loud to see whether they make sense.
5. Have students mix up their own joke and return it to the envelope. Save jokes for another day and let students do this activity by themselves in their free time. This activity develops reading comprehension skills as well as sequencing skills.

JUMBLED JOKE

"He isn't hungry."
The rabbit ordered lettuce, carrots, and spinach.
The surprised waiter said, "What's the matter?"
The rabbit answered, "If he were hungry, I wouldn't be here."
The rabbit answered for the lion.
The waiter then asked the lion what he wanted to eat.
A rabbit and a lion were having lunch together.

Repeat this activity using other kinds of writing such as clearly sequenced songs, rhymes, jingles, or condensed fables. Try the jumbled fable that follows.

JUMBLED FABLES

She opened her mouth to sing.
Don't be fooled by flattery.
Then a clever fox came along.
A crow had stolen a piece of cheese.
He wanted the cheese for his supper.
"You look beautiful today. Your feathers are so shiny."
The crow was very flattered with his words.
The Fox and the Crow
She carried the cheese to a tree and sat on a branch.
"Good morning, Miss Crow," he said.
"I bet you sing beautiful songs too."
The cheese dropped out and the fox snatched it.

EXTENSION 2   Ask the students to write their own version of any fable. The student versions can then be used for follow up activities for other students who might need extra practice.

Irrelevant Sentences

OBJECTIVE   To sequence relevant sentences in paragraph.

MATERIALS   Sample paragraphs: each sentence on a separate strip of oaktag.

PROCEDURE   1. Choose a paragraph and write each sentence from paragraph on a separate strip of oaktag. Add one irrelevant sentence. Put all sentences in envelope in mixed up order.

Example   It is important to take good care of your teeth.
Be sure to brush them at least two times a day.
When you cannot brush them, rinse your mouth.
It is very cold in Alaska most of the year.
Use dental floss, too.
Visit your dentist twice a year.
Remember, too many sweets cause cavities.

2. Pass out one envelope to each student.
3. Ask students to read all the sentences, identify the irrelevant sentence, remove it, then sequence the sentences to rebuild the paragraph.
4. Check paragraphs for accuracy. If correct, have students mix up their paragraphs and irrelevant details, and return them to envelope.
5. Pass envelope to another person and repeat the activity.

EXTENSION   Have students write paragraphs with one or two irrelevant details deliberately added. Have them copy each sentence of their paragraph on a separate strip of paper, put all of the strips in an envelope in mixed up order, then switch with another person in the room.

This activity not only helps students identify irrelevant sentences (to alert them to identify irrelevant ideas in their own writing), but also helps to improve reading comprehension.

Sentence Sort (Main Ideas and Details)

OBJECTIVE   To group and sequence related ideas under topic heading (main ideas and details).

MATERIALS   Strips of oaktag with sample sentences and topics (see examples).

PROCEDURE
1. Choose two factual paragraphs on different topics. Copy each sentence of each paragraph on a separate strip of paper. Or, write the sentences in mixed up order on a ditto and have students cut strips apart.
2. Mix two sets of topics and sample sentences together. Put them in an envelope.
3. Give an envelope to each student. Have students first locate the two title cards and put them at the top of the desk. Next have students sort sentences under the corresponding title, sequence the sentence strips in meaningful order, then copy one paragraph on a piece of paper and read it out loud to see whether it makes sense.
4. Have students reshuffle topic and sentence strips and put them back in envelope. Continue the activity on another day by giving students different envelopes with different paragraphs.
5. Control the level of difficulty by using appropriate reading vocabulary levels and a smaller number of sentence strips (two, three, or four at first). Or, just use one paragraph if students have difficulty sorting and sequencing the sentences.

SENTENCE SORT

Some snakes are very dangerous.
The giraffe is a strange-looking animal.
There are only seven bones in the giraffe's neck.
The largest and most dangerous is the diamondback rattlesnake.
It has the same number of bones that a mouse's neck has.
It can grow to be eight feet long.
This snake is easily identified.
The giraffe's thin legs are much stronger than they appear.
It can run at a speed of thirty miles an hour.
It has a rattle at the end of its tail.
Only the lion, the giraffe's only enemy, can run faster.
However, the giraffe can kill a lion with one kick from its hoof.
When people or animals approach the rattlesnake, it rattles its tail as a warning.
But the mouse's neck is much, much shorter.
Giraffes
Snakes

Mixed Up Stories

OBJECTIVE   To sequence a series of related paragraphs.

MATERIALS   A collection of articles cut from student workbooks (e.g., *New Practice Readers*, or *Reading for Concepts*); index cards.

PROCEDURE   1. Choose five or six multiparagraph selections from a student workbook. Cut selections into paragraphs. Put one paragraph on each index card. Then put each story in a separate envelope. Or, copy selections on a ditto with paragraphs in mixed up order. (Keep each selection on a separate ditto to avoid confusion.)

2. Give each student an envelope. Explain that there is a selection inside but that it is mixed up. Have the students take out the paragraphs, read them, and sequence them according to the context of the story.

3. To check, have each student read his or her selection out loud. Ask other students to listen for correct sequence.

4. Discuss the clues that students can use to help sequence the paragraphs (topic paragraph, key words, time).

5. When stories have been checked for accuracy, have students put cards back in envelope and pass to a person near them to repeat the activity.

6. Make a game out of this by dividing the class into groups. Give each group selections for each member in the group to sequence. The first group with stories in the correct sequence is the winner. Students may help each other.

EXTENSION 1 Mix paragraph cards from three or four different stories together and put in one envelope. Have students sort paragraphs into appropriately related groups and then sequence the paragraphs into stories.

EXTENSION 2 Try this activity another way. Divide the class into groups and give each group three or four sets of related paragraphs all mixed up. Ask each group to sort out their paragraphs and sequence them properly. The first group to sequence all paragraphs correctly wins.

EXTENSION 3 Students may want to cut up some of their own stories for their classmates to read and sequence.

RESOURCES

Be A Better Reader *Series*
Nila Banton Smith
Prentice-Hall

Multiple Skills Series
Barnell-Loft

New Practice Readers
Reading for Concepts
Webster Division
McGraw Hill

Sequence Words

OBJECTIVE To sequence stories using key words that represent time sequences.

MATERIALS Sentence strips that tell a short story, or ditto sheet with mixed up story (see examples).

PROCEDURE

1. Write each sentence of the story on a separate strip of oaktag, or on a ditto with each sentence on a separate line.

2. Explain to students that key words often help to sequence events in a story or paragraph. Ask students to suggest some "key words" that relate to time sequences. Give a few examples to get them started. Write suggestions on board.

Examples:

first	morning	after
then	afternoon	afterwards
finally	evening	immediately
next	last year	soon
last	next year	suddenly
second	now	previously
later	then	
earlier	before	

3. Give each student some mixed up sentences. Have students read sentences, then arrange in correct order using key words as a guide.
4. Have students read stories out loud to check for accuracy.
5. Have students write a time sequence story using key words. Let them write their stories on strips of oaktag after the stories are checked, or write on a ditto in mixed up order. Mix up the strips and let classmates arrange them in correct order.

EXTENSION 1 Explain that another group of words can help to order sequence in writing: words that refer to arrangement of things in space. List a few key words and ask students to suggest additional words.

> in, on, under
> in front of, in back of, next to, behind
> above, below, beyond, beside
> next to, to the right of, to the left of
> near, far

Have students write a description of the classroom. Next ask a number of students to read their descriptions while class members listen for words that provide spatial clues.

EXTENSION 2 Have students locate setting descriptions in their reading material, then list words used that show spatial sequence. Read the selection from Chapter 10 of *Tuck Everlasting* by Natalie Babbitt (Farrar, Straus & Giroux, 1975) which demonstrates the use of spatial words in description.

FIRST, THEN, FINALLY

Then he ran downstairs and ate a quick breakfast.
First he looked at the clock.
It said 8 a.m.
It was 8:30 a.m.
Finally, he looked at the school clock.
Phew!
Jim realized that his clock at home was wrong.
Jim woke up.
He got dressed in three minutes.
He was late for school.
He ran to school as fast as his legs could carry him.

Spotting Details

OBJECTIVE To identify specific details in writing a description of an item.

MATERIALS Paper and pencil.

PROCEDURE
1. Have each student choose an item in the classroom to describe. Have students write down as much descriptive information as possible. Encourage them to include information on color, size, shape, texture, movement, location, and last, function. *Do not* name the item.
2. Have each student read his or her written descriptive information to the class without naming the item.
3. Ask class members to try to identify the item as the description is read.

4. Continue reading descriptions until all items are found.

5. Do this activity in a different setting, perhaps outside in the school yard, or in the library, or the lunchroom, on another day.

EXTENSION   Have students write descriptions of "things" not found in the schoolroom. Have students put *least* important clues first, and most important clues last. See how long it takes students to guess the answer.

Task Analysis

OBJECTIVE   To analyze the sequence of steps in a common task.

MATERIALS   Slips of paper with specific tasks written on them (e.g., "Make Scrambled Eggs").

PROCEDURE

1. Ask students to help you analyze the steps in making scrambled eggs. Encourage students to suggest steps. Write these on the board as they are suggested. Do not attempt to rearrange steps as you go along.

2. Help students identify missing steps. (They generally say "put eggs in a bowl, beat them up, add milk, then cook them.") Add in missing steps (e.g., get eggs from refrigerator, crack egg shells against side of bowl, split egg shells apart, let eggs drop into bowl).

3. Ask students to identify the correct sequence of steps. Write these on another section of the board. Have one or more students pantomime the process of scrambling eggs.

4. Have students choose a slip of paper with another task listed on it. Ask them to analyze the task, listing as many steps as possible, then arrange the steps in appropriate sequence.

5. Ask some students to volunteer to read their directions out loud. Have several other students pantomime the actions. Caution students to do only what the directions say. Point out when they "fill in" steps for the writer.

Sample Tasks

put up and trim a Christmas tree
make chocolate chip cookies
bake a cherry pie
wash the car
build a fire in the fireplace
change a flat tire
brush teeth
put on a belt
tie a tie
plant a bush
tie shoes
iron a shirt
prepare dinner
change sheets on a bed
make lemonade from frozen concentrate
make lemonade from lemons
polish a pair of shoes
make popcorn
make a cake
make a salad
make a bed
repot a plant
sew on a button
make a kite

EXTENSION Write some of these directions on a ditto in mixed up order. Ask students to arrange correctly.

RESOURCES

Carving: How to Carve Wood and Stone
Harvey Weiss
Addison Wesley, 1976

Step-by-step illustrations and directions are given for carving fish, birds, heads, eagles, figures, animals, wooden masks, and totem poles.

Mr. Weiss has written other books in this Beginning Artist's Library. Topics include print-making, sculpture, crafts, ceramics, photography, and others.

The Gadget Book
Harvey Weiss
Crowell, 1971

Directions are given for a number of interesting gadgets. Want to make a "Sunbeam Alarm Clock"? Well, the directions are here.

Other projects included in this book are: "A Mysterious Rolling Can," "A Burglar Alarm," "A Muscle Coordination Tester," and lots of things to do with the insides of an alarm clock, including my favorite, "The Shifty-Eyed Spy."

Easy to Make Puppets
Frieda Gates
Harvey House, 1976

Gives good, clear directions and illustrations for making hand puppets, rod puppets, string puppets, shadow puppets, and even directions for making a stage. A play entitled "The Sad Princess" is included in the book.

Rube Goldberg: His Life and Work
Peter C. Marzio
Harper and Row, 1973

Rube Goldberg is best known for his fantastic cartoons which made fun of modern technology as well as quirks of people, events, and social movements.

This book includes 190 of his greatest cartoons. Students will enjoy studying some of Professor Lucifer Gorgonzola Butts's inventions, such as the Simplified Can Opener (seventeen steps); Simplified Pencil Sharpener (eleven steps); The Automatic Window Closer (sixteen steps); and the Automatic Mosquito Bite Scratcher (fifteen steps).

The Best of Rube Goldberg's Inventions
Charles Keller, editor
Prentice-Hall, 1979

This book presents some of Rube Goldberg's fantastically complex inventions designed to resolve some of the simplest problems.

Time Machine: Past

OBJECTIVE To describe an object, device, or mechanism.

MATERIALS Pictures of means of transportation, household appliances, furniture, garden or yard machines.

PROCEDURE
1. Tell students that they are going into a time machine that will take them to past eras of history (e.g., prehistoric days, medieval times, colonial America). Choose one item and have students explain it in terms that would be understood (e.g., can opener, vacuum cleaner, automobile, motorcycle, stove).
2. Do a sample with the class. Follow the outline presented below. Go through whole process *orally* and make notes on the board.
    I. Name of object, device, or mechanism
        A. Basic definition (description)
        B. Purpose/function
        C. How does it work?
            1. Parts and how related to whole
            2. How made

3. How it operates

4. Results

3. Have students choose another object, device, or mechanism and complete the outline given above. You may want to have students work in pairs or small groups.

4. Have students write a short report on their object, device, or mechanism based on their outline.

5. Have students read their results to classmates.

6. Discuss the kinds of problems that students had when trying to explain object or device. (Frequently many vocabulary words need to be explained.)

EXTENSION 1   Tell students they are going into the future time machine. Ask them to design a mechanism to perform one of the following purposes: personal transportation, or public transportation.

EXTENSION 2   Have students look in magazines for advertisements featuring historical figures using modern equipment (e.g., Benjamin Franklin using a Xerox machine.) Put these advertisements on the bulletin board and use as examples for this activity.

RESOURCES   **The Time Machine, and Other Stories**
H. G. Wells
Scholastic Book Co.
This time machine provides journeys into the far distant future.

Tunnel Through Time
Lester del Rey
Scholastic Book Co., 1970
Two boys become familiar with dinosaurs and other features of the Ice Age after the time machine sends them back millions of years.

What's the Big Idea?

OBJECTIVE   To identify main idea, details, and conclusion in paragraphs.

MATERIALS   Outline format (topic, details, conclusion), overhead transparency of outline format, copies of paragraph selections for students.

PROCEDURE   1. Put copy of the outline format on an overhead projector.

2. Point out that paragraphs or groups of related paragraphs generally have the same basic parts: an introduction or topic sentence which makes a general statement; details, facts, or examples which provide proof for that statement; and a summary or conclusion which quickly reviews the topic sentences. Also point out that this type of arrangement helps the reader understand the content of the paragraph more easily.

3. Explain that you will read a selection and that the students must listen for topic, details, and conclusion. Give students a copy of the paragraph so they can follow along.

4. Read paragraphs to students.

5. Ask students to identify the title and topic of the paragraphs. Write this information on the transparency.

6. Ask students to underline the details on their copy of the paragraph. List these under details.

7. Ask students to underline the conclusion. Write it on transparency.

8. Review the whole outline with students.

9. Repeat the procedure with several other paragraphs.

10. Save the outlines for several days, then ask students to write a paragraph using the outlines as a guide.

EXTENSION 1   Continue this activity with several paragraphs for several days. Gradually ask students to complete worksheet on their own. Save completed worksheets for a week or so, then return them to students and ask them to write paragraphs from the outlines.

The delay of a week after making the outline forces the students to rely on the outline, rather than on their memory for information. In addition, if any outlines are incomplete, students will have difficulty completing the paragraph. Frequently this forces them to pay closer attention to the actual outline making.

EXTENSION 2 Assign a different paragraph to each student to outline. When outlines are complete, ask each student to trade his outline with another student. Ask the second student to write a paragraph using the first student's outline. Students very quickly realize the importance of making their outlines clear when someone else has to write a paragraph from them. Ask the students to comment on problems they had on this activity and suggest ways to alleviate the problems.

Repeat this activity with multiple paragraph selections.

MAIN IDEA, DETAILS, CONCLUSION

Title: _____

Main Idea: _____
_____

Details: 1. _____
_____

2. _____
_____

3. _____
_____

4. _____
_____

Conclusion: _____
_____

Questions

OBJECTIVE To restate questions in the form of statements (topic sentences).

MATERIALS List of suggested questions.

PROCEDURE
1. Write a question on the board. Ask students to rewrite the question as a statement using as many words from the question as possible.
   Question: What were the causes of the American Revolution?
   Restatement: There were several causes for the American Revolution.
2. Have students compare and note the words from the question that were included in the restatement (causes for the American Revolution).
3. Have students note the words that were added to the question (There were several).
4. Ask students to identify the type of information that would be needed in a paragraph to answer the question.
5. Point out that the restated question becomes the first sentence in a paragraph answer. The remainder of the paragraph provides additional information about the topic sentence.
6. Continue changing questions to restatements and asking for the kind of information needed to answer the questions.
7. Have students choose one restatement (topic sentence) and write a short paragraph which answers the question.

Examples

It is best to use questions directly related to the topics being studied in social studies, history, or science classes. The following questions are representative of questions that could be asked in a history class.

What	What were the causes of the American Revolution?
	What did the first American flag look like?
	What did the stars and stripes of the flag represent?
Who	Who attended the first Constitutional Convention?
	Who was the first president of the United States?
	Who designed the first American flag?
Which	Which battles of the American Revolution did the British win? Which did the colonists win?
When	When was the American Revolution fought?
	When was the last battle of the American Revolution?
How	How were candles made in colonial America?
Why	Why was independence so important to the colonists? If you were a colonist, why would independence be important to you?
	Why did the colonists want to have a constitution?

Listen for the Details

OBJECTIVE To listen to a factual paragraph and recall details.

MATERIALS Selections from student workbooks (see resource list for Mixed Up Stories activity).

PROCEDURE
1. Ask students to listen for details in the selection that you read orally. (Adjust number according to ability of students. At first ask them to listen for two or three details. Gradually build up the number required.)
2. Read the paragraph to students twice.
3. Ask students to recall details. Write details on the board as students suggest them. If some details are omitted, read selection again. Ask students to listen for omitted facts.
4. Ask students to write a summary of the paragraph using the information on the board.
5. Have students read completed paragraphs out loud. Compare results.
6. Repeat this activity on another day with a different paragraph.

EXTENSION This activity is especially useful in content subject areas such as social studies, science, and history. Read a factual paragraph from the class text and ask students to listen for and write down details.

Outline Match

OBJECTIVE To make factual paragraphs with prepared outlines.

MATERIALS Short detailed paragraphs, outlines of paragraphs, 3" x 5" index cards, envelopes.

PROCEDURE
1. Select a number of factual paragraphs from student workbooks. Outline each paragraph. Cut out and tape each paragraph and outline on a separate 3" x 5" card.
2. Shuffle several paragraphs and outlines together and put them in an envelope.
3. Give an envelope to each individual or small group of students. Ask students to read the paragraphs and outlines and match them appropriately.
4. Check results.
5. Make this activity harder by preparing a set of paragraphs and *incomplete* outlines. Have students match paragraphs and outlines, then fill in the blanks on the outline.
6. Let students choose one paragraph outline several days later and have them write a paragraph. Then pass out the original paragraphs and have students compare their results with them.

Use multiparagraph articles with partially filled in outlines. Ask students to match paragraphs and outlines, then complete the outlines. Save the outlines for several days. Return outlines to students and have them write a multiparagraph article using the outline as a guide. Have students compare their results with original paragraphs.

Prove It!

OBJECTIVE To provide descriptive details that support a generalization.

MATERIALS List of generalizations.

PROCEDURE
1. Write a generalized statement on the board. Ask students to suggest details that would prove the generalization. Write suggestions on the board.
   Example: The man was very poor.
   Proof: His clothes were faded and ragged.
   He wasn't wearing a coat, even though it was very cold.
   His shoes were very scuffed and had large holes.
2. Ask students to suggest behavioral clues that would suggest poverty.
   Proof: He sat in the park every day.
   He slept on a park bench every night.
   He didn't have a job.
   He asked people for money.
3. Have each student write a description of the man that shows he was poor.
4. Continue this activity on another day with another sample generalization.

EXTENSION Other examples to use:

"The weather has been horrible this week."

"Mr. Jones was very angry."

"The citizens of Brownsville were disturbed about the new taxes."

"The boys got very dirty playing football yesterday."

Example: The weather has been horrible this week.
Proof: The temperature dropped to 20 degrees.
It has been foggy and damp every day.
Visibility has been very poor.
Winds reached 35 miles per hour.
The airport was closed because of fog and strong winds.
A lot of snow fell in the mountains, closing roads and causing accidents.

Broad and Narrow

OBJECTIVE To narrow topics that are too broad.

MATERIALS Sample topics, sample broad and narrow chart.

PROCEDURE
1. Explain that sometimes writers have difficulty with reports because the topics they choose are too broad. For most reports, it is best to choose a narrow topic because all relevant facts and/or generalizations can be easily covered.
2. To demonstrate the broadness of some topics, put an example on the board. Ask students to suggest as many possible subtopics as they can for the following example.
   Example: Animals

   Subtopic Suggestions
   How Animals Protect Themselves

How Animals Find Food
What Animals Eat
Animal Homes
Animal Habits
Dangers that Animals Face
Unusual Looking Animals
Farm Animals
Wild Animals

3. Point out that even these subtopics are too broad. Ask students to suggest a narrower topic for each one. For example, choose specific animals to narrow the topic.

Example

How
{ Antelopes
  Rabbits
  Eagles }
{ Hunt for Food
  Protect Themselves
  Make Their Homes }

4. Ask students to choose one narrow topic and write a short report. Encourage them to use reference sources (encyclopedias) as well as nonfiction library materials.
5. Repeat the activity on another day using a different broad topic.

EXTENSION   Give students a copy of the Broad and Narrow Topics chart. Ask them to fill in at least two additional narrow topics for each broad topic suggested.

Figure 4-1
Broad and Narrow Topics

Too Broad	Still Broad	Narrow
Animals	Eating Habits of Animals	Eating Habits of Guinea Pigs
Plants	Unusual Plants	The Strange World of Insect-Eating Plants
Occupations	Careers in Communications Industry	Duties of a T.V. News Reporter
Fishing	Fresh Water Fishing	Trout Fishing
School	School Activities	Drama Club Activities
The Universe	The Solar System	Jupiter

Hasty Generalizations

OBJECTIVE   To identify inaccurate generalizations.

MATERIALS   Sample generalizations.

PROCEDURE	1. Tell students that sometimes people make "hasty generalizations"—statements that are very broad and not always true. Give the example "Winters are always cold," and ask students to suggest times when this might not be true.
	2. Ask students to identify the word that makes the statement untrue ("always"). Ask students to suggest places where it might be hot in winter.
	3. Ask students to revise the statement to make it true. This can be done by adding the names of specific places where it is cold or by adding a qualifier to the sentence.

"Winters in the Artic are cold." (specific place)

"Winters are cold in Alaska." (specific place)

"Winters are cold in *some* places." (qualifier)

4. Read other hasty generalizations to the class. Identify the words in each that make them untrue and put these words on a chart. Show parallel modifiers or specific details in chart.

General Words	*Qualifiers*
Always	Sometimes
Never	Occasionally
	Usually
	Generally
All	Some
Everybody	Most
Everyone	Many
Every	

5. Rewrite the hasty generalizations with the students and add either a qualifier or a specific detail that modifies the sentence. Develop several modified versions of each hasty generalization.

EXTENSION Have students deliberately write some hasty generalizations, then switch papers with partners who read and add words to correct the statement. Read before and after results out loud to whole class. Have students try to think of exceptions to the modified generalizations.

SAMPLE GENERALIZATIONS

Generalizations	*Exceptions*
Everybody sleeps at night.	(Nightwatchmen usually don't.)
	(But even they sometimes fall asleep on job.)
All dogs are friendly.	(Dobermans are mean.)
	(Are *all* Dobermans mean?)
All apples taste delicious.	(Rotten apples taste awful.)
It never rains on Sunday.	(Sometimes it does.)
All Mexicans love hot food.	(Maybe some don't.)
Mexican food has chili peppers in it.	(Not all dishes.)
All students are lazy.	(Some are not.)

Fact or Fiction

OBJECTIVE To separate paragraphs of fact from paragraphs of fiction.

MATERIALS Four inch by six inch index cards, paragraphs from newspapers and/or workbooks, encyclopedias, fictional books.

PROCEDURE
1. Cut paragraphs of fact and fiction from newspapers and/or workbooks. Copy additional paragraphs from encyclopedias or other nonfiction materials, and also fictional library materials. Mount each paragraph on a 4" x 6" index card.
2. Mix up cards. Choose one card and read it to students. Ask students to decide whether the paragraph is fact or fiction.
3. Ask students to identify the differences between fact and fiction. Make a chart on board to summarize differences.

Fact	Fiction
• based on facts which can be checked	• based on ideas which cannot be checked
• related details grouped together	• details not grouped together
• no main characters	• characters identified
• no setting	• setting identified
• no plot	• character problem (plot development)
	• builds up suspense

Is That So? (Fact or Opinion?)

OBJECTIVE   To identify statements of fact and opinion.

MATERIALS   List of statements: some factual, some opinion (see examples).

PROCEDURE
1. Read a statement and have students decide whether it is a fact or an opinion. Does everyone agree with the statement? Can it be proved? If not, it must be an opinion.
    Examples: Ford Motor Company makes the best cars.
    Ford Motor Company makes Mustangs.
2. Make a chart on the chalkboard. List factual statements on one side and opinion statements on the other side. Notice how many opinions use "hasty generalizat'ons." Notice the ways opinions were modified. (Specific examples or details were added to make the statement true.)
3. Give students a factual statement and have them write an opinion statement on the same topic.
    Fact: "It is raining today."
    Opinion: "The weather today is great. I love rain."
4. Have students read their opinions out loud to the class. Ask other students to identify the words that changed the statement from fact to opinion.

EXTENSION   Save all fact and opinion statements and copy them on a ditto or index cards in mixed up order. Students can sort fact and opinion statements as an independent activity on another day.

EXAMPLES: FACT AND OPINION

I waited exactly six minutes and thirty seconds to get my lunch.

We have to wait a long time to get our lunch. (How long is long?)

All cars need gasoline in order to run. (What about cars that use Diesel fuel—Mercedes?)

My car, a 1977 Chevrolet, uses no-lead gas.

Pancakes make the best breakfast. (I like scrambled eggs.)

Pancakes are made out of flour, water, and eggs.

All students are lazy.

John did not do his science homework.

The temperature is 92 degrees today.

Phew, it's really hot today. (How hot is hot?)

That kid is really tall. (How tall? Taller than my father?)

That kid is 5 foot 10.

Our product, Fluffy Flour, is the best.

You use flour to make bread.

A new Cadillac is very expensive. (Even for a millionaire?)

That Cadillac cost $10,000.

Cadillacs cost more than Volkswagens.

Every family needs two cars. (My mother doesn't drive. The kids don't drive yet, either.)

That dress was very cheap. (How cheap? For me or the millionaire?)

That dress cost $249.50.

This book is too long to read. (What's too long? 100 pages? 800?)

This book has 545 pages in it.

We had a terrible lunch today.

The menu for today is hamburgers and french fries.

VOCABULARY The selection and arrangement of vocabulary control interest, meaning, and effectiveness of written expression. Experienced writers use a variety of word types while poor writers tend to overuse a limited number of commonly used words. As a result, their writing lacks clarity and precision and frequently fails to interest the reader.

The use of poor or inappropriate vocabulary in written expression may be due to any of several factors. Some students simply do not have a good command of vocabulary in oral expression, while other students, who do have a broad speaking vocabulary, may use simpler words in writing because they are easier to spell. The first student needs more emphasis on building vocabulary comprehension and usage in *oral expression*, while the second needs more practice in *spelling the words he or she uses in oral expression.*

The activities in this vocabulary development section are based on the premise that students can broaden their command of vocabulary and spelling by working and playing with words in a variety of ways.

The following specific vocabulary skills are developed in this section.

1. *Using Specific Vocabulary.* Developing an awareness of alternative vocabulary choices to the most commonly used words is essential to increasing effectiveness in writing. Emphasis is placed on identifying specific nouns, verbs, synonyms, and antonyms to replace those overused, nonspecific words.
2. *Using Descriptive Words.* Examples of beautiful imagery in poetry, fiction, and nonfiction help students visualize images. These serve as a stimulus for students' own writing.
3. *Using Abstract Words.* Defining abstract words encourages students to provide specific facts, details, or examples.
4. *Playing with Words.* Arranging words in interesting patterns according to sounds creates interesting poetic effects in writing. Activities that emphasize alliteration and onomatopoeia allow students to play with words.
5. *Making Original Comparisons.* Students frequently use stereotyped phrases in their writing without stopping to think of different ways that the same idea could be expressed. Playing with these stereotypes and rephrasing them with precise vocabulary choices draw students' attention to the problem.

FEELINGS ABOUT WORDS

Some words cling
as ice in drink.
Some move with grace
A dance, a lace.
Some sound thin:
Wail, scream and pin.
Some words are squat:
A mug, a pot,
And some are plump,
Fat, round and dump.
Some words are light:
drift, lift and bright.
A few are small:
A, is and all.
And some are thick,
Glue, paste and brick.
Some words are sad:
"I never had. . ."
And others gay:
Joy, spin and play.
Some words are sick:
Stab, scratch and nick.

Some words are hot:
Fire, flame and shot.
Some words are sharp,
Sword, point and carp.
And some alert:
Glint, glance and flirt.
Some words are lazy:
Saunter, hazy.
And some words preen:
Pride, pomp and queen.
Some words are quick,
A jerk, a flick.
Some words are slow:
Lag, stop and grow,
While others poke
As ox with yoke.
Some words can fly—
There's wind, there's high;
And some words cry:
"Goodbye. . .Goodbye. . ."

"Feelings About Words" from WORDS, WORDS, WORDS by Mary O'Neill. Copyright © 1966 by Mary O'Neill. Reprinted by permission of Doubleday & Company, Inc.

Using Specific Nouns

OBJECTIVE   To list specific nouns in different categories.

MATERIALS   Chart paper and magic markers.

PROCEDURE
1. Choose a category word and ask class members to suggest specific nouns that would fit this category. Write suggestions on the board (e.g., *dogs:* Great Dane, Beagle, Poodle, Cocker Spaniel, Irish Setter, Elk Hound, Terrier, Sheep Dog).
2. Explain the reason for this activity: Very often we use common nouns in our writing when we really could use very specific nouns. This activity will alert students to other possible word choices.
3. Divide the class into small groups and let each group choose a category. Ask them to list specific nouns in their category on the chart. Dictionaries or other reference materials may be used.
   Suggested categories: states, countries, cars, trees, flowers, desserts, vegetables, fruits, zoo animals, birds, occupations, sports, tools, meats, toys, and games.
4. Have each group write five sentences using specific nouns from their categories, then read sentences to the class. Ask class to identify the specific nouns used and name the category.
5. Put finished charts with specific nouns and sample sentences on bulletin board as a reminder to students to use specific nouns in writing whenever possible.

EXTENSION 1   Let students choose a category and illustrate specific nouns from that group.

EXTENSION 2   *Categories*

Have students make a grid on their paper, then list some category words along the side of the grid and their name across the top of the grid. The students must fill in each box with a word from the category that begins with the specific letter at the top of the column. Students may use a dictionary to help find appropriate words.

You can use scoring procedures with this activity. Give five points for each block that is filled in. The student with the highest score wins. Use the same word across the top of the grid when using scoring procedures because some names have more difficult letters. An open time allowance will allow slower students to compete with faster students. To shorten the time necessary to complete this activity, pair students of different ability levels. The better student can help the poorer student.

EXTENSION 3   See "Grocery List" Activity in Organization Skills section.

Figure 4–2
Category Word Grid

	N	A	N	C	Y
animals *newt*					
food *noodles*					
clothes *necktie*					
countries *New Zealand*					
states *New York*					

Using Specific Verbs

OBJECTIVE   To identify specific verbs that can be used in place of overused verbs.

MATERIALS   A beginner's thesaurus (*In Other Words*), drawing paper, crayons, overused verb list.

PROCEDURE
1. Explain that students frequently rely on very common overused verbs in writing. The purpose of this activity is to alert students to the words that are overused and to identify specific verbs to use in their place.
2. Select one overused verb and ask students to suggest other words that could be used instead.

Example: "said"

answered	responded	argued
mentioned	discussed	explained
chattered	sighed	asked
described	protested	called
whispered	repeated	
cried	yelled	

If students cannot think of any, have them look in a thesaurus or in their current library book to see what the author used in place of said.
3. Divide the class into groups. Give each group an overused verb (see chart on page 116). Have students look up a verb in the thesaurus and list alternative words on a chart.
4. Have each student draw a picture that demonstrates his specific verb, and write a sentence to go with the picture.
5. Have students share their illustrations and sentences with class members. Have class members guess the original overused verb.
6. Make a class verb thesaurus by putting all of the illustrations and sentences in a notebook binder.
7. Encourage students to add pictures and sentences to the binder during free periods.

8. Keep a list of overused verbs on the bulletin board as a reminder of which verbs to avoid.

EXTENSION   Repeat this activity using overused adjectives.

SYNONYMS (VERBS)

Be sure to use words in context!

ask

query	beg	coax	request
inquire	demand	interrogate	

come

appear	arrive	approach	attend
enter	visit	reach	

eat

consume	devour	feed	gnaw
gobble	nibble	swallow	chew
digest	dine	feast	

get

receive	obtain	fetch	earn
procure	capture	purchase	collect
acquire			

give

donate	supply	present	dispense
dole out	distribute	deliver	bequeath
contribute	consign		

go/went

depart	disappear	escape	leave
retreat	vanish	vacate	flee
retire			

hate

detest	dislike	abhor	disapprove
despise	loathe	shun	denounce
resent	disfavor	condemn	

have

possess	own	control	treasure
hold	keep	guard	maintain

help

assist	aid	cooperate	support

keep

preserve	conserve	protect	guard
retain	hoard	maintain	

laugh

roar	howl	guffaw	snicker
giggle	chuckle	grin	smile
chortle	smirk		

like

enjoy	admire	love	prefer
favor	be fond of	treasure	

make

assemble	build	construct	create
establish	invent	manufacture	originate
produce	develop	compose	fabricate

put

place	lay	deposit	arrange
spread	plant	situate	install
lodge			

run

bolt	chase	flee	gallop
jog	lope	race	sprint
trot	dash	scurry	scamper

said

added	agreed	began	commented
continued	cried	declared	exclaimed
observed	shouted	shrieked	stated
announced	related	answered	suggested
questioned	bragged	discussed	sighed
yelled	mentioned	explained	argued
chattered	responded	described	

see/look

observe	view	glance	gaze
stare	glare	peer	peek
watch	examine	scrutinize	inspect
behold	review		

start

originate	introduce	establish	initiate
commence	launch		

stop

halt	pause	discontinue	terminate
conclude	finish	cease	quit

take/bring

carry	deliver	transport	tote
steal	borrow	capture	seize
confiscate	dispossess	clutch	appropriate
procure			

talk

converse	discuss	communicate	speak
chat	gossip	chatter	argue
quarrel			

think

suppose	imagine	believe	wonder
guess	consider	ponder	plan
muse	cogitate	contemplate	ruminate
meditate	speculate	deliberate	

walk

amble	hike	hobble	limp
lurch	march	saunter	shuffle

stalk	step	stride	stroll
stumble	tiptoe	traipse	trudge
tramp	stagger	promenade	meander

want

| desire | aspire | covet | |

work/do

toil	slave	labor	perform
practice	produce	accomplish	function
operate	execute	act	complete

bad

| naughty | harmful | evil | dangerous |
| belligerent | | | |

beautiful

| lovely | attractive | handsome | appealing |
| charming | resplendent | impressive | magnificent |

better/best

superior	favored	premium	supreme
paramount	incomparable	matchless	superlative
inimitable	choice		

big/fat/large

mammoth	titanic	immense	vast
enormous	monstrous	giant	tremendous
massive	gargantuan	colossal	gigantic
stout	plump	obese	husky
corpulent	brawny		

easy

| simple | obvious | manageable | facile |

enough

| sufficient | abundant | adequate | ample |
| satisfactory | plentiful | suitable | |

fantastic

| extravagant | outlandish | ridiculous | exotic |
| preposterous | | | |

fast

| speedy | brisk | accelerated | hasty |
| rapid | racing | | |

funny

hilarious	laughable	humorous	comical
amusing	witty	ludicrous	whimsical
droll			

good (food)

| delicious | tasty | flavorful | appetizing |
| luscious | tempting | excellent | savory |

good (person)

honest	loyal	respectable	conscientious
reliable	ethical	decent	pleasant
kind	generous		

happy

joyful	merry	cheerful	contented
cheery	jovial	good-humored	jubilant
high-spirited	mirthful	gleeful	jolly

hard

difficult	arduous	tricky	tedious
complex	abstract	puzzling	troublesome
laborious			

important

significant	paramount	considerable	momentous
essential	critical	primary	principal
influential	substantial	vital	famous
necessary	valuable		

interesting

stimulating	arresting	fascinating	absorbing
satisfying	impressive	captivating	refreshing
attractive			

little/small

microscopic	diminutive	miniature	dwarf
undersized	wee	puny	skinny
gaunt	slender	minute	petite
emaciated			

many/a lot

numerous	multitudinous	sundry	innumerable
numberless	countless	prevalent	plentiful
abundant			

new

newfangled	fresh	modern	faddish
contemporary	fashionable	latest	current
innovative			

old

obsolete	old-fashioned	aged	elderly
enfeebled	decrepit	patched	dilapidated
antiquated	decayed	historical	antediluvian

really

actually	certainly	absolutely	positively
authentically	legitimately	precisely	literally
unmistakably			

right

accurate	precise	certain	exact
factual	proven	valid	suitable
proper	appropriate	reasonable	rational
legitimate	equitable	lawful	

sad

sorrowful	miserable	melancholy	downcast
forlorn	mournful	gloomy	depressed
anguished	grieving	despairing	morose
moody			

slow

sluggish	diminish	leisurely	overdue
lazily	inactive	creeping	crawling

terrible

terrifying	appalling	horrifying	shocking
unfortunate	disastrous	petrifying	

too

additionally	furthermore	exceedingly	excessively
extremely			

ugly

homely	unattractive	hideous	horrid

very/quite

extremely	exceedingly	particularly	emphatically
extraordinarily	substantially	extensively	remarkably
noticeably	conspicuously	excessively	enormously
intensely	exceptionally	severely	seriously
infinitely	uncommonly	totally	entirely
positively			

wonderful/good/nice

useful	valuable	excellent	pleasant
likeable			

Synonym Call

OBJECTIVE   To identify synonym meaning.

MATERIALS   Blank cards, magic marker, master list of synonyms.

PROCEDURE
1. Choose four or five groups of synonyms from the master list. (Use list from previous activity. Write one synonym on each card. Shuffle cards and pass them out to students. Have students spread cards on desk. (Or prepare a ditto which has a number of sets of synonyms listed in columns. Leave one empty space at the top.)

   Example: _____

   roar
   giggle
   chuckle
   snicker
   guffaw

2. Call out synonyms in mixed up order from one group on the master list ("snicker, giggle, guffaw, chuckle, chortle, grin").
3. Ask students to pick up words (or circle them on ditto) as they are called and to identify the synonym most commonly used as soon as they can identify it (e.g., "laugh"). Add any synonyms that students suggest to the list.
4. Put a sample sentence for each group of words that you use in the lesson on the board. Substitute synonyms that the students have on their desks and discuss variations of meaning.

   The class *laughed* at the joke.
   The class *snickered* at the joke.
   The class *guffawed* at the joke.
   The class *giggled* at the joke.

5. Encourage students to make up additional sentences using a selected set of syn-

onyms. Look up terms in *In Other Words* to read more about distinctions in word meanings.

EXTENSION   Keep all synonym cards together in one envelope. Individuals or small groups can shuffle them up, then sort them during free periods.

RESOURCES

Word Links
Creative Teaching Press
    Word Links is a domino-type game that helps develop students' awareness of word relationships. Two to four players can play at one time. Emphasis is on synonyms, antonyms, or both. Eighty words are included on forty-two dominoes. For intermediate grades.

Synonym Poster Cards
Milton Bradley
    Thirty cards, 11¼" x 14", show sixty pairs of synonyms in isolation and in sentence contexts.

In Other Words
W. Cabell Greet, William A. Jenkins, Andrew Schiller
Scott, Foresman
    Two levels of *In Other Words*, designed for upper elementary grades, enable young readers and writers to explore synonyms and antonyms of the most commonly used words. Sample sentences and pictures help to explain the distinctions between closely related words. A valuable resource for every classroom.

Synonym Pass and Sort

OBJECTIVE   To sort synonyms according to meaning.

MATERIALS   Small blank cards, magic markers, a beginner's thesaurus (*In Other Words*).

PROCEDURE
1. Divide class into small groups. Give each group some blank cards, magic markers, a thesaurus, and five overused words chosen from their writing or from the charts in previous activities.
2. Have the students look their five words up in the thesaurus (*In Other Words* is the best source for elementary grades), find synonyms, then write one synonym on one side of the card and a clue sentence on the other side. Encourage students to make as many cards as possible using all the synonym possibilities for each overused word.
       When the period is finished, take a tally of the following points:

   • Which word had the most synonyms?
   • Which word had the fewest synonyms?
   • Which group found the most synonyms?

   Have students read the word and its synonyms when answering these questions.
3. On another day, have each group shuffle their words and pass them to another group. The second group must sort out the synonyms in piles according to meaning. If the meaning is unknown, they must look the word up in the dictionary or thesaurus. Set a time limit. The winning group is the one that matches all the cards first. Give bonus points for any group that can think of an additional synonym and write a sample sentence to show its meaning.
4. Continue the activity by switching cards between groups and repeating the process.

EXTENSION   Keep cards together in an envelope. Individuals or small groups can sort them during their independent activities time.

Antonym Concentration

OBJECTIVE   To match antonym pairs.

MATERIALS   Small blank cards, magic markers, list of antonyms.

PROCEDURE   1. Divide the class into small groups. Give each group twelve different antonym pairs and twenty-four small cards. Have students write one word per card.
2. Shuffle the card set and place cards face down in four columns—six words in a column. Have players take turns and turn up two cards at a time. If the cards are antonyms, the player keeps the pair and takes another turn. This player continues until she or he fails to turn up a match. The second player then takes his or her turn.
3. To keep the word pairs, the student must use each word correctly in a sentence.
4. The player with the most cards at the end of the game is the winner.
5. Have groups exchange card sets and play another round with new words.

EXTENSION 1   Have students make an illustrated antonym dictionary. Let each student choose several antonym pairs and illustrate them. Complete the page with a sentence that correctly uses one of the antonyms. Collect class papers and put them in binder.

EXTENSION 2   *Unusual Opposites*

Get the book *Opposites* by Richard Wilbur (Harcourt Brace Jovanovich). You may find it in the children's section of your school or local library. Read several of the questions found in the book to your students (e.g., "What is the opposite of a prince?"). Let students give their suggestions before you read the rest of the selection. Write student suggestions on the board, then read Wilbur's answer. Your students may be surprised by the answers! Continue by trying out other selections from the book. Next, let students choose some words and write some of their own "unusual opposites."

What Is The Opposite of a Prince?

What is the opposite of a prince?
A frog must be the answer, since,
As all good fairy stories tell,
When some witch says a magic spell,
Causing the prince to be disguised
So that he won't be recognized,
He always ends up green and sad
And sitting on a lily pad.

From OPPOSITES, copyright © 1973 by Richard Wilbur. Reprinted by permission of Harcourt Brace Jovanovich, Inc.

ANTONYMS

Set 1

work–play	wet–dry	hard–easy
day–night	young–old	noisy–quiet
old–new	early–late	lost–found
take–give	brother–sister	fat–thin
now–then	front–back	laugh–cry
go–come	dirty–clean	asleep–awake
go–stop	yes–no	mother–father
boy–girl	big–little	push–pull
up–down	hard–soft	under–over
hot–cold	loud–quiet	run–walk
happy–sad		

Set 2

city–country	giant–midget	appear–disappear
aunt–uncle	fix–break	beautiful–ugly

grandmother–grandfather
top–bottom
good–bad
off–on
fast–slow
light–dark
light–heavy
floor–ceiling

bright–dull
sharp–dull
true–false
inside–outside
right–wrong
right–left
friend–enemy
answer–question

begin–end
beginning–ending
start–stop
always–never
first–last
before–after
near–far

Set 3

for–against
rich–poor
lead–follow
whole–part
swiftly–slowly
hate–love
cheap–expensive
sour–sweet
dead–alive
black–white
smooth–rough

crooked–straight
add–subtract
multiply–divide
above–below
strong–weak
empty–full
near–far
tight–loose
sloppy–neat
north–south

east–west
sick–well
narrow–wide
evening–morning
wild–tame
remember–forget
safe–dangerous
brave–cowardly
wise–foolish
husband–wife

Set 4

bright–dim
victory–defeat
agree–disagree
fresh–stale
difficult–easy
same–different
gentle–rough
public–private
coarse–fine
cautious–reckless

raw–cooked
deep–shallow
bold–timid
lengthen–shorten
succeed–fail
entrance–exit
loan–borrow
arrive–depart
simple–complicated
help–hinder

thoughtful–thoughtless
common–unusual
whisper–shout
conceal–expose
flimsy–sturdy
friend–enemy
gather–scatter
reward–punish
beneath–above

Set 5

inner–outer
length–width
idle–busy
accept–reject
imprison–free
wise–ignorant
profit–loss
cause–effect
demolish–construct
deliberate–accidental
deserted–crowded

assemble–disassemble
passive–active
patient–impatient
necessary–unnecessary
encourage–discourage
appropriate–inappropriate
gradual–sudden
inferior–superior
enthusiastic–indifferent
polluted–pure

descend–ascend
descent–ascent
hasty–sluggish
boisterous–subdued
diminish–increase
unite–separate
united–separated
former–latter
strengthen–weaken
advance–retreat

Set 6

vertical–horizontal
maximum–minimum
optimistic–pessimistic

progress–regress
naive–sophisticated
harmony–discord

include–omit
positive–negative
abundant–scarce

create–destroy	deposit–withdraw	villain–hero
accept–reject	tentative–permanent	reluctant–enthusiastic
convex–concave	analysis–synthesis	illegal–lawful
abstract–concrete	asset–liability	authentic–imitation
simple–complex	epilogue–prologue	literal–figurative
modern–obsolete	intermittent–continuous	irrelevant–pertinent
hazardous–safe		

RESOURCES

Antonym Poster Cards
Milton Bradley
Thirty cards, 11¼" x 14", show sixty pairs of antonyms in isolation and in sentence contexts.

That's Good, That's Bad
Joan M. Lexau
Dial Press, 1963
"Boy" gets out of one jam and immediately gets into another one. Kids love the switch from "That's good," to "That's bad." Read this story to them and let them think up some more good-bad stories. Easy reader.

Example

Tell students the story of the pilot who went up in his airplane one day. It was a beautiful day.
"That's good."
A sudden thunderstorm came up.
"That's bad."
No, the thunderstorm was twenty miles away.
"That's good."
But the airplane engine conked out.
"That's bad."
But the pilot had a parachute.
"That's good."
But the parachute wouldn't open.
"That's bad."
But he was falling toward a haystack in the field.
"That's good."
But there was a pitchfork in the haystack.
"That's bad."
But he missed the pitchfork.
"That's good."
He missed the haystack, too.
THAT'S BAD.
YEAH!

Substitution

OBJECTIVE   To substitute specific words for general words.

MATERIALS   Sample sentences.

PROCEDURE
1. Write a sample sentence on the board or overhead transparency.
2. Underline one word at a time and ask students to suggest a *more specific word* that would make sense in the sentence (the words do not have to be synonyms). Rewrite the sentence with the new word.

   The <u>old</u> man walked slowly.

   The <u>comical man</u> walked slowly.

   The comical clown <u>walked</u> slowly.

   The comical clown tumbled <u>slowly</u>.

   The comical clown tumbled awkwardly.

3. Read completed sentences. Compare first sentences with the last sentence. What happened?
4. Continue this activity by using a new sample sentence. Some students may wish to continue the activity on their own, while others may need more practice with the group.

   Examples
   1. The little girl played a game.
   2. My puppy chewed something.

3. David quickly climbed the tree.
4. The thing was big and black.
5. The football player threw the football.
6. That big elephant ate the grass.
7. Several children played a game.
8. A little old lady sang a song.

EXTENSION
1. Use only *synonyms* in the new sentences: The elderly gentleman ambled awkwardly.
2. Use only *antonyms* in the new sentences: The teenage football player dashed briskly.

Repetitive Words

OBJECTIVE   To substitute specific words for repetitive words.

MATERIALS   Sample paragraphs with repetitive words (following).

PROCEDURE
1. Read a sample paragraph to the students and ask them to identify the problem (in this case the repeated use of the word "nice"). Emphasize the repeated word as you read.
   Example: "nice"

   > It was a *nice* warm day in April. I was wearing my *nice* new clothes that I had just bought at the *nice* store. A *nice* breeze was blowing *nice* leaves across the *nice* street. There were *nice* children playing in the *nice* yard with their *nice* dog. I could hear the *nice* chirping of the birds who were perched on the *nice* branches of the *nice* oak tree. It was really a *nice* day.

2. Give students a copy of the paragraph and let them suggest alternatives for the repeated word. Read the corrected paragraph to the class.
3. Give students another paragraph to do on their own. Encourage them to use a thesaurus to find alternatives to the repeated word.
4. Have individual students read their original paragraph, then their corrected paragraph to the class. Make a list of different words used by the students.
5. Place corrected paragraphs on the bulletin board.

REPETITIVE WORD STORIES

"said"

> "I want to go to the park," *said* the little girl.
> "Not now," *said* her mother. "I'm getting dinner ready."
> "Please take me to the park. I want to see my friends," *said* the girl.
> "I told you I am busy," *said* the mother.
> "If you don't take me to the park, I won't eat dinner," *said* the girl.
> "Well, if you don't stop complaining, you'll go to your room without any dinner," *said* the mother.
> "O.K.," *said* the girl.

"good"

> Yesterday was a *good* day for a picnic. Early in the morning I telephoned my *good* friend Larry and asked him whether he wanted to join me. He said a picnic was a *good* idea. We decided that a *good* time to meet would be twelve

o'clock in front of the park entrance. I brought some *good* roast beef sandwiches and a jar of *good* potato salad. Larry brought some *good* lemonade, which he carried in his father's *good* thermos. He also brought along some *good* homemade chocolate cake. When we found a *good* spot to eat near a stream, we spread out my *good* picnic blanket and unpacked the *good* food. After having a *good* feast we went on a *good* long walk. Larry and I left the *good* park at four o'clock. We both felt *good*.

Mary Had a Little Lamb

OBJECTIVE   To rewrite nursery rhymes using *specific* nouns, verbs, and adjectives.

MATERIALS   Several nursery rhymes that have nouns, verbs, and adjectives omitted.

PROCEDURE
1. Choose a nursery rhyme and write it on an overhead transparency, leaving blanks for all nouns, verbs, and adjectives (see sample following).
2. Tell students that they are going to help write a nursery rhyme by suggesting *specific* words for categories that you call out. Encourage the use of proper nouns in order to get extremely specific responses. *Do not* give students a copy of the ditto sheet yet.
3. Read the first category and ask for suggestions for the blank (e.g., "girl's name"). Encourage students to think of uncommon responses (e.g., Melody, instead of Mary). Write the response in the blank on the transparency. Do not put transparency on the overhead projector until it is completely filled in.
4. Put completed transparency on overhead projector and have a student read the final version.
5. Ask students to guess the name of the original nursery rhyme.
6. Have students write additional original nursery rhymes by using the word substitution method.

SAMPLE NURSERY RHYME

(Mary Had a Little Lamb)

_____ had a _____ _____ (girl's name)   (size—adj.)   (noun—animal name)
Its _____ was _____ as _____ (noun—body part)   (color)   (noun—weather word)
Everywhere that _____ the _____ (repeat girl's name)   (repeat animal name)
was sure to _____. (verb—action word)
It followed her to _____ (noun—place)   (when phrase)
to _____ _____ (repeat place)   (repeat when phrase)
to _____ _____ (repeat place)   (repeat when phrase)
It made the _____ _____ and _____ (collective noun)   (verb—action word)   (verb—action word)
To see a _____ at _____. (repeat animal name)   (repeat place)

RESOURCES   Mad Libs,
Monster Mad Libs,
Son of Mad Libs,
Sooper Mad Libs,
and others.
Price, Stern, Sloan Publishers, Inc.

"Mad Libs" are published collections of poems and short stories in which words have been left out. Students suggest words to fill in these blanks with the appropriate part of speech. The results are usually quite humorous.

Descriptive Words

OBJECTIVE   To pick out descriptive phrases in reading material.

MATERIALS   Several books that have very good descriptive selections.

PROCEDURE

1. Read to students several pages from a book that contains vivid descriptions. Ask students to listen for descriptive phrases and sentences that help them form a specific visual picture in their mind.
2. Write phrases on the board as students recall them. Talk about different ideas that students had as they heard the descriptive words.
3. Ask students to identify the way the author helped them to imagine the scenes or picture (e.g., specific words, colorful words, concrete images, comparisons). Write these ideas on the board.
4. Read several more pages and continue to identify and talk about the descriptive phrases.
5. Ask students to select one descriptive phrase or sentence to illustrate. Have them write the phrase under the illustration.
6. Or, have students illustrate without labeling the picture. Let other students match phrases and illustrations.

EXTENSION   Have students look for interesting descriptive phrases as they read on their own. Keep an ongoing bulletin board for these phrases. Have students illustrate the phrases and add them to the bulletin board. Share new phrases during group discussions.

RESOURCES

Have You Seen Trees?
Joanne Oppenheim
Addison Wesley, 1967
Specific details and varied vocabulary are used to describe trees.

The Clean Brook
Margaret Bartlett
Crowell, 1960
The author uses specific details when describing objects and settings.

The Brook
Carol and Donald Carrick
Macmillan, 1967
Many beautiful watercolor illustrations along with beautiful usage of words help form visual images.

Poems Make Pictures,
Pictures Make Poems
Giose Rimovelli and Paul Pimsleur
Pantheon, 1972
Each poem in this collection makes a picture. The book will give students all kinds of ideas about the many different forms that poems can take. Some of the poems form the shape of a shoe, a boat, or a building.

First Voices, *Vol. 1 and Vol. 2*
Geoffrey Summerfield
Random House (Singer School Division), 1971
This four volume anthology presents an *outstanding* collection of original and traditional rhymes and poems by poets from around the world. Some of the material included is written by children. Photographs and illustrations provide added interest.

There Is No Rhyme for Silver
Eve Merriam
Atheneum, 1962
This collection includes invented words.

Ounce, Dice, Trice
Alistair Reid
Little, Brown, 1958
Like to make up new words and

definitions? You will enjoy some of the invented vocabulary and definitions in this book. Kids will really get the idea of "playing with words" after hearing some samples from this book.

Silly Songs and Sad
Ellen Raskin
Crowell, 1967
Here is another good collection of poems. Ellen Raskin's poems are delightfully written and give students some excellent samples of ways to "play with words."

I'm Nobody!
Who Are You?
The Poems of Emily Dickinson
for Children
Stemmer House Publishers, Inc., 1978
This edition of Emily Dickinson's poems features illustrations of the cos-
tumes and settings of nineteenth century New England and contains such familiar poems as "Hope is the Thing with Feathers," and "There is no Frigate Like a Book."

I See the Winds
Kazue Mizumura
Crowell, 1966
Kazue Mizumura captures the many forms of wind through the seasons in free verse and beautiful illustrations.

Wind, Sand, and Sky
Rebecca Caudill
Dutton, 1976
Caudill uses beautiful phrases of imagery in her writing, and gives us a romantic view of the desert. The illustrations by Donald Carrick add tone and depth to this beautiful book. Many beautiful comparisons are made.

Make It Real

OBJECTIVE   To list concrete details for abstract words.

MATERIALS   Paper and pencil.

PROCEDURE   1. Tell the class that specific details often make abstract words seem very real to the reader. List some abstract words on the board. Have students suggest others.

fear	loneliness	bravery	love
sadness	happiness	solitude	friendship
hate	anger	beauty	contentment

2. Have each student write a phrase or sentence about "happiness" on a piece of paper. Collect the papers and read the phrases. Write them on the board in the form of a poem.

Happiness is. . .
   getting a new little kitten for a birthday
   sharing an ice cream cone with a friend
   playing jump rope with friends
   playing baseball after school

3. Choose another abstract word and have students think of concrete experiences to represent the word. Students may want to write a poem completely on their own.

EXTENSION   Collect the abstract "poems" and put them in a notebook. Let students add to them as they come across new abstract words.

Strange As It Seems

OBJECTIVE   To illustrate literal interpretations of common cliches.

MATERIALS   List of cliches, drawing paper, crayons or magic markers.

1. List several cliches on the board and discuss their meaning. Have students give examples of how each cliche is commonly used.
2. Ask students to suggest other cliches that they have heard or used. List these on the board and discuss their common meaning.
3. Have each student choose one or several cliches to illustrate. Ask them to draw the *literal* interpretation of the words. (For example: "It's raining cats and dogs" might show dark rain clouds overhead and cats and dogs falling from the clouds to the ground.)
4. Ask students to make up a story which explains the way their unusual events (e.g., cats and dogs falling from the rain clouds) occurred. Encourage them to use their wildest imaginations.
5. Share stories and illustrations by reading out loud. Bind the stories in a booklet entitled *Strange As It Seems*, or *Believe It or Not*.

EXTENSION   Remind students to avoid cliches in their own writing.

Have students look for othe cliches to add to the list and to the Believe It Or Not books.

RESOURCES

Raining Cats and Dogs
Myra Shulmen Auslin
Dormac, 1978

This workbook, originally designed for hearing impaired students, is quite useful with other students who have difficulty understanding idioms. Idioms are presented with literal pictures, then in written situations in which the idioms are used in context. Guide questions help students identify the figurative meaning of the idioms.

Chocolate Moose for Dinner and the King Who Rained
Fred Gwynne
Windmill Books, 1970

Two children's storybooks that illustrate some literal interpretations of phrases using homonyms. Good samples for students to get ideas from. For younger readers.

It Doesn't Always Have to Rhyme
Eve Merriam
Atheneum, 1964

"A Cliché"

A cliché
is what we all say
when we're too lazy
to find another way

and so we say
warm as toast
quiet as a mouse
slow as molasses
quick as a wink.

Think!
Is toast the warmest thing you know?
Think again, it might not be so,
Think again: it might even be snow!
Soft as lamb's wool, fleecy snow.

Listen to that mouse go
scuttling and clawing,
nibbling and pawing.
A mouse can speak
if only a squeak.

Is a mouse the quietest thing you know?
Think again, it might not be so.
Think again: it might be a shadow.
Quiet as a shadow,
quiet as growing grass,
quiet as a pillow,
or a looking glass.

Slow as molasses,
quick as a wink,
Before you say so,
take time to think.

Reprinted by permission of Atheneum Publishers from IT DOESN'T ALWAYS HAVE TO RHYME by Eve Merriam. Copyright © 1964 by Eve Merriam.

SAMPLE CLICHÉS

a finger in every pie
a little bird told me
alive and kicking

all thumbs
apple of my eye
apple pie order

as the crow flies

at the end of the rope

at wit's end

a wolf in sheep's clothing

ax to grind

barking up the wrong tree

beating around the bush

be at loose ends

bite your tongue

blind leading the blind

blow off steam

blue blood

born with a silver spoon in one's mouth

building castles in the air

bull-headed

bury the hatchet

button your mouth

by hook or by crook

by the skin of his teeth

can't carry a tune in a bucket

can't get over it

caught red-handed

chip off the old block

chip on his shoulder

cook one's goose

cost a pretty penny

crocodile tears

cut a long story short

cut corners

cut it out

done to a turn

down in the dumps

drive a hard bargain

drop a line

eat your heart out

eat your words

egg one on

elbow grease

face the music

fall head over heels in love

feather in your cap

fit as a fiddle

flying high

frog in your throat

full of baloney

full of hot air

get it straight from the horse's mouth

give a hand

go fly a kite

gone to the dogs

food for thought

grease my palm

handle with kid gloves

have a green thumb

heart of stone

he's a fence sitter

he's a fish out of water

he's a square peg in a round hole

he's a walking encyclopedia

in a nutshell

in hot water

in the bag

in the nick of time

kick the bucket

learn by heart

like two peas in a pod

long arm of the law

my hair is standing on end

not my cup of tea

once in a blue moon

on cloud nine

on edge

one foot in the grave

on pins and needles

on the up and up

on the wagon

out of the woods

over the hill

pain in the neck

pass the buck

pie in the sky

pin a rap on

pipe down

play second fiddle

pound the pavement

pull a fast one

pulling up stakes

pulling your leg

pull strings

put wool over his eyes

rack one's brains

raining cats and dogs

read between the lines

scratch the surface

seal your lips

second thoughts

see eye to eye

shell out (money)

skeleton in the closet

spill the beans

take place

teach an old dog new tricks

the cat's got your tongue	tip off
the time is ripe	took the words right out of my mouth
through and through	
tied to apron strings	under the weather
tie the knot	watch your tongue
time flies	your name will be mud

Happy As a Lark

OBJECTIVE   To write original comparisons.

MATERIALS   List of worn-out comparisons (clichés).

PROCEDURE   1. Ask students whether they have heard phrases like:

happy as a lark	cross as a bear
quick as a wink	quiet as a mouse
brave as a lion	stubborn as a mule
funny as a monkey	lazy as a dog
nervous as a cat	cute as a button
cold as ice	

2. Ask students to add more to the list if they can.
3. Explain to class that these are worn-out phrases or clichés that are frequently used in speech or writing. Choose one phrase and ask the students to suggest some original comparisons. Try to get four or five different examples from the students.

"nervous as a cat" can become

"nervous as a mexican jumping bean in a hot hand"

"nervous as a bird being stalked by a hungry cat"

4. Choose another example and try to think of additional examples.

"as quiet as a mouse" can become

"as quiet as a leaf falling from a tree"

"as quiet as a cloud floating in the sky"

Point out that a specific action added to the comparison helps the reader visualize more clearly.
5. Read the poem "It Doesn't Always Have to Rhyme," by Eve Merriam. Put a copy on the bulletin board.
6. Have students write some original comparisons on their own to share with the class. Students may want to illustrate them and put them on the bulletin board.
7. Point out that original comparisons make writing much more interesting.

EXTENSION   1. Have students watch for original comparisons in their reading. Have them copy the comparisons down on an index card and put them on the bulletin board.
2. Have students collect clichés from their reading and make a class chart labeled "Avoid these Clichés."

black as ink	cold as ice
black as night	cute as a button
blind as a bat	dead as a doornail
busy as a bee/beaver	deep as the ocean
clean as a whistle	dry as a bone
clever as a fox	fit as a fiddle
cool as a cucumber	flat as a pancake

free as a bird	quick as a wink
fresh as a daisy	red as a beet
green as grass	scarce as hen's teeth
happy as a clam	sharp as a tack
high as an elephant's eye	sick as a dog
hungry as a bear	slippery as an eel
large as life	slow as molasses
mad as a hatter	snug as a bug in a rug
nutty as a fruitcake	soft as butter
old as the hills	sour as a pickle
pale as a ghost	strong as an ox
plain as the nose on your face	sweet as sugar
poor as a churchmouse	thin as a rail
pretty as a picture	tough as nails
proud as a peacock	warm as toast
quick as a flash	white as a sheet

The Sun Is a Golden Earring

OBJECTIVE To recognize and write original comparisons (metaphors).

MATERIALS Library books: *The Beautiful Things, The Sun is a Golden Earring.*

PROCEDURE
1. Read either of the suggested books to the students and ask them to listen for descriptive comparisons.
2. Ask students to list some of the comparisons that were just read. Write these comparisons on the board. Read the comparison from the book again if students cannot remember the whole sentence. Here are a few examples:

   "The tree is a cloud of leaves anchored to the earth by its roots." (*The Beautiful Things*)

   "The moon is a white cat that hunts the gray mice of the night." (*The Sun is a Golden Earring*)

3. Write one phrase (e.g., The wind is . . . .) on the board and have each student finish the comparison on a slip of paper. Collect slips of paper and read comparisons anonymously. Write them on the board with the other comparisons.
4. Continue the activity by writing more phrases on the board and having students write more comparisons.

EXTENSION Illustrate the metaphors and put them on the bulletin board. Keep a chart of interesting comparisons that students find in their reading.

RESOURCES

The Sun is a Golden Earring
N. Belting
Holt, Rinehart, and Winston, 1962

The Beautiful Things
T. McGrath
Vanguard Press, 1960

Orange is a Color: A Book About Colors
Sharon Lerner
Lerner Publications, 1970
   Although this book starts out telling about the changes that occur when colors are mixed, it finishes with some interesting and colorful metaphors.

Words, Words, Words
Mary O'Neill
Doubleday
   Mary O'Neill presents poems about parts of speech, punctuation, abstract words, as well as some interesting interpretations of such words as "memory," "forget," "thoughts," and others.

Hailstones and Halibut Bones
Mary O'Neill
Doubleday, 1961

Have You Seen Roads?
Joanne Oppenheim
Addison Wesley, 1969

Sound Poems

OBJECTIVE   To write a "sound poem."

MATERIALS   Sample "sound poem."

PROCEDURE
1. Write a "sound poem" on the board and have students read it out loud together (e.g., "Thunder").
2. Ask students to comment on the way the poem was written. (It's a list of words that tell about the title.)
3. Write a different sound word on the board (e.g., Rain) and ask *each* student to write down three words that tell what sounds or actions the word uses. Have students read these words out loud when everyone is finished. Write words on the board in a list. Read the new "sound poem" in unison. Ask students whether they would like to rearrange any words to make the poem sound smoother.
4. Repeat this activity with another word.
5. Put a list of suggested words on the board and let each student choose a title word for a "sound poem." Students may want to suggest additional words for this list.

rain	wind	motorcycles	quiet
snow	breeze	cars	loud
lightning	ocean waves	machines	noise
laughter	trucks	planes	

6. Have students write their own "sound poem" and then read their results to the group.
7. Have students copy and illustrate their "sound poems" on another day. Bind poems and their illustrations in a "Sound Book."

EXTENSION   Make a book of sounds. Have each student draw a picture of something that makes a sound and then write the sound somewhere on the picture. Show Peter Spier's book, *Crash! Bang! Boom!*, as an example.

Example: Sound Poem

THUNDER

rumbles,
tumbles,
rolls,
bangs,
booms,
bumps,
bounces,
cracks,
snaps,
crackles,
echoes.
LOUD NOISE!!!

JKH

RESOURCES

Crash! Bang! Boom!
Peter Spier
Doubleday, 1979

Here is whole book of things and actions that make sounds. Each item or action and the sound are illustrated. Show this to students as an example of a "Sound Dictionary."

Street Poems
Robert Froman
McCall Publishing Co., 1971

Mr. Froman writes his poems in shapes. Along with sound poems, he has sad poems about city problems (pollution, traffic, and loneliness) and funny ones about skyscrapers, buildings, and garbage trucks.

Something Special
Beatrice Schenk DeRegniers and Irene Haas
Harcourt Brace Jovanovich, 1958

Did you ever hear
a rabbit biting a lettuce leaf?
a cow switching her tail?
a tiny baby breathing?

Klippity Klop
Ed Emberley
Little, Brown, 1974

Prince Krispin and Dumpling go for a ride. All the sound effects are spelled out. "Krunch, krinch, krunch, klick, klack, klick, klick," etc.

Alphabet Antics

OBJECTIVE   To write sentences using alliteration.

MATERIALS   Book: *A Twister of Twists, A Tangler of Tongues,* dictionaries.

PROCEDURE
1. Read the following tongue twister to students and ask what they notice about it.

   "A pale pink proud peacock pompously preened its pretty plumage." (p. 26, *A Twister of Twists*)

2. Explain to students that use of one letter or letters on the beginning of each word in a group of words is called "alliteration." Ask students whether they know any other tongue twisters that use alliteration. List student suggestions on the board.
3. Have each student choose a letter of the alphabet. (They may want to use the first letter of their names.) Have them write down words that begin with their chosen letter. Encourage them to use a dictionary to find additional words.
4. Ask students to create a sentence using only words on their list. They may use articles and conjunctions.
5. Have them read their finished sentences to classmates. They may illustrate their sentences if they choose.

EXTENSION   Read "Shrewd Simon Short" (p. 50, *A Twister of Twists*). Every word in this three-page story begins with "s." Ask students to write longer pieces using only one letter. Share results with the class. (See *The Knight, the Knave, and the Knapsack* for another example.)

THE KNIGHT, THE KNAVE, AND THE KNAPSACK

The knight left his knapsack of knives on the knotty tree on the knoll. A knave wearing knitted knickers noticed the knapsack and knelt on his knees on the knoll. He tried his knack at unknotting the knot on the knapsack. As he did, he cut his knuckle on a knife in the knapsack. The knight-errant soon returned and knocked the knife-stealing knave down on the knoll. The knave had learned some new knowledge: never kneel on a knoll and try to take knives from the knight's knapsack!

List all *kn* words:

kna	*kne*	*kni*	*kno*	*knu*
_____	_____	_____	_____	_____
_____	_____	_____	_____	_____
_____	_____	_____	_____	_____
		_____	_____	
		_____	_____	

Now put them in alphabetical order:

kna	*kne*	*kni*	*kno*	*knu*
_____	_____	_____	_____	_____
_____	_____	_____	_____	_____
_____	_____	_____	_____	_____
		_____	_____	
		_____	_____	

RESOURCES

My Tang's Tungled and Other Ridiculous Situations
Sara and John Brewton and G. Meredith Blackburn III
Crowell, 1973
　　"Tongue twisters twist tongues twisted"

Tongue Tanglers
More Tongue Tanglers and a Rigamorole
Charles Francis Potter
World Publishing Co., 1962 and 1964

Letters, Sounds and Words: A Phonic Dictionary
Linda Hayward
Platt & Munk Publishers, 1973

　　Amusing sentences and illustrations demonstrate different phonetic principles for kids. Use this as an idea starter. Let students create additional phonics lessons for younger kids.

A Beastly Collection
Jonathon Coudrille
Frederick Warne & Co., 1975
　　A compendium of alphabetical animals complete with illustrations.

A Beastly Circus
By Peggy Parish
Simon & Schuster, 1969
　　Announcing another anthology about alphabetical animals actually acting and ad-libbing additional amusing antics!

SENTENCE STRUCTURE

The use of a variety of sentence patterns increases the effectiveness of written expression. The inexperienced writer, however, tends to rely most heavily on simple sentence structure, with the most common vocabulary. Awkward constructions appear in the work of those writers who *do* attempt to vary sentence structure. Omission of words and phrases, inappropriate wording (verb tense, pronoun agreement), and missing or inaccurate punctuation cause some of this awkwardness. The original ideas of the writer are thus lost in the inability to communicate clearly through accurate and interesting sentences.

Good ideas are the starting point for written expression. Beyond that, a well developed "sentence sense" which allows the student to use a variety of sentence patterns is essential. The purpose of the activities in this section is to provide opportunities for students to experiment with techniques for building different kinds of sentences. Students who have poor sentence sense will need to start at the beginning of the sequence and work carefully through the activities over a period of time. Others who have some degree of sentence sense can move more quickly through the sequence and focus on sentence combining and reducing activities.

Several principles form the basis for this sequence of activities.

1. *Sentences have two basic parts; the naming part and the action part.* It is *not* necessary for students to remember the terms "subject" and "predicate" as long as they can understand the purpose for each part of the sentence: the subject *names* the participant(s), while the predicate provides the *action*. At first focus strictly on physical action verbs (e.g., jumping, running), then move on to "brain work" verbs (e.g., thinking, knowing), to linking verbs (e.g., is, are).

2. *Sentences can be expanded by:*
   - adding descriptive detail, and
   - adding when, where, how, and why phrases.

3. *Sentence arrangement can be varied by:*
   - changing sequence of who/what, when, where, how, and why phrases.

4. *Sentences can be combined to:*
   - eliminate excess words;
   - replace short, choppy sentences; and
   - develop longer, more interesting sentences.

5. *Sentences can be reduced to two basic parts by:*
   - deleting descriptive detail; and
   - deleting when, where, how, and why phrases.

By building and expanding kernel sentences, by constructing compound and complex sentences, and by combining sentences, students gain familiarity with constructions they would not ordinarily use. Reducing sentences of all types to their basic components will help students to eliminate awkwardness in longer sentences, fragments, and run-on sentences.

Although the emphasis in this section is on building and writing longer sentences, *the ultimate goal is to have students use a variety of sentence types and lengths in their writing.* Keep in mind that writing skills are developmental. Do not rush students into writing highly complex sentences before they have mastered the simpler types, and do not expect a student to go from writing basic simple sentences to writing complex sentences in a short time. "Sentence sense" develops gradually, over a period of time, as students have experience writing sentences.

Remember it is better to have many short practice sessions on sentence building, rather than one occasional long one. If specific sentence problems in student writing persist, try some of the activities in "Tackle the Troublespots."

Kernel Sentences

OBJECTIVE To develop a list of kernel sentences for use in subsequent activities.

MATERIALS Samples of kernel sentences, paper, and pencils.

PROCEDURE *Part One*

1. Write the following words on the board in a column:
   <u>D</u>ogs <u>C</u>ats <u>B</u>ears <u>B</u>irds

2. Ask students to identify the way all these words are alike.
   - all words name *living and moving* things
   - all begin with capital letters
   - all have an "s" to indicate more than one
   (It is *not* necessary to identify these as *nouns*, although you may if you wish.)

3. Ask students to name other words which would fit into this category. Write suggestions on the board.

   giraffes, snakes, witches, boys, teachers

4. Have students fold their paper in half and number side **1** and side **2**.

1	2

5. Have students write five words in column 1 that would fit in the category. Encourage students to think of other words that are not listed on the board if they can. Do not say words out loud. Fold papers so words cannot be seen.

Part Two

6. Write the following words on the board and ask students to identify how they are alike.

    eat.   run.   climb.   sing.

    - all *action* words (you may also identify them as *verbs*)
    - all followed by a period

7. Ask students to suggest other words that would fit in this category. Write suggestions on the board.

    whistle, giggle, dance, climb, wiggle

8. Have students pass their folded papers to another student so that the first group of words cannot be seen. Ask the second student to write five words that would fit in category 2 in column 2 on their papers.
9. Have students open papers and read the resulting kernel sentences.

**IMPORTANT

10. *Review* with students that kernel sentences have *two basic parts—a naming word* and an *action word*. Check to see whether all sentences had a naming word and an action word.
11. Ask students to write more kernel sentences as a follow-up exercise.
12. *Save all kernel sentences for future activities.*

KERNEL SENTENCES

Set 1 (present tense—living and moving things)

Level 1		Level 2	
Dogs	eat.	Soldiers	march.
Cats	run.	Dentists	drill.
Bears	climb.	Horses	gallop.
Birds	sing.	Customers	buy.
Fish	swim.	Umpires	shout.
Babies	cry.	Teachers	teach.
Boys	read.	Parents	work.
Girls	play.	Students	study.
Horses	eat.	Secretaries	type.
Lions	roar.	Detectives	investigate.
Owls	hoot.	Astronauts	explore.
Mice	run.	Voters	vote.
Children	play.	Carpenters	build.
People	work.	Termites	chew.
Snakes	wiggle.	Leaves	flutter.
Flowers	grow.	Parrots	talk.
Kings	rule.		

Set 2 (present tense—non-living things)

Level 1		Level 2	
Boats	sail.	Candles	flicker.
Trucks	rumble.	Snowflakes	fall.
Clocks	tick.	Bombs	explode.
Saws	cut.	Whistles	blow.
Planes	fly.	Rivers	flow.
Rockets	blast.	Winds	blow.
Rocks	fall.	Raindrops	fall.
Balls	roll.	Spaceships	explore.
Stars	shine.	Nutcrackers	crack.
Seeds	slide.	Waves	splash.
Guns	shoot.	Marbles	roll.
		Mirrors	reflect.

Dogs Eat (Descriptive Detail)

OBJECTIVE To add descriptive detail to kernel sentences.

MATERIALS List of kernel sentences from kernel sentence activity.

PROCEDURE
1. Write a kernel sentence on the chalkboard or transparency (e.g., "Dogs eat.").
2. Ask students to suggest size words that might describe a dog. If students suggest common words, e.g., "big", encourage them to think of more specific synonyms. Continue the activity by asking for color words, then personality words (friendly, mischievous).

    Encourage students to use very specific words. When someone suggests "big" say, "What's another word for big?" When someone suggests a common color, such as brown, ask "How brown?" Chocolate brown? Cocoa brown? Continue to ask "What's another word for _____?" for any common words that are suggested. Write all suggestions on the board.
3. Put the following sentence pattern on the board and have students suggest sample sentences which incorporate some of the words previously suggested.

    _____, _____, _____dogs eat.
4. Have students write some descriptive sentences on their own using the above pattern. Remind them that commas are needed when words are listed in a series.
5. Have students read results to the class. Have classmates listen for interesting vocabulary.

EXTENSION 1 Continue this activity for several weeks, using one or two kernel sentences a day, brainstorming details, and writing expanded sentences. *Save the descriptive sentences for the following activities.*

EXTENSION 2 Use the expanded sentences and substitute more specific nouns and verbs:

"Large, slender, rusty-colored *Irish Setters* eat."
"Large, slender, rusty-colored Irish Setters *munch*."

EXTENSION 3 Use expanded sentences and add objects. Add descriptive detail to the object.

"Large, slender, rusty-colored Irish Setters munch *bones*."
"Large, slender, rusty-colored Irish Setters munch *crispy, crunchy* dog bones."

EXTENSION 4 Use expanded sentences and add adverbs:

"Large, slender, rusty-colored Irish Setters *quickly* munch crispy, crunchy dog bones."

EXTENSION 5 When students become familiar with this expansion process, they quickly learn to add descriptive detail to subject and object, and to add adverbs all in one step.

Use this pattern sentence:

_____, _____, _____ <u>dogs eat</u> _____ ,
_____, _____, <u>bones</u> _____ .

(how)

EXTENSION 6   To vary the activity on different days, choose sample kernel sentences from different sets provided. All sentences are divided into *sets* to control for verb consistency within a lesson. All sets are divided into *levels* to accommodate different reading levels of students. Choose the level most appropriate to the needs of your students.

Building Simple Sentences

OBJECTIVE   To build simple sentences.

MATERIALS   Two sets colored cards: set 1 (green), noun phrases; set 2 (red), verb phrases. **Keep verb tense consistent within each set. (See sample phrases.)

PROCEDURE

1. Pass out *noun phrases* to students and have them read cards out loud to class. List phrases on the board as students read them. Ask: "How are these cards alike?"

   That boy scout

   A girl scout

   A working mother

   A busy father

   (They are all naming phrases.) Ask students to suggest other phrases that would fit in this group. Add these to the list on the board.

2. Pass out verb phrases and ask, "How are these phrases alike?"

   chopped some wood.

   fixed some dinner.

   baked some bread.

   washed the dishes.

   (They are all action phrases.)

3. Remind students that a simple sentence is composed of two parts: a *naming phrase* and an *action phrase*. Have students note the difference between kernel sentences and simple sentences. (Kernel sentences have two words: a naming word and an action word. Simple sentences have additional words, articles, adjectives, noun objects.)

4. Ask students to build several sentences with the cards they have on their desk. Ask individual students to read their completed sentences to the class.

5. After each sentence is read, ask: "Does that sentence have a naming phrase? What is it? Does it have an action phrase? What is it?"

6. Collect cards. Shuffle each deck. Let students build and read additional sentences.

EXTENSION 1   Prepare a worksheet on which you have arranged noun phrases in one group and verb phrases in another group. Follow procedure outlined in main activity sequence. Let students cut up worksheet, arrange phrases in complete sentences, then paste them on another sheet of paper. (To make this activity easier, choose phrases with basic sight vocabulary. Capital letters and periods provide clues to sentence parts.)

Sample using controlled vocabulary:

The pig	My mother
A monkey	That cat
The girl	The frog
is eating.	is hopping.
is singing.	is sleeping.
is jumping.	is playing.

Use more difficult vocabulary to make activity harder.

EXTENSION 2 To make this activity harder mix noun and verb phrases up on worksheet and eliminate capital letters and periods. Students will first have to sort phrases into two groups (noun phrases, verb phrases) before they can build their sentences.

EXTENSION 3 *Sentence Building Game*

Object: To build as many simple sentences as possible.
Directions: Shuffle both decks of cards together. Pass out three cards per student. Ask students to build and read the sentence if they can make one. Next, each student draws two more cards and tries to make a sentence. Game continues until cards or time runs out.
Winner: Who has the most sentences?

SIMPLE SENTENCES

Set A—present tense: is + verb + ing

Level 1		Level 2	
The workman	is walking.	That child	is screaming.
The zookeeper	is working.	A singer	is whistling.
The teacher	is laughing.	The student	is memorizing.
The witch	is flying.	The professor	is lecturing.
The girl	is writing.	My brother	is listening.
My cat	is sleeping.	The horse	is galloping.
My mother	is singing.	That soldier	is marching.
The frog	is jumping.	An alligator	is snapping.
The mouse	is squeaking.	That gorilla	is growling.
The bug	is climbing.	This grasshopper	is hopping.
The pig	is eating.	The leopard	is hunting.
The bird	is flying.		

Set B—simple past tense

Level 1		Level 2	
That turtle	crawled.	That pupil	sneezed.
That frog	jumped.	That magician	performed.
That boy	played.	The rhinoceros	charged.
This bear	growled.	The goose	honked.
A monkey	climbed.	The dinosaur	explored.
A rabbit	hopped.	The donkey	kicked.
The bee	buzzed.	The owl	hooted.
The queen	yelled.	The porcupine	chewed.
The goat	gobbled.	The chicken	clucked.
That duck	quacked.	The dancer	waltzed.

Set C—noun phrases and verb phrases

Level 1	
That boy scout	chopped some wood.
A girl scout	fixed some dinner.

A working mother	baked some bread.
A busy father	washed the dishes.
The airplane pilot	fixed the plane.
My big brother	climbed the tree.
My little sister	played a game.
A new born baby	cried and cried.
The newspaper boy	delivered the paper.
A truck driver	changed a flat tire.
A race car driver	crashed his car.
The bus driver	washed the bus.
That firefighter	started the fire engine.
A friendly police officer	waved her hand.
A first grade teacher	looked at a book.
The school doctor	checked my teeth.
The little pig	gobbled the food.

Level 2

The United States President	prepared a speech.
Our school librarian	read an encyclopedia.
The apartment house owner	painted the building.
A police sergeant	arrested a robber.
The radio engineer	watched television.
The television news broadcaster	announced the news.
A famous astronaut	photographed the moon.
The telephone repairman	climbed the telephone pole.
A meteorologist	prepared a weather report.
The bank teller	cashed a check.
A busy electrician	fixed the toaster.
The professional basketball player	scored two points.
An architect	designed a mansion.
The neighborhood pharmacist	sold some medicine.
The forest ranger	noticed a fire.
A supermarket cashier	checked the price.
A furniture maker	hammered on a table.
An oil well driller	discovered some oil.
A private investigator	followed the spy.
An insurance salesman	visited the neighbors.
The riverboat captain	maneuvered the boat.
The school custodian	raked the leaves.
A meter maid	ticketed a car.
The friendly florist	arranged the flowers.
The beautician	styled my hair.

What's Going On?

OBJECTIVE   To listen for "who," "did what," "when," and "where" phrases in expanded sentences.

MATERIALS   Four index cards for each student, labeled <u>who</u> <u>did what</u> | when | <u>where</u>; sample sentences.

1. Give each student a set of who, did what, when, where cards.
2. Read a sentence, one phrase at a time, to the students.

>   Yesterday morning   the starving puppies
>   gobbled up their food   from their dish in the kitchen.

3. Ask students to listen to the phrase and hold up the category card that identifies the phrase. Check student repsonses and discuss any differences.
4. Continue in this manner until five or six sentences have been read. Repeat the activity on different days as it reinforces reading skills.
5. Change the activity to a reading task when students gain proficiency at the listening level. Make a ditto sentence with phrases widely spaced. Have students mark the phrases in the following manner.

>   <u>who</u>   <u>did what</u> | when | where
> | Last night | some quiet campers   <u>heard a strange noise</u>   near their campsite.

6. Gradually reduce the spacing between phrases. Students must then determine the phrasing on their own.

Put phrases from sample sentences on index cards. Have students read and sort cards into piles according to category. Have students build new sentences by choosing a phrase from each category.

Have students write sentences with when and where phrases. Prepare for this activity by writing kernel sentences on index cards or on a worksheet. Have each student choose four or five kernel sentences and write appropriate when or where phrases.
Have students read their completed expanded sentences to the class.
Ask students to rearrange phrases in sentences.

<u>WHO</u> <u>DID WHAT</u> | WHEN | WHERE SENTENCES

Set one

1. Last night
   heard a strange noise
2. Last week,
   spun a huge web
3. The ambitious student
   in the library
4. An old army sergeant
   on the train platform
5. Yesterday morning
   gobbled up the food
6. Last month
   climbed the old oak tree
7. Many foreigners
   in the United States
8. At three a.m. this morning
   knocked noisily

some quiet campers
near their campsite.

the black widow spider
in the dark, dusty attic.

wrote a book report
two weeks ago.

marched back and forth
just before the parade.

the starving puppies
from their dish in the kitchen.

John and Jerry
in the back yard.

travel freely
every year.

a mysterious stranger
on my door.

Set two

1. An angry bee
   around the picnic table
2. After the game
   moaned quietly
3. The magnificent magician
   from a black, satin hat

buzzed noisily
at lunch time.

the injured football player
in the hospital emergency room.

pulled a rabbit
during intermission.

4. Before presidential elections must register to vote   American citizens at city hall.
5. The mournful guitar player after work   sang a sorrowful song at the corner of Maple Street.
6. After the game threw rotten tomatoes   the angry crowd at the umpire.
7. Last week the ancient volcano   in Hawaii erupted violently.
8. Two jazzy sports cars during the race   crashed suddenly at Indianapolis Speedway.

Set three

1. On Saturday, caught some trout   two excited fishermen in the swift river.
2. At midnight, chased the fire engine   the howling dog down the street.
3. A frightened child through the haunted house   walked slowly on Halloween night.
4. At dawn flew silently   a single sea gull near the deserted beach.
5. Out in the garage let the air out of some tires   two mischievous boys near midnight.
6. The grumpy waitress on the customer   carelessly spilled coffee during the noon rush hour.
7. At the air show opened their chutes   a group of skydivers after their free fall.
8. Before the final attack watched the enemy   the brave astronauts from inside their spaceship.

Zany Sentences

OBJECTIVE   To build expanded sentences using "who," "did what," "when," "where," and "why" phrases.

MATERIALS   Five sets of colored cards, one set for each category; e.g., "who" phrases on red cards; "did what" on green cards, etc.

PROCEDURE

1. Divide the class in small groups and give each group five sets of cards with phrases. Do not mix the piles. If you do not have colored cards, put phrases on a ditto and mark each phrase in a different manner; e.g., draw a line under the "who" phrase, a double line under the "did what" phrase, a rectangle around the "when" phrase, and a wiggly line under the "where" phrase. Have students cut phrases apart and separate into appropriate piles.
2. Ask students to rearrange the phrases within the sentence and read to the group again and decide whether the sentence sounds right. Encourage students to try additional phrase arrangements.
3. Continue the activity by having students choose new phrase cards.
4. To make this task more difficult, put all phrases on white cards or on a ditto without special markings. The students must then read and sort phrases into categories before building sentences.

EXTENSION   *Zany Sentence Card Game*

Shuffle *all* cards together. Deal out five cards per person. Students must try to build a five-phrase sentence. Cards are placed face up on the table until a complete five-phrase sentence is made. Two additional cards may be drawn on each turn. *Winner:* the person with the most complete sentences.

ZANY SENTENCES: WHO-DID WHAT-WHEN-WHERE-WHY

Primary Level

Who	*Did What*
a singing bird	walked the dog
a friendly frog	jumped off the roof
a big dragon	caught a turtle
a fat snowman	kicked the ball
the sloppy pig	sang a song
a wicked witch	hugged a seal
the lazy dog	planted some seeds
a very fat man	followed footprints
a boy with mumps	jumped for joy
a rotten egg	laughed out loud
a skinny snake	got lost
an ant with big feet	took a bath
a purple turtle	did the dishes
a pink elephant	ate an egg
a crazy fox	cast a spell
a jolly giant	kissed a frog
a tiny kitten	caught a rabbit
a tired tiger	found a peanut
a happy hippo	beat up a boxer
a playful puppy	jumped off the roof

Where	*When*
in the desert	on Christmas Day
at the zoo	yesterday morning
on a mountain	late last night
in a cave	before lunch
in a shark's mouth	at breakfast time
in a department store	when the stars were out
in the city jail	at midnight
on a ship	at high noon
on the beach	ten minutes ago
in a tree house	ten years ago
six miles away	one hundred years ago
on top of a tall building	at two a.m.
in the barn yard	on New Year's Day
in the car	on a school day
in the classroom	at dinner time
on the street	before sunrise
in an elevator	as the sun went down
in a telephone booth	early in the morning
in a spaceship	after school
on Mars	after T.V. time

Why

because he/she was tired	because it was so cold
since it was so easy	because she/he heard a loud noise
because she/he was hungry	because the T.V. was on

because mother was angry
since it was so late
because the joke was funny
since she/he couldn't sleep
because he/she was crazy
because the telephone rang
because it was so cold

because dinner was ready
because the bell rang
because the floor was wet
because the car had a flat tire
because he/she ate a spider
because the teacher yelled
because the eggs were broken

Advanced Vocabulary Level

Who

a reckless robber
a trembling trapeze artist
a phony fisherman
a methodical meteorologist
your calculating cashier
my diabolical dentist
a soft-spoken spook
this pious pioneer
the grandma goblin
a devoted daydreamer
your bungling bugler
a jazzy gentleman
this wandering minstrel
that jealous judge
my bargaining barber
a scheming scholar

the broken-hearted broadcaster
this tight-fisted tourist
that sober sailor
an ingenious inventor
that pale, puny poltergeist
our proud, praiseworthy president
that discourteous disc jockey
that science fiction writer
the patriotic parachuter
the wicked wishy-washy witch
an absent-minded ad writer
her terribly timid teacher
Sam's sullen servant
the impatient patient
the single scientist
the gargantuan gourmet

Did What

sauntered slowly
clawed clumsily
bragged bravely
yelled yearly
cruised craftily
hurried hungrily
knocked knowingly
poisoned politely
cried hysterically
defended defiantly
complained constantly
haggled hopefully
jumped jubilantly
gambled gallantly
called cautiously
polished politely

drooped drearily
plunged pleasantly
promised profoundly
insulted insistently
studied sufficiently
graduated gratefully
recruited recently
vaccinated valiantly
announced acrimoniously
balanced believably
haunted haphazardly
invited enthusiastically
rehearsed relentlessly
tripped triumphantly
dawdled deliberately
triggered tragedy

When

during dinner
in early evening
while waiting
as time ran out
later and later

ages and ages ago
before sailing south
at the last moment
during the dance
at breakfast time

ahead of schedule
before breakfast
many minutes ago
at break of day
before sunrise
while whistling whimsical tunes
at 10:20 p.m.
after Sesame Street
at approximately 8:08
in the Middle Ages
as cymbals sounded

during dawn's early light
in prehistoric times
while Christmas caroling
during the last speech
as the ticker ticked away
at the stroke of midnight
while riding in a rickshaw
as the last bell rang
before being elected
yesterday morning
as the sun sank slowly in the west

Where

in a terrible tenement
at a patriotic party
on a funny farm
in a deep, dark dungeon
across the continent
beneath the bristling bear
in the flaming forest
around the reading room
among primitive people
at a raging rebellion
under an amber umbrella
around arguing diplomats
between the fighting fans
on a foreign freighter
in a cluttered classroom
in the dry, deserted desert

on a capsizing catamaran
on a purple picket fence
near the threatening throng
in a tiny telephone booth
at the Singing Society Sale
behind the battered battleships
around a round, rotating room
among the amiable amateurs
below billions of bubbles
in a hospitable hospital
on the second secret safari
beneath the border bridge
beside broken-hearted bystanders
between belligerent believers
in a dilapidated apartment
above a balanced barricade

Why

because the apple had worms
because the knife slipped
since the payment was late
since it was so easy to do
since you've gone away
since the homework was done
because mother was angry
because she/he was brainwashed
since it was so late
because bugles were blowing
unless he/she got his/her own way
unless her/his shoes were shined
so the boss wouldn't fire him/her
since money was hard to get
because she/he wanted to be alone
so he/she wouldn't be alone

because the ship sailed for Singapore
so the diamonds could be delivered
so the news could spread
because the natives were restless
so the bills could be paid
because her/his brain wasn't functioning
because he/she had a vivid imagination
in order to earn some money
in order to maintain her/his way of life
because the teacher was on a tirade
because everyone was so bored
since the stagecoach had already left
if conditions weren't exactly right
if not allowed to do what he/she wanted
so that the noise would stop
because the room was empty

Reducing Expanded Sentences

OBJECTIVE   To reduce expanded sentence to kernel elements (subject and verb).

MATERIALS · Sample expanded sentences. (Use sentences developed by students from kernel sentence activity, page 136, or sample sentences provided here.)

PROCEDURE
1. Tell students that you want them to reduce expanded sentences to two words. (Note: At first limit the sentence reduction activity to expanded sentences. Compound and complex sentences should be avoided until after completion of the following activities.
2. Write one expanded sentence on the chalkboard and ask students to identify all descriptive words. Circle descriptive words as students identify them. See example below #4.
3. Ask students to identify all "where," "when," "how," and "why" words and phrases. Circle them as they are identified.
4. Ask students to identify the kernel sentence elements. (There may be a few words remaining; i.e., objects of verb, determiners.) Draw a line under the subject and a double line under the verb.
   Example: When it is dinner time, that large, slender, rusty-colored Irish Setter noisily and swiftly gobbles crispy, crunchy dog bones in the kitchen.
   Write the remaining subject and verb on the board.

   Irish Setters gobble.

   Point out that this is a kernel sentence and that all sentences, no matter how long, can be broken down into kernel sentences.
5. Repeat this activity with the students using another expanded sentence before asking students to do some on their own.

Pass It On

OBJECTIVE
To write expanded sentences using "who," "did what," "when," "where," and "why" phrases.

MATERIALS
Pencil and paper.

PROCEDURE
1. Divide the class into groups of five.
2. Have students fold their paper down like an accordion five times and number each section.

3. Have the first person in each group write a "who" phrase on the paper, then fold the paper over and pass it to the next student without exposing their phrase.
4. The second student writes a "did what" phrase without looking at the "who" phrase. The paper is passed to the third student. Students continue in order, writing "when," "where," and "why" phrases.
5. Have the student open the paper and read all five phrases to the class. Ask students to rearrange phrases within the sentence.
6. Continue the activity by changing the starting place in the group. Have the second student start the second set and write a "who" phrase. Continue the activity until everyone in the group has had a chance to start a new sentence.
7. Continue the activity by changing the sequence of phrases; e.g., when, where, who, did what, why; or where, who, did what, when, why.

Whisper

Divide the class into groups of five. Have one student whisper a "who" phrase to the second student. The second student must repeat the "who" phrase and add a "did what" phrase to the third student, and so on. The last student must repeat the entire sentence out loud, or write it down and read it.

Example:

| 1 A wicked witch |
| 2 caught a rabbit |
| 3 in an elevator |
| 4 as the sun went down |
| 5 because she couldn't sleep. |

Building Compound Sentences

OBJECTIVE   To form compound sentences by combining related sentence pairs.

MATERIALS   List of sentence pairs (independent clauses).

PROCEDURE
1. Write two sample sentences on the board and ask a student to read them out loud.
   Example: Betty washed the dishes.
   Ann dried them.
2. Point out that two short sentences can be combined into one longer one by using a joining word called a conjunction. The most commonly used conjunctions are:

   and   for   so
   but   or   yet

   (Write these on the board.)
3. Ask students to form a new sentence by joining the two sample sentences using the conjunction "and."
   Example: Betty washed the dishes, and
   Ann dried them.
   Note: A comma usually follows the first clause in a compound sentence. It can be omitted if the first phrase is very short.
4. Draw a square around the conjunction for emphasis.
5. Continue with other sample sentences pairs that require the use of other conjunctions.
   Examples: We lost our money.   (so)
   We went home.

   It rained hard.   (but)
   We stayed dry in the tent.

   John will do his homework.   (or)
   He will stay after school.

   Sally ate four candy bars.   (yet)
   She was still hungry.

   He did not pay for the coat. (for)
   He did not have his money.
6. Draw a square around each conjunction for emphasis.

EXTENSION   Have students form compound sentences with the following sentence pairs and the joining word (conjunction) that makes the most sense.

   and   for   so
   but   or   yet

1. The circus came to town. All the children wanted to go.
2. The bus came on time. I wasn't ready.
3. The landlord will lower the rent. We will move anyway.
4. It had been a hard day. Benjamin was tired.
5. There was a terrible blizzard yesterday. School was cancelled.
6. The students planted the seeds. They didn't grow.
7. John will get his way. He will cry.
8. You can buy new dungarees. You can patch your old dungarees.
9. The teacher gave the assignment. The students did it.
10. Charlotte wanted to go. Her mother wanted her to stay home.
11. Vic likes ice cream. Jan likes cookies.
12. At the basketball game, John scored ten points. Bill scored two.
13. I have a long fur coat. I never wear it.
14. The weather might change. It might stay nice and sunny.
15. The toast is in the toaster. The butter is on the table.
16. Ten fire engines came to the fire. The building burned down anyway.
17. Everyone was going to the football game. I had to stay home.
18. Turn the radio off. Turn the T.V. off.

Sentence Combining

OBJECTIVE   To combine related sentences and eliminate excess words.

MATERIALS   Pairs of related sentences.

PROCEDURE   1. Write a sample sentence pair on the chalkboard or overhead transparency. Ask the students to combine them in one short sentence. (Some students try to combine the sentence simply by adding "and." Remind them to make the sentences *shorter* than the two previous sentences combined.)

   The baby was happy. He was laughing.
   The happy baby was laughing.

2. Write the revised sentence on the board. Ask students to identify the changes that were made. Illustrate by drawing arrows to indicate a change in a word's position and circling unnecessary words.

   The baby was happy. He was laughing.

3. Continue the activity by using four or five additional sentence pairs. Then have students combine the remaining sample sentence pairs independently. Read results to the class. Write the combined sentences on the board, noting how each sentence was changed.
   - words rearranged
   - extra words eliminated
   - sentence reduced in length
4. Remind students that the overall goal in sentence development is to write efficient sentences that vary in length. This activity helps to eliminate the use of short, choppy sentences and excess words.)

Sentence Combining: examples of simple sentence pairs

1. The boys are angry. The boys are fighting.
   (The angry boys are fighting.)
2. The newspaper boy is cheerful. He is earning some money.
   (The cheerful newspaper boy is earning some money.)
3. The child is frightened. He hears a strange noise.
   (The frightened child hears a strange noise.)
4. The boys are hungry. They want to eat their sandwiches.
   (The hungry boys want to eat their sandwiches.)
5. The student is forgetful. He didn't do his homework again.
   (The forgetful student didn't do his homework again.)

6. That bear is angry. She can't find her cubs.
   (That angry bear can't find her cubs.)
7. The cows were hungry. They began to moo.
   (The hungry cows began to moo.)
8. The pig is dirty. He is wallowing in the mud.
   (The dirty pig is wallowing in the mud.)
9. That businessman is jubilant. He just received a raise.
   (That jubilant businessman just received a raise.)

EXTENSION 1   *Simple sentences changed to descriptive detail*

1. James got a new bike.
   It is a shiny, red bike.
   It is a ten-speed bike.
   He got it for his twelfth birthday.
   ** James got a new, shiny, red, ten-speed bike for his twelfth birthday.
2. Mr. Brown bought a new Cadillac.
   The Cadillac was huge.
   The Cadillac was shiny.
   The Cadillac was green.
   He bought it for his wife.
   ** Mr. Brown bought a new, huge, shiny, green Cadillac for his wife.
3. Mrs. Jones bought a new dress.
   She is going to wear it to a party.
   It is a beautiful dress.
   It is a green dress.
   It is a long dress.
   ** Mrs. Jones bought a beautiful, new, green, long dress to wear to the party.
4. The boys are going to camp.
   It is a small camp.
   It is a boy scout camp.
   The camp is in the mountains.
   The boys are young.
   ** The young boys are going to a small boy scout camp in the mountains.
5. We have a new teacher.
   The new teacher has beautiful hair.
   It is very long.
   It is very shiny.
   It is dark brown.
   It is curly.
   ** Our new teacher has beautiful, long, shiny, dark brown, curly hair.
6. My grandfather owns a Model T Ford.
   It is a very rare model.
   It is shiny black.
   It is an antique.
   ** My grandfather owns a very rare, shiny black, antique Model T Ford.
7. The kitten chased the pretty butterfly.
   He chased the busy bee.
   He chased the bouncing ball.
   He chased the piece of string.
   He is a silly kitten.
   ** The silly kitten chased the pretty butterfly, the busy bee, the bouncing ball, and the piece of string.
8. I like to grow things in my garden.
   I like to grow tomatoes.
   I like the tomatoes to be juicy.
   I like to grow peppers.
   I like the peppers to be hot.
   I like to grow onions.
   I like the onions to be fat.
   ** I like to grow juicy tomatoes, hot peppers, and fat onions in my garden.

EXTENSION 2 *Simple sentences changed to "when," "where," and "why" phrases*

1. It is dawn.
   Many ducks are quacking.
   They are looking for food.
   They are near the pond.
   ** Many quacking ducks are looking for food near the pond at dawn.
2. The soldier is tired.
   He is on guard duty.
   He is working near the campground entrance.
   He will work until midnight.
   ** The tired soldier will be on guard near the campground entrance until midnight.
3. It was the first game of the season.
   The Red Sox played the Cardinals.
   The Red Sox won the game.
   The game was played in Fenway Park.
   Fenway Stadium is in Boston.
   ** The Red Sox beat the Cardinals at the first game of the season in Fenway Park in Boston.
4. That old man is tired.
   He sits on a bench.
   The bench is in the park.
   He sits there every afternoon.
   ** The tired old man sits on a bench in the park every afternoon.

Make It Parallel

OBJECTIVE   To write sentences using parallel structure.

MATERIALS   Sample sentence patterns.

PROCEDURE
1. Put a sample sentence pattern on the chalkboard or overhead transparency. Ask students to identify the pattern.

   The woman sings, dances, skips, shouts, whistles, hums, and claps.

   Point out the verbs used are present tense and all end with "s."
2. Ask students to repeat the pattern with the following phrase·

   The man _____ , _____ , _____ , _____ , _____ , and _____ .

3. Put a second sample sentence on the chalkboard or transparency. Ask students to identify the pattern.

   The women are singing, dancing, skipping, shouting, whistling, humming, and clapping.

   Point out that all verbs are present tense and have an "ing" ending.
4. Ask students to repeat the pattern with the following phrase:

   The boys are _____ , _____ , _____ , _____ , _____ , _____ , and _____ .

5. Point out that it is important to keep verb tense consistent within sentences.
6. Write another sample sentence on the board in the following pattern. (This time phrases are used.)
   Dogs can eat a bone,
      chase a cat,
      chew a slipper,
      chase a car,
      bite a child, and
      kill a rat.
7. Ask students to repeat the pattern using the following sentence.

Boys can climb a tree,

_____,

_____,

_____,

_____, and

_____.

Help

OBJECTIVE   To deliberately write excessively worded sentences.

MATERIALS   Sample sentence, kernel sentences.

PROCEDURE   1. Write the sample word sentence on the board or on an overhead transparency.

"I am in desperate need of assistance because cold water is rushing very rapidly into my lungs and it is difficult for me to breathe so please send the required assistance as soon as poss... BLUB...BLUB...BLUB..."

2. Ask the students to translate the message to one word. (Help!)
3. Emphasize to students the need to have a *variety* of sentence lengths in their writing and to avoid writing excessively long sentences that could be more effective if shortened.
4. Put a word on the board and ask students to elaborate on it and deliberately build an excessively long sentence. "Danger!" Have students read their long sentences to classmates.
5. Ask students to develop another excessively long sentence on their own. Have them read their sentences to the class and let class guess what the single word should be. "Stop!" "Run!" "Fire!" "Go!" "Eat!" "Wait!" "Danger!" "Stop, Look, Listen!"

Tackle the Troublespots

Several persistent errors, or "troublespots," are found in the written expression of poor writers. Run-on sentences, incomplete sentences, incorrect punctuation, incorrect subject–verb agreement, and confusing noun–pronoun usage are among the most troublesome. Errors are made by three basic groups of students:

1. students who think faster than they write and do not proofread;
2. students who proofread, but just do not know what to look for (these students read the passage as it was intended, rather than as it was actually written); and
3. students who have weak basic writing skills because of a lack of training and/or motivation.

The sentence development section presented activities for building up completely new sentences by combining words and phrases; this section builds sentence skills through analyzing sentences or stories that are already written and that isolate one type of error. These activities generally focus on mechanical problems and attempt to develop proofreading and editing skills. Responsibility for identifying and correcting errors is placed on the student, although the number of errors in an assignment may be given as a clue. Important points in this process are:

1. *Focus on specific problems in students' writing as the need arises*, rather than teaching the rules of grammar in a predetermined sequence. *Avoid* isolated exercises (workbook type) that bear no relationship to the students' immediate problems.
2. *Identify and remediate errors in order of importance.* A student who is writing run-on or incomplete sentences does not need to work on parallel structure or complex sentences.
3. *Isolate one persistent type of error at a time.* Require students to proofread for and correct only this one kind of error. If a student has a great deal of difficulty proofreading her or his own paper, present some of the activities in this section that isolate one type of problem. Students must be able to recognize the problem before they can correct it in their own work. Provide oral practice so that students can "hear" their own errors.

4. *Recognize that as students master simpler forms and attempt higher levels of written expression, they will make different kinds of errors.* The student has to feel free to experiment with more difficult forms before he or she can master them. (The student who is using a variety of sentence structures in his or her writing, but who is making a few errors on compound or complex sentences, is developing more skill than a student who consistently uses *only* simple sentences.) Again, isolate the error category and use specific teaching strategies to help the student recognize, identify, and correct these errors.

MECHANICS

This section of the manual includes activities on capitalization, punctuation, sentence problems (run-ons and fragments), verb tense and agreement, and pronoun agreement. Spelling and handwriting are covered in separate sections. Tables 5-1 and 5-2 review the rules for capitalization and punctuation. See Table 2-4 in Chapter 2 for a review of sentence types.

Table 5-1   Capitalization

Capitalize. . . . .

BASIC	first word in sentences	Zebras have stripes.
	names of people, nicknames	Susan, Tom, Mike, Mr. Jones, Mrs. Hall
	the pronoun I	I
AVERAGE	days, months, holidays	Sunday, July 24th, Christmas, New Years Day
	streets, roads	Woodside Road
	cities, states, countries	San Francisco, California United States of America
	other *specific* places (names of schools, parks, oceans)	Grand Canyon, Rocky Mountains Lincoln School, Fenway Stadium, Atlantic Ocean
	first word in quoted speech	John exclaimed, "Wait, I want to go."
	title of books, plays, poems, magazine articles, student papers	*The Black Stallion* *The Mixed-up Files of Mrs. Basil E. Frankweiler*
	(Not: a, an, the; and, but, or; or prepositions)	
	abbreviations	Mr., Mrs., Dr.
ADVANCED	titles of persons and organizations	Queen Elizabeth, President Carter United States Marines, Peace Corps
	races, nationalities	Caucasian, Negro French, Mexican, Spanish
	religions	Protestant, Catholic, Jewish
	words pertaining to deity,	God, the Father, the Creator
	sacred writings	Bible, Torah, Koran
	saints	Saint Peter
	historical periods	Middle Ages, Renaissance
	events	World War II, Battle of the Bulge
	documents	The Constitution, Magna Carta

Capital Contest

OBJECTIVE   To review rules of capitalization.

Table 5-2   Levels of Punctuation Usage

BASIC	*period* at end of sentence	The weather is nice today.
	question mark after question	How are you today?
AVERAGE	*period* after abbreviations and initials.	Mr. Mrs. Jan. Nov. Dr. Jr. Sr. M.D.
	commas	
	in dates	July 29, 1977
	in addresses (city, state)	San Francisco, California
	after greeting in letter.	Dear Vic,
	after close in letter.	Sincerely,
	after words in series	Skip ate a hot dog, a hamburger, and a banana split for lunch.
	after introductory words.	Well, he was hungry.
	before, after, or around speaker tag.	David announced, "It's time to go." "But I'm still hungry," said Skip. "O.K.," said David, "eat some more."
	quotation marks for direct quotes.	"Hurry up, it's time to go."
	exclamation point after word or phrase expressing strong emotion	Let's go! Help! Fire!
	apostrophe	
	to show possession.	Mary's typewriter Tom's office
	to show plurals	3's p's and q's
	to show contractions	can't won't don't
ADVANCED	*comma* after introductory clauses before a conjunction in a compound sentence	When you stand up on the hill, you can see the lovely sunset. The train finally arrived, but everyone had gone home. Mr. Jones, who is the mayor, is a very friendly person.
	semicolon between two main clauses NOT joined by and, but, or, nor, or for	The train finally arrived; everyone had gone home.
	colon	
	to introduce a list	Sandy wanted a lot of things: a new car, a new house, and a boat.
	after greeting in business letter.	Dear Mr. Jones:

MATERIALS   Sample paragraph, overhead projector, acetate sheet, marking pen, atlas, maps of the United States and the world.

PROCEDURE   1. Review rules of capitalization with the students by having them suggest when capital letters are needed. Make a chart as they make suggestions. Post chart in the classroom.

2. Announce that you are going to have a "Capital Contest." Show sample story on overhead projector. Have students note where capital letters should be and let them write them in on the transparency.

3. Ask students to write a short story using as many capital letters as possible. Remind them to use as many of the rules from the chart as they can. Ask for suggestions of the kinds of stories that could be written.

   Possible Suggestions: Travel Story

   Sports Stories with names of teams, players, and cities visited

Leisure Time Activities (movies, T.V. programs, books, magazines)

Students may use reference sources to get correct spelling (atlases, maps, encyclopedias, etc.).
4. Have students share their stories when finished. Count the number of capitals in each story. Give the person with the highest number a rousing cheer and a funny prize.

EXTENSION   Save completed capital stories for review practice on another day. Let each student carefully copy her or his story on a transparency or a ditto, omitting the correct capital letters. Let the student lead a discussion on where capital letters should go.

CAPITAL CONTEST CHECKUP

the rotary club was organizing a three-week trip to europe for its club members during september. mr. and mrs. harry jones were extremely excited about the trip and were among the first to sign up to go. mr. jones had always dreamed of going to paris, france, so he started to practice his french lessons right away. he had a special interest in french history and was eager to visit the sites of world war II battles. he was also interested in visiting the french museums, especially the louvre, and seeing some of the work of the famous artists: renoir, monet, cezanne, and toulouse-lautrec.

mrs. jones shared her husband's enthusiasm for the trip. she went to the boston public library and got the following books to read:

the sun king   by nancy mitford,

the french revolution   by douglas johnson,

art centers of the world—paris   by alexander watt.

soon august 5th arrived and mr. and mrs. jones went to logan international airport in boston to meet their group. They boarded trans world airlines flight #65 to england. they discovered that another group, the massachusetts teachers association, had also chartered space on the same flight. everyone had high expectations for an interesting and exciting trip.

Run-on Sentences

OBJECTIVE   To identify and correct "run-on" sentences.

MATERIALS   Several paragraphs with punctuation replaced with "and," "and then," or "so."

PROCEDURE   1. Read a paragraph and emphasize the repeated word or words. Ask students to identify the repeated word.
2. Put a written copy of the paragraph on an overhead transparency. Have students locate the repeated words and draw a box around each one, then draw a big X through the box.
3. Have the students put a period in the sentence before the box and a capital letter on the first word after the box.
4. Read the corrected story out loud.
5. Put another run-on story on a ditto and give out to students. Let them find the "run-ons" by themselves, then put boxes around the repeated words, and insert correct capitalization and punctuation. Ask them to copy the paragraph correctly if it is not too long.

EXTENSION   Have students write run-on paragraphs deliberately, then switch papers with another student. The second student must then locate all the run-ons, eliminate them, and correct capitalization and punctuation. The first writer checks the work for accuracy.

Examples: "Run-On" Stories

The Strange Event

The little girl heard a big noise and she went up on the roof to see what happened and she saw something and it looked like a fireball and then she went to bed and when she got up the next morning she listened to the news on the radio and then she heard that the big noise was really a rocket taking off.

The Turtle Race

The turtle race is held every year at the pool and everyone is invited to bring a fast turtle and each person holds his turtle at the starting line and somebody yells, "Let them go!" and everybody lets go and some turtles start walking very fast and some turtles start going off in the wrong direction and everyone starts yelling and finally one turtle crosses the finish line and everybody cheers some more and they give a prize to the owner of the winning turtle.

Making Cookies

Geraldine wanted to make some cookies and so she went into the kitchen to get everything ready and she read the cookie recipe and it told her she needed eggs, flour, milk, and sugar and then she began to mix the flour with the milk and then she added some nuts and then she finished mixing the other stuff in the bowl and then she put the cookies on the cookie sheet and then she put the cookies in the oven to bake and then when the cookies were done she gave them to her friends.

Sentence Fragments

OBJECTIVE   To distinguish between sentences and fragments.

MATERIALS   List of sentences and fragments; 2 blank cards for each student, labeled | yes | | no |

PROCEDURE
1. Remind students that a simple sentence has two parts: a naming phrase and an action phrase. Give several samples.
2. Read several sentences and fragments to students (one at a time).
3. Ask students to hold up | yes | card if you read a sentence, and | no | if you read a fragment.
4. Ask students to complete sentences that are incomplete.
5. Give out a practice sheet after students have had sufficient oral practice. Tell students to write | yes | if the sentence is complete, and | no | if the sentence is incomplete. Have them finish incomplete sentences.
6. Share results by having students read their completed sentences aloud.

Sentence Collage

OBJECTIVE   To make "sentence" and "fragment" collages.

MATERIALS   Magazines, scissors, paste, poster paper.

PROCEDURE   1. Review the meaning of "sentence" and "fragment" by reading samples to the class.

Remind students that a complete sentence must have a "naming phrase" and an "action phrase," and may have "when" and "where" phrases added.

2. Have students cut out whole sentences and sentence fragments from brightly colored pages from magazines.
3. Ask students to separate the sentences and fragments, then paste them on posters labeled "sentences" and "fragments."
4. Encourage students to form a message, letter, or short poem with the phrases and sentences found.
5. Display complete posters around the classroom or hallways.

Hidden Sentences

OBJECTIVE To locate and punctuate hidden sentences.

MATERIALS A series of words that contains a hidden sentence.

PROCEDURE
1. Write a series of words that contains a hidden sentence on the board.
   "ring circus the lion tamer jumped into the lion's cage whip zoo"
2. Have students read the sample and locate the sentence that is hidden. Next underline it, then point out the type and location of capitalization and punctuation needed.
3. Pass out a worksheet that contains some hidden sentences. Have students locate and underline the hidden sentences.
4. Have student copy the "found" sentences with correct capitalization and punctuation.

EXTENSION Ask each student to write some "hidden sentences" for a classmate. Switch papers when completed and have the second student locate and correct the hidden sentences. Save the papers for review practice on other days.

SAMPLE HIDDEN SENTENCES

Set One

1. song please turn off the record player noise music record now
2. that painter dropped his paint bucket on the floor sloppy mess
3. husky happy most people enjoy football and basketball gym yell
4. workman that workman fell in a huge manhole street working water
5. once upon a door dogs that zoo keeper wanted to eat his lunch
6. trip suitcase train that tourist packed his clothes and left
7. red warm woolen mittens are used on cold days winter blizzard
8. little pictures have big chief has small muscles indian teepee
9. holiday joyful a plump turkey was sizzling in the oven roast
10. noisy jets fly above the clouds airport weather is leave

Set Two

1. crowds of people were at the train station ticket money good-bye
2. tinsel packages pretty lights christmas is not coming this year
3. a painful toothache my dentist will remove the decayed tooth
4. black furry gorillas weigh four hundred pounds dangerous cage
5. growl angry a gorilla had a thorn in his foot painful aspirin
6. hunters trap young gorillas are caught and tamed for the zoo
7. when you go on vacation in the summer you can swim fish and play
8. look at the bright side of things be happy smile more often more
9. watch out the sky is falling said chicken little its time to go
10. hurry up and finish your work so we can go outside to play soon

Set Three

1. terrific smile sour a smile will brighten your entire face happy
2. television commercials are too long interrupt good programs and
3. sneakers baseball hockey soccer and tennis are exciting games
4. fire call the fire department throw on some water it's out now
5. many many years ago yesterday history teaches us many lessons
6. water swimming pool help I can't swim sink butterfly stroke
7. science social students match homework is your homework done
8. impending disaster tornadoes hurricanes the weather is nice
9. magazines newspapers and television provide up to date news
10. furniture carpenters appliances salesman we need a new T.V.

Sentence Scramble

OBJECTIVE   To arrange scrambled words into sentences.

MATERIALS   Scrambled sentences from students' writing, or from the following examples.

PROCEDURE
1. Copy some sentences from students' writing on strips of paper. At first, write capital letter on first word and period after last word. Later, write sentences with no capitalization or punctuation clues.
2. Cut each sentence into individual words. Shuffle order of words. Keep each shuffled sentence in a separate pile or envelope.
3. Have students choose an envelope or pile of words, read the words, and then rearrange the words in a meaningful sentence. Have students read the sentence out loud to see whether it is complete and makes sense.
4. Have students trade envelopes with other students and continue unscrambling sentences.
5. Give students some of the scrambled sentences that do not have capitalization and punctuation clues and have them arrange the words in order, then copy and put in correct capitalization and punctuation.

Cats

nice are Cats pets.
neat are They clean. and very
they lazy. But are very
sleep like They sun the in day. all to

Dogs

a kind favorite my dog pet is of
tricks teach like I to them
shake them teach can I to hands
sit them also can up teach I to
cats can't teach but I chase them to
do themselves that by all they

Growing vegetables

own grow is vegetables it to easy very your
soil first must prepare the you
shovel dig plant use area and a the up want you where to
rocks the and rake all stones out big
fertilizer soil add to prepared the
plant ready are you now the seeds to
seed the the read packet on directions
to it you tell will how seeds plant deep the

Tackle the Troublespots   **159**

to the the sow directions seeds according
dirt seeds the with cover
water with the sprinkle area
see moist keep sprout the until the to area you seeds start

EXTENSION Give students a ditto copy of scrambled sentences. Let them decide on correct word order, copy sentence, and put in correct capitalization and punctuation. Start with easier sentences first and gradually move on to harder sentences when students are ready.

Foolish Questions

OBJECTIVE To use question marks at the end of questions.

MATERIALS Sample questions.

PROCEDURE
1. Write several "foolish questions" on the board.
   Examples: Is a 50 pound canary heavy?
   Do hyenas laugh?
   Do bears live in the woods?
   Do giraffes have long necks?
2. Ask students to suggest other "foolish questions." Write suggestions on the board. Emphasize the use of the question mark at the end of the question.
3. Ask students to write five or ten foolish questions on a piece of paper.
4. Have student volunteers read the questions to the class. Have the class decide on the most foolish question.
5. Ask students to think of original answers to some of the foolish questions.

EXTENSION *The Question Game*

Have each student choose a partner. Explain the rules of the game: one person must ask a question; the second person must answer the first question by asking another question; the first person must answer the second question by asking a third question, and so on. (Have students write their conversations down. Remind them to use question marks and quotation marks.)

Example:

First student: "Want some lunch?"

Second student: "Do you have any tuna fish?"

First student: "Would you like mayonnaise on it?"

Second student: "Do you have to put mayonnaise on it?"

First student: "Would you like something else instead?"

Second student: "Do you have any peanut butter?"

First student: "Do you want a peanut butter sandwich?"

Second student: "Do you have any milk to go with it?"

First student: "Want some chocolate milk?"

Second student: "Is it fresh?"

etc., etc., etc.

Which students created the longest conversation that stays on the topic?

RESOURCES **Mind Your A's and Q's:**
Useless Questions to Dumb Answers
Jack Stokes
Doubleday, 1977

Here is a collection of a different kind of joke: the answer comes first and you have to figure out what the question should be.

For example:

A. Zub-zub-zub.

Q. What sound does a bee make when it backs up?

Rube Goldberg: His Life and Work
Peter C. Marzio
Harper and Row, 1973

"Foolish Questions" was a popular Goldberg cartoon series. In this series, Goldberg made fun of some of the questions that people ask in obvious situations. Foolish Question No. 40,976 shows a father who asks, "Son, are you smoking that pipe again?" The son, who *is* smoking a pipe responds, "No, Dad, this is a portable kitchenette and I'm frying a smelt for dinner."

Ask or Tell

OBJECTIVE To distinguish between questions and statements.

MATERIALS List of questions and statements; 2 cards for each statement, labeled ask? tell

PROCEDURE
1. Review the difference between a statement and a question with the class: i.e., a statement tells something, and a question asks something. Remind them that a question always need a response.
2. Read a few samples and ask students to note changes in voice patterns.
3. Read a sentence to the class. If it *asks* something, tell the students to hold up the ask? card. If the sentence *tells* something, have the students hold up the tell. card.
4. Have students give an appropriate answer to the questions that you use.

Examples: Statements and Questions

1. Is your class going on a picnic?
2. The students were playing different games on the playground.
3. What is your favorite game?
4. Did you see the boy fall down the stairs?
5. Jane always complains that her work is too hard.
6. Would you like to go to the movies with me?
7. Giraffes have long necks so they can reach the high leaves.
8. Why does a monkey climb a tree?
9. A monkey climbs a tree to keep away from other animals.
10. Did you finish your homework?
11. Yesterday, Ann had two ice cream cones after school.
12. Everyone in my family likes music.
13. What would you like to do on your vacation?
14. The vendor on the corner was selling hot pretzels.
15. The principal of our school came into our class today.
16. Was Pam invited to the party?
17. What do you want for Christmas?
18. What do you want for your birthday?
19. How many people are in your family?
20. Five people are in my family.

EXTENSION Put these *ask/tell* sentences on strips of paper and keep in an envelope. Have individual students sort them into two groups during independent activity time.

Ask, Tell, Exclaim!

OBJECTIVE To identify statements, questions, and exclamations.

MATERIALS List of statements, questions, and exclamations; three small cards per student, labeled ask? tell. exclaim! .

1. Give each student a set of three labeled cards.
2. Review the difference between asking and telling sentences by giving students some samples and having them hold up the card that corresponds.
3. Give students the ⎡exclaim!⎤ card if students are accurate with ⎡ask?⎤ and ⎡tell.⎤ cards.
4. Explain that an exclamation shows excitement or emphasis. Give several examples.
       Wait! Stop thief! Fire!
5. Continue by reading a variety of sentences. Ask students to hold up the appropriate response card. Discuss any differences of opinion. Be sure to read exclamations with extra emphasis.
6. Ask students to suggest other sentences that would be exclamations.

EXTENSION Put these ask, tell, and exclaim sentences on strips of paper and put them in an envelope so students can sort them during free periods.

Examples: Statements, Questions, Exclamations

Sample Exclamations: an exclamatory sentence shows excitement!

   1. Fire!
   2. Help!
   3. Watch out!
   4. Don't do that!

Statements, Questions, and Exclamations

   1. The snow kept falling all through the night.
   2. Do you know what tomorrow's weather will be like?
   3. Wow! What a hit!
   4. Watch out! That's hot!
   5. The first game of the baseball season will be on Thursday.
   6. Can we go to the first baseball game?
   7. Don't run in the halls! Take your time!
   8. He hit a homerun!
   9. The long freight train pulled into the station.
   10. Did you do your homework last night?
   11. Do you have any money?
   12. That's a poison snake! he yelled.
   13. The newspaper boy threw the paper on the porch.
   14. Did you ever catch a fly ball at a baseball game?
   15. The Red Sox won! What a game!

Conversations

OBJECTIVE To write dialogue with quotation marks.

MATERIALS Two different colored felt tip pens, list of topics.

PROCEDURE 1. Ask students to work in pairs and choose a topic from the topic list, or think of another topic to write a dialogue about.
2. Tell each student to choose a different colored pen to use. Write one person's conversation in one color and the responses in another color. Skip lines between each person's speech, and put quotation marks before and after each statement.
3. Read the conversations to the class.
4. Add names of characters and response words. Try to avoid the repetitive use of "said" by making a list of alternatives with the class. Remind students to use commas after the character introduction (e.g., Amelia yelled,).
5. Try to vary the placement of the tag by placing it at the beginning, end, or middle of the sentence. Show students samples, or put samples on the bulletin board for reminders.

Examples: Topic List

One teacher discussing a hard day with another teacher.
Two invaders from space on their first visit to earth.
The newspaper boy talking to an angry customer.
Two boys arguing over a baseball.
Two mischievous boys planning a camping trip.
Two girls going to a gymnastics meet.
Two housewives complaining about the price of groceries.
A news reporter and the fire chief at the scene of a fire.
A student and a parent talking about a good/bad report card.
Two old-timers chatting about the weather.
A mechanic and an owner of an old broken down car.
A police officer and a motorist stopped for speeding.
A sales representative trying to sell a vacuum cleaner to a home owner.
A farmer talking to his cow.
Two girls planning a shopping trip.

EXTENSION   See activity on "Telephone Conversations."

Punctuation Dictation

OBJECTIVE   To identify required punctuation in an unpunctuated paragraph by listening to vocal intonation.

MATERIALS   Unpunctuated paragraphs (at first eliminate only capital letters and periods from paragraphs, gradually exclude other types of punctuation).

PROCEDURE
1. Give each student a copy of the unpunctuated paragraph. Tell them that you will read the paragraph through once at a normal rate and then you will repeat it at a slower rate.
2. Point out the type of punctuation that is omitted from the paragraph. Or, ask students to identify the type of punctuation missing. At first use paragraphs from which you have omitted only periods and capital letters; later use paragraphs without quotation marks, commas, and question marks.
3. Have students write a goal at the top of the paper.
   Example: Find missing capital letters and periods.
4. Read paragraph to students twice.
5. Put unpunctuated copy of paragraph on overhead projector. Ask students to identify where omissions are. Have students check their papers against the corrected copy on the overhead projector.

Add the Ending (Verb Tense)

OBJECTIVE   To identify and add omitted endings on verbs.

MATERIALS   Incomplete stories with endings omitted on verbs.

PROCEDURE
1. Read one incomplete story to the class. Tell them that something is wrong and ask them to listen to see whether they can identify the error. (Consonants have been doubled or final "e" vowel dropped when necessary to avoid confusing the lesson by introducing additional rules.)
2. Have students state the error. (The endings are missing from the action words.)
3. Give students a copy of the story and have them state the goal of the activity on the "Goal line."
   Goal: Put endings on action words.

4. Have students read and correct incomplete story, then add an ending to the story.
5. Have students share their different endings by reading them out loud to their classmates.

EXTENSION After students have done several of these, have them write stories with endings omitted deliberately. Put these stories on dittos and give out to the rest of the class for correction. Let the person who wrote the story be the corrector.

Example 1

Boston Bruins versus_____

"The last period of the Bruins versus the hockey game is about to begin! What an excit____ game this is. The score is 2 to 2. The fans are scream_____ in the stands. In just a few minutes, we will know who the championship playoff winners will be.

There they go. Both teams are skat_____ back on the ice after the quarter break. Wow, look at that! Phil Esposito is break____away and is skat_____ down the ice like mad. _____ is chas_____ him. Oops, now_____ is knock_____ him with his stick. Phil is fall_____down.

Wait! Bobby Orr is skat_____ up on the side. Look at that! He's sav_____ the puck and now he's shoot_____ right for the net. Fantastic! It's go_____ right in. Listen to the fans. They are really scream_____ now. The score is 3 to 2.

The _____ are really feel_____ the pressure now. Only sixty seconds to go. Wait! _____ is break-_____ away. He's_____

_____
_____
_____
_____

Example 2

The Gymnastics Meet

Yesterday Geraldine, Kelly, and Wendy went to the gymnastics meet. They perform_____ many difficult acts for the audience. Wendy tumbl_____on the mats and did somersaults on the trampoline. Geraldine perform_____ on the parallel bars. Kelly walk_____ , jump_____, and roll_____ on the high balance beam. The audience clapp_____ and yell_____ after every act. The girls were very proud of their performance.

Then everyone turn_____their attention to the ropes. Kelly climb_____to the very top of the ropes and start_____ to do fancy movements with her hands and feet. Suddenly her right hand slipp_____ and _____

_____
_____
_____
_____

Example 3

The Undersea World

Yesterday, Cindy and her two friends want_____to go scuba diving. They need_____ rubber suits, goggles and air tanks. They collect_____ all their equipment together, then check_____ the air tanks to make sure they were fill_____ with air. They load_____ their equipment in the car and start_____off.

At the beach, they unload_____ the car and pil_____ the equipment on their blanket. Then, they dress_____ in their rubber suits, hook_____ up their oxygen tanks, and climb-_____ on the boat.

A mile out in the ocean, the boat stopp_____ . The girls jump_____ off into the water and explore_____ the undersea reef. Cindy was near a large jagged rock, when suddenly her air hose caught on the rock and it was cut open. She_____

_____

_____

_____

_____

Sports News (Verb Tense)

OBJECTIVE   To write sports news articles using present and past tenses.

MATERIALS   Sports pictures from newspaper or magazines.

PROCEDURE
1. Collect interesting action pictures from the sports section of newspapers or magazines. Ask students to help you collect them.
2. Let students choose a picture and write an "on the spot" news report using an announcer point of view. Read sample to class. This activity encourages the use of present tense verbs.
3. Encourage students to use short sentences loaded with action verbs and exclamations of excitement.
4. Read results to class.
5. On another day, have each student rewrite the "on the spot" report as a report for the daily news. Remind students that newspaper reporting is more objective than "on the spot" type reporting and generally does not include the exclamations of excitement or statements of opinion. This time the story will be written in past tense.
6. Read results to the class. Compare the difference in style between the "on the spot" report and the follow-up newspaper report.

EXTENSION 1   Have students listen to televised sports news programs. These programs generally use quite precise verbs in their descriptions of games. Ask students to jot down some of the descriptions and bring them into class.

EXTENSION 2   Have a student follow one team or sports hero through a period of time by collecting pictures from the newspaper and writing short reports on each picture. Bind all of the articles and pictures in book format. Newspaper pictures xerox very well, so many students can use the same pictures.

EXTENSION 3   Present some catchy titles found in the sports section of the newspaper. Also present an outline of information which provides who, did what, when, and where. Let students write an article to match the title and information. Encourage them to describe an interesting scene in the game.

I, We, He, She, They, It

OBJECTIVE   To use pronouns correctly in sentences.

MATERIALS   Small cards for each student, labeled:

| I | we | she | he | they | it |

list of sentences (Example 1)

1. Give each student a set of pronoun cards. Read a sentence and ask students to identify the word card that would replace the *name* in the sentence. Have them hold up the appropriate card.

    "George needs a new winter coat."

2. Let several students add on a second sentence starting with the appropriate pronoun.

    "He will go to the store to buy one."

    "He will buy a fur coat."

3. Continue with several more practice sentences.

4. Give extra practice in using pronouns by providing a worksheet of sentence pairs, omitting pronouns. (See Example 1.)

Give students a copy of "The Haunted Mansion" (Example 2) and have them fill in the correct pronouns and complete the story.

Or, try "The Circus Comes to Town" or "The Case of the Missing Cookies."

Example 1: Sample Sentences—Pronoun Usage—I, We, He, She, They, It

Set One

1. Ann just baked some cookies.	(She. . .)
2. Charlotte and Jack are planning a trip to India.	(They. . .)
3. The children were rehearsing for the school play.	(They. . .)
4. George lost his lunch on his way to school.	(He. . .)
5. The circus is coming to town.	(It. . .)
6. The penny rolled down the drain.	(It. . .)
7. Mary, Jane, and I are hungry.	(We. . .)
8. The teacher gave the assignment.	(He or She. . .)
9. Mother wants me to go right home after school.	(She. . .)
10. My father just bought a new car.	(He. . .)

Set Two

1. Birds fly south for the winter.	(They. . .)
2. Bears hibernate every winter.	(They. . .)
3. Mother wants to go shopping.	(She. . .)
4. The dog was lost in the woods.	(It. . .)
5. Esther and George live in a big, brick house.	(They. . .)
6. Friends are always around when you need them.	(They. . .)
7. The farmer just plowed his field.	(He. . .)
8. Sam, Harry, and I want to play baseball.	(We. . .)
9. Kathy, Lynn, and Mary want to play baseball, too.	(They. . .)
10. The boys don't want to play with the girls.	(They. . .)

Example 2

THE HAUNTED MANSION

1. The old mansion on Clark Street had been deserted for years.
2. _____ was supposedly inhabited by ghosts.
3. The ghosts were very mischievous.
4. _____ liked to scare people at night.
5. Mr. Brown lived near the mansion.
6. _____ didn't believe in the story of the ghosts.
7. Mrs. Brown *did* believe the story.
8. _____ was afraid to go near the mansion.
9. One night, Mr. and Mrs. Brown heard a strange noise coming from the mansion.
10. This time, _____ both were frightened. Richie, Steve, and Jill were afraid, too.
11. But Mr. Brown decided to investigate.
12. _____ quietly walked to the front door of the mansion.

13. The noise was getting louder and louder.
14. _____ sounded like chains dragging, bones rattling, and teeth chattering.
15. Mr. Brown opened the front door very carefully and. . . .

_____

_____

_____

Example 3

THE CIRCUS COMES TO TOWN!

1. Mom!
2. The circus is coming to town!
3. _____ will arrive on Friday at 10 A.M.
4. The first show will be on Saturday afternoon.
5. _____ will last four hours!
6. Acrobats and clowns will entertain the audience first!
7. _____ will do a lot of funny tricks and stunts.
8. The tiger trainer will be here, too.
9. _____ will put his hand in the tiger's mouth!
10. The trapeze artist is a young girl!
11. _____ will do her tricks without a net!
12. The jugglers will juggle bats, balls, and bottles.
13. _____ won't even break any of the bottles!
14. Twenty elephants will be in the parade!
15. _____ will carry many of the acrobats.
16. The fat man will eat lots and lots of popcorn.
17. _____ will get even fatter.
18. Please Mom, Michael, John, and Eddie are going.
19. _____ want me to go, too.
20. Can _____ go! Please!
21. _____ all want to go together.

Example 4

THE CASE OF THE MISSING COOKIES

1. Lori baked some good chocolate chip cookies.
2. _____ put them on the windowsill to cool.
3. Bobby, Richie, and Steve had just finished their ball game.
4. _____ smelled the cookies. Yummy! Yummy!
5. _____ each took two.
6. Ellen saw the boys near the window.
7. _____ went to see what they were doing.
8. The boys saw Ellen coming.
9. _____ ran away fast!
10. Ellen saw the cookies on the window, too.
11. _____ took two.
12. Scott and Brian were playing tag and ran around the house.
13. _____ saw the cookies.
14. _____ each took three.
15. Jill, Cheryl, Brenda, and Alisha came along.
16. _____ saw the cookies, too.
17. _____ each took two. Yummy!
18. Kevin came along.
19. _____ took four cookies. Yummy! Yummy!
20. Kim came along next.
21. _____ thought, "That's strange, why is that empty dish on the windowsill?"
22. Rob, Mark, Joy, and Todd didn't get any cookies.

Mixed Up Stories

OBJECTIVE   To detect pronoun inconsistency.

MATERIALS   Short story with pronouns used incorrectly; ditto copy of story.

Example 1

THE PICNIC

Yesterday, Joe, Robert, Susan, and Ruth went on a picnic.
He met at the entrance to the town park.
Susan told the others that he knew the perfect spot near a lovely little pond.
She all agreed that would be a terrific place for the picnic.
When he all reached the pond, he spread the blanket, unpacked the food, and ate lunch.
After lunch, he suggested that everyone go for a walk.
It started to walk around the pond.
While taking the walk, she tripped over a twig and he landed in the pond.
What a sight they was!
The others started to laugh and so did he.
He were sure that she would always remember his first picnic.
She was a perfect day and everyone had a wonderful time.

Example 2

THE PICNIC

Yesterday, Joe, Robert, Susan, and Ruth went on a picnic.
_____ *met at the entrance to the town park.*
Susan told the others that _____ *knew the perfect spot near a lovely little pond.*
_____ *all agreed that would be a terrific place for the picnic.*
When _____ *all reached the pond,* _____ *spread the blanket, unpacked the food, and ate lunch.*
After lunch, _____ *suggested that everyone go for a walk.*
_____ *started to walk around the pond.*
While taking the walk, _____ *tripped over a twig and* _____ *landed in the pond.*
What a sight _____ *was!*
The others started to laugh and so did _____.
_____ *were sure that* _____ *would always remember* _____ *first picnic.*
_____ *was a perfect day and everyone had a wonderful time.*

1. Give students a ditto copy of "The Picnic."
2. Tell the students that something is wrong with the story. Ask them to try and identify the problem as you read it and they follow along on the ditto.
3. Read "The Picnic." Emphasize the pronouns as you read.
4. Ask the students to state the problem. (It is not necessary for them to say that the "pronouns" are incorrect. They may say that the he's, she's, they's, etc., are all mixed up.)
5. Give students a copy of the story with pronouns omitted. Have them fill in the correct pronouns.
6. Have one student read the corrected story to the class.
7. Continue this activity on another day with another "mixed up" story. Or, have students write some mixed up stories for the class to correct.

SPELLING

Students need specific phonics instruction on a frequent basis if they are to learn to read and write with a measure of skill. At the same time, they need practice on sight words that occur in reading and writing. Spelling should *not* be treated only as a separate strand of instruction, but should be part of an integrated language arts experience as well. The approach presented in this book emphasizes greater written production (quantity) rather than complete accuracy in spelling. Errors should not be totally ignored, and specific time should be set aside for correcting them.

Students who fear making spelling mistakes tend to use very limited word choice in their writing. Specific strategies to circumvent this problem can be initiated at *three* different points in the writing process: pre-writing, during writing, and post-writing. Remember that communicating ideas is the first focus of the writing program. Students should be encouraged to write freely without worrying about perfect spelling. Once the ideas are down on paper and reviewed, then spelling errors can be corrected.

Pre-Writing

1. Write key words and phrases on the board as students discuss topic.
2. Have students suggest any additional words they might need to complete their writing assignment. Write these on the board. Students can refer to them as needed during the writing session.

During Writing

1. Encourage students to sound out as much as possible of the unknown word, then draw a line to indicate that help is needed (e.g., ani_____). This keeps the students writing and prevents them from getting bogged down while waiting for spelling help.
2. Write the needed words on a piece of paper for the student. Or ask a second student to write the words out.
3. Give positive reinforcement for every word attempted.

Post-Writing

1. Do not circle errors in red!
2. Have students proofread their papers and circle all words that they think might be wrong. (They may *not* find all errors—that's O.K.) This method reduces teacher judgment of spelling errors and gives the students more responsibility for finding their own errors. If students cannot find all of their misspelled words, write the misspelled words correctly on a separate piece of paper. Ask students to go back over the writing and find the misspelled words, then substitute the correctly spelled words.
3. *Write* needed words on a separate piece of paper for students.
4. After the students correct their spelling, have them keep the needed words in an alphabetized notebook or index file. You may want to add other words to the page or card if it is a pattern word. This will help reinforce correct spelling.

Example: sound
              found
              hound
              mound, etc.

The students may also write sentences using the words on the page or card.

5. Pair students up periodically for review of spelling words.

Specific Techniques for Improving Auditory Skills

A. Problem: Substitution of letters.
1. Confusion between voiced and unvoiced (breath) sounds:
   Teach the students to distinguish between voiced sounds and unvoiced or breath sounds. Have the students *feel* the puffs of air coming out of the mouth on breath sounds and *feel* the vibrations in the throat on voiced sounds.
2. Confusion on similar sounds and vowel sounds:
   Teach the child to *feel* the difference between the sounds as they are formed in the mouth. Do this by having the child imitate mouth movements that you make as you form the letter. Verbalize the mouth movements. "Stick your tongue out between your teeth when you see the letter 'th'."

B. Problem: Omissions of letters and syllables on phonetically regular words, omission of endings or suffixes, mixed sequence of letters or syllables.
1. Encourage the students to listen through the whole word as you say it slowly.
2. Have the student count the sounds in the one-syllable words.
3. Have the student count the syllables in multisyllable words.
4. Dictate slowly and have students write one sound or syllable at a time.

Note: Children with auditory problems may learn best through a visual approach to spelling. Use flashcards and concentration games so that phonetic patterns can be seen and heard at the same time. This provides visual reinforcement for auditory activities. A child may understand rhyming much faster and be able to spell the words easier, if she or he can see the patterns visually (*look, book, cook, took*).

Provide time for review and reinforcement of auditory skills. A child with auditory discrimination problems must "overlearn" phonetic elements.

Specific Techniques for Improving Visual Skills

1. Keep a chart of the most commonly misspelled words in the classroom.
2. Make flashcards of the most commonly misspelled words. Have the students play concentration games with the cards. As the students turn over the cards, have them spell the words orally. Limit the game to about six word pairs at a time.
3. Have the student look at the word card, spell the word, turn the word card over, and then write the word from memory on his paper. Repeat this procedure daily until the word is mastered. Give a pretest and posttest.
4. Keep alphabetized spelling boxes or notebooks. Have the students add new words as they need them.
5. Keep a chart of mnemonic devices that aid in spelling difficult words.

Note: Children with visual problems may learn best through an *auditory approach.* Use activities that involve oral spelling with written reinforcement.

Additional Suggestions for Spelling Improvement

1. Keep a list of student errors to see whether an error pattern exists (e.g., student consistently misses vowel sounds, or blends, or mixes sequences on letters). If you do see a pattern, try to develop a series of lessons that teach that particular skill.
2. Encourage students to identify their own learning style. Some students learn best by saying letter names out loud as they write; others by writing the words many times; and still others by looking at the word and then trying to write it from memory.
3. Have the class make a chart of mnemonic devices that are useful in spelling difficult words. Keep the chart visible in the room.

Spelling Interviews

OBJECTIVE   To develop lists of difficult words.

MATERIALS   Pencil and paper.

PROCEDURE

1. Ask the students to name the words that they have difficulty spelling. Put these on a chart.
2. Next have different class members interview students in other classrooms and find out which words they have difficulty spelling. Add these words to the chart.
3. Tally the number of times each word was mentioned. Keep the chart posted in the classroom.
4. Sponsor a "Spelling Mastery Contest" based on the list of words collected in the interviews.

EXTENSION   Point out that teachers have some spelling troublespots, too. Have students interview other teachers and make a list of words that they have trouble spelling. Add these to the "Spelling Mastery Contest" and see whether everyone can learn all of the troublespots.

Visual Dictation

OBJECTIVE   To develop visual memory of spelling words.

MATERIALS   Sentences or short paragraphs slightly above the students' level of spelling ability.

PROCEDURE

1. Write a sentence or short paragraph on the board or overhead projector. At first use only one sentence, but gradually build up to short paragraphs. (This activity works best with small groups of students.)
2. Ask the students to read the sample out loud several times. Ask them to pick out the words that they think might be hard to spell. Spell these out loud as a group, then write them down on a scrap piece of paper.
3. Read the sample one more time, then ask the students to take one last careful look before you cover it up.
4. Dictate the sample slowly in short phrases and have students write down what you say. Repeat several times or until all students are finished.
5. Have students proofread their papers and underline any word they had trouble with or they think they have misspelled.
6. Expose the sample again and ask students to compare their version with the original. Focus specific attention on any words that were misspelled. Have students spell them out loud and write them down (one at a time).
7. Repeat the Visual Dictation Exercise a second time. Ask students to compare their second copy with the sample. Then compare the second copy with the first. Which one was better?
8. Repeat this activity frequently for students who are making errors on basic sight words.

The Bare Bear

OBJECTIVE   To illustrate and write sentences with homophones.

MATERIALS   Drawing paper, crayons, colored pencils, or magic markers.

PROCEDURE

1. Explain the meaning of "homophone" to the students (i.e., words that sound the same, but have different spellings and different meanings). *Note:* The term homonym is frequently substituted for homophone. Homonyms are words that sound

a	him	school
about	his	see
after	home	she
all	house	so
am	I	some
an	if	that
and	in	the
are	into	them
around	is	then
as	it	there
at	just	they
back		think
be	know	things
because	like	this
but	little	time
by	man	to
came	me	too
can	mother	two
could	my	up
day	no	us
did	not	very
didn't	now	was
do	of	we
don't	on	well
down	one	went
for	or	were
from	our	what
get	out	when
go	over	will
got	people	with
had	put	would
have	said	you
he	saw	your
here		

The ten most frequently used words. . . .in order of frequency:
   I   and   the   a   to   was   in   it   of   my
The first three words account for 11.8% of the words identified in Hillerich's study. The first five account for 18.2%; the first ten account for 26.1%. The 100 words make up 60% of words used by children in their writing.

Source: Hillerich, R.L., A Writing Vocabulary of Elementary School Children. *Springfield, Illinois: Charles C Thomas, 1978. Used with permission of the author and publisher.*

   the same, have the same spelling, but different meanings. Sometimes homonyms
   are called homographs because they are written with the same spelling.
2. Write several pairs on the board for examples.
       nose-knows   pair-pear   plane-plain   beat-beet
3. Ask students to suggest other pairs. Add them to the chart as they are suggested.
   Give students clues if they have trouble thinking of words.
       "The post office delivers the ＿＿＿＿＿＿＿."
4. Read one of the suggested resources that use homophones aloud to the class.
   Have students listen for homophones to add to the list.

Table 5-4   Dolch Word List

a	eat	jump
above	eight	just
after	every	
again		keep
all	fall	kind
always	far	know
am	fast	
an	fight	land
and	find	laugh
any	first	let
are	five	like
around	fly	little
as	found	look
ask	for	long
at	four	
ate	from	made
away	full	make
	funny	many
be		may
because	gate	me
become	gave	most
been	get	much
best	give	my
better	go	myself
big	goes	
black	going	never
blue	good	nine
both	got	no
bring	green	not
brown	grow	now
but		
buy	has	of
by	had	off
	have	old
call	he	on
came	help	once
can	her	one
carry	here	only
clean	him	open
cold	his	our
come	hold	over
could	hot	own
cut	how	
	hurt	pick
did		play
do	I	please
does	if	pretty
done	in	pull
don't	into	put
down	is	
draw	it	read
drink	it's	red
		ride
		right

Table 5-4   Dolch Word List

rode	that	was
round	the	wash
run ____	them	warm
said	then	we
saw	their	well
say	there	went
seven	these	were
shall	they	what
she	think	when
show	this	where
sing	those	which
sit	three	white
six	to	who
sleep	today	why
small	together	will
so	try	wish
some	two ____	with
soon	under	work
start	up	would
stop ____	upon	write ____
take	us	yellow
tell	use ____	yes
ten	very ____	you
than	walk	your
thank	want	

Source: "Dolch Basic Sight Vocabulary" by E.W. Dolch. Garrard Publishing Co. Champaign, Ill. 61820

5. Ask students to choose some pairs of homonyms to use in sentences and to illustrate.
6. Ask individual students to read their sentences to the class. Have class members decide on the correct spelling to fit the sentence meaning.
7. Put illustrated homonyms and sentences on bulletin board.

EXTENSION 1   Encourage students to add homonym pairs to the charts and sentences and illustrations to the bulletin board.

EXTENSION 2   Have students check the library for books that use homonyms. (See Resources.)

EXTENSION 3   Play Homophone Concentration. Put homophones on separate cards (see suggested sets). The sets increase in difficulty. Two or more students can play at one time.

RESOURCES

How a Horse Grew Hoarse on the Site Where He Sighted a Bare Bear
Emily Hanlon
Delacorte Press, 1976
   The tale of an odd assortment of characters and their sail on the high seas, all based on the use of homonyms.

Your Art is a Which: Fun With Homophones
Bernice Kohn Hunt
Harcourt Brace Jovanovich, 1976
   Presents homophones in rhyme.

Homonyms: Hair and Hare and Other Words That Sound the Same but Look As Different As Bear and Bare.
Joan Hanson
Lerner Publications Co., 1972

A delightfully illustrated book on "hair and hare and other words that sound the same but look as different as bear and bare." Students could make a similar collection of illustrated homonyms.

Would You Put Your Money in a Sandbank?
(Fun with Words)
Harold Longman
Rand McNally, 1968

Another good book which builds on common homonyms, rhymes, and riddles.

Show and Tell
Helen Jill Fletcher
Platt & Munk

A mixed collection of puns on homonyms and clichés. Each pun is delightfully illustrated.

Homonym Cards
Developmental Learning Materials

Forty cards show words that are spelled alike but have different meanings, such as checker/checker, chest/chest, etc.

Homophone Cards
Developmental Learning Materials

Forty picture–word cards show cards that sound alike, but have different spellings and meanings, such as pear/pair, flour/flower, and toe/tow.

The Hoarse Horse

OBJECTIVE   To identify the correct spelling of homophones when used in context.

MATERIALS   A list of sentences that use homophones, index cards.

PROCEDURE
1. List specific homophone pairs and sample sentences using those homophones on the board. Ask students to copy one word on each index card in letters about one inch high.
2. Read a sentence containing a homophone to the students. Ask students to listen for the homophone, then choose the correct spelling, and hold the correct index card up in the air.
3. Check all cards to see whether all students chose the correct spelling. If there are discrepancies, *write* the sentence on the chalkboard. Underline the homophone and have a few students spell it out loud.
4. If all students are in agreement, go on to another sentence.
5. *Caution:* Limit this activity to five or six pairs of homophones at a time. Keep sample sentences on the board for homophones that are consistently confused. Overemphasize the homophones that are more commonly used until students make no errors.

EXTENSION   Have students write pairs of sentences using homophones. Duplicate some of these sentence pairs leaving a blank for the homophone. Ask students to read and fill in the correct homophone for the sentence context. Have the original sentence writer be the checker.

Set One

ate – eight	be – bee	beat – beet
bear – bare	blew – blue	dear – deer
flower – flour	hair – hare	here – hear
hour – our	knew – new	know – no
made – maid	meat – meet	one – won
pail – pale	pair – pear	peel – peal
right – write	road – rode	rows – rose
sea – see	sew – so – sow	son – sun

some – sum   tail – tale   too – to – two
tow – toe   we – wee   week – weak

Set Two

brake – break	buy – by – bye	clothes – close
days – daze	die – dye	doe – dough
dying – dyeing	eye – I – aye	flee – flea
for – four	forth – fourth	hall – haul
heard – herd	higher – hire	its – it's
hole – whole	in – inn	or – ore – oar
knows – nose	mail – male	red – read
pane – pain	peak – peek	sent – cent – scent
reed – read	rain – rein – reign	wood – would
whale – wail	which – witch	who's – whose

Set Three

ant – aunt	arc – ark	bale – bail
band – banned	boy – bouy	chews – choose
earn – urn	feet – feat	find – fined
fir – fur	great – grate	groan – grown
guest – guessed	him – hymn	hoarse – horse
knot – not	main – mane	nay – neigh
neckless – necklace	need – knead	night – knight
prints – prince	real – reel	seam – seem
seen – scene	stake – steak	sale – sail
sore – soar	tied – tide	tier – tear
their – they're – there	through – threw	thrown – throne

Set Four

aid – aide	aloud – allowed	base – bass
berth – birth	board – bored	brows – browse
build – billed	capital – capitol	coarse – course
cord – chord	cymbal – symbol	dew – due
ewe – you	foul – fowl	frees – freeze – frieze
gate – gait	hail – hale	heal – heel – he'll
hoes – hose	jam – jamb	laps – lapse
leak – leek	lesson – lessen	lie – lye
lo – low	mints – mince	mist – missed
morn – mourn	morning – mourning	nun – none
pass – past – passed	paws – pause	peer – pier
please – pleas	plain – plane	pedal – peddle
rap – wrap	rapped – wrapped – rapt	rays – raise – raze
ring – wring	rote – wrote	sheer – shear
side – sighed	stare – stair	steal – steel
Sunday – sundae	tax – tacks	tacked – tact
teas – tease	time – thyme	wade – weighed
wait – weight	way – weigh	waste – waist

Set Five

adds – ads	aisle – I'll – isle	alter – altar
baron – barren	bard – barred	beer – bier
boar – bore	boarder – border	bolder – boulder

brewed – brood	cannon – canon	cause – caws
ceiling – sealing	cell – sell	cellar – seller
chute – shoot	clause – claws	colonel – kernel
creak – creek	fort – forte	gambol – gamble
gild – guild	gilt – guilt	idle – idol – idyl
knave – nave	lacks – lax	liar – lyre
links – lynx	maize – maze	mantel – mantle
mode – mowed	ode – owed	packed – pact
pore – pour	presence – presents	pries – prize
quartz – quarts	rack – wrack	roomer – rumor
rung – wrung	rye – wry	scull – skull
serf – surf	sighs – size	slay – sleigh
soared – sword	sold – soled	sole – soul
seize – sees	peace – piece	praise – prays – preys
principal – principle	profit – prophet	root – route

Set Six

ascent – assent	born – borne	borough – burrow
bough – bow	bouillon – bullion	bridal – bridle
canvas – canvass	carat – carrot – caret	cereal – serial
choir – quire	choral – coral	complement – compliment
correspondence – correspondents	council – counsel	currant – current
phrase – frays	dependence – dependents	fisher – fissure
heroin – heroine	hoard – horde	guise – guys
marshal – martial	medal – meddle	manner – manor
might – mite	miner – minor	mews – muse
mustard – mustered	naval – navel	missile – missal
penance – pennants	populace – populous	patients – patience
stationary – stationery	straight – strait	precedence – precedents
troop – troupe	taught – taut	tracked – tract
vice – vise	vial – vile	vale – vail
waiver – waver	ward – warred	waive – wave
wore – war	you'll – yule	weather – whether

HANDWRITING Cursive writing is most commonly taught using one of several commercially available writing programs. While there is general agreement on a number of areas in these programs (e.g., the need for legibility, the need for purposeful practice, etc.), there are surprising differences in letter formation, letter sequencing, and teaching practices among the programs (Otto, McMenemy, and Smith, 1973). The biggest drawback to the use of commercial programs is that letters are introduced very quickly and without sufficient practice allowed for mastery before new letters are introduced. Some students may be able to handle this, but others, especially those with fine motor problems, need much more practice before mastery is obtained. Ideally, the teacher should provide additional practice both before and after the exercises are completed in the workbook.

By third or fourth grade, most students begin to make the transition from manuscript to cursive writing. The average student makes the transition with little difficulty when practice and teacher supervision are part of the program. Other students, who have immature fine motor co-ordination, may need program adjustments. Suggested adjustments follow.

1. *Use evaluation procedures outlined in Chapter 1.* If students have been using cursive writing, check different writing samples to identify specific problems

in letter formation, size, or slant. Ask the student to identify the letters that are most difficult to write.

2. *Introduce cursive writing at a slower pace.* This might mean allowing the student to use manuscript writing for a longer period of time. For extreme cases, it might mean allowing the use of a typewriter as an alternative to handwriting.

3. *Give frequent, short, guided cursive writing practice sessions.* It is essential that the teacher provide specific handwriting lessons in which emphasis is placed on correct letter formation and correct spacing. This is particularly important during the transitional stages of changing from manuscript writing to cursive writing, Without careful instruction and supervision, students may learn to form letters incorrectly, and through repeated practice of the incorrect formation, establish a pattern that is difficult to break. A minimum of ten minutes a day should be spent in guided handwriting practice.

4. *Teach letters with common formations.* The letters with the simplest formations should be taught first. (See Table 5-5.) In addition, all of the vowels, except "y," should be taught quickly since these letters form the basic shape of the more difficult letters. Once the basic forms are taught, the more difficult letters with their "families" can be taught. As these patterns become automatic, speed will increase. Verbalize the movements as they are made. Ask a student who has mastered the letter formation in question to demonstrate and verbalize the sequence of movements to the rest of the group or class.

5. *Practice letters in isolation until they are mastered.* When the letter has been mastered, it can be integrated and used with previously learned letters through writing short words, phrases, sentences, and paragraphs.

6. *Allow the student to write in a comfortable style during creative and other writing sessions.* This will prevent overloading (requiring the use of too many new skills at one time). This might mean a return to the manuscript style for the first draft of a story or report. As students become more comfortable with cursive writing, they will be able to use it more effectively and effortlessly.

7. *Encourage students to evaluate their own letter formations.* Have students make quality comparisons of their work. Provide copies of the Handwriting Checklist and evaluation scales from commercial programs so that students may compare their own writing. When all letter formations are known, have student copy one of the following sentences in order to make a weekly or biweekly comparison.

   1. The quick brown fox jumps over the lazy brown dog.
   2. Pack my box with five dozen jugs of liquid.
   3. The five boxing wizards jump quickly.

   At the bottom of the paper put these sentences:

   I have trouble with the following letters: _____
   I write these letters the best: _____

8. *Emphasize the importance of posture, paper placement, and pencil grasp.* These factors can affect the consistency, slant, and legibility of writing. Generally, for right-handed cursive writers, the paper should be slanted slightly toward the left so that the lower *left* corner points toward the belt buckle. For left-handers, the paper should be slanted to the right so that the lower *right* corner points to the belt buckle. This arrangement of paper allows left-handers to keep their hand below the line of writing instead of above and hooked around as is frequently seen. If this hooked position has developed, it is inadvisable to attempt to change it (Wiederholt, Hammill, and Brown, 1978).

   Be sure that the student has the appropriate size chair and desk while completing writing tasks.

9. *Establish realistic expectations.* Recognize that cursive writing instruction is time-consuming, but that eventually the results will show that the effort

Table 5-5 Sequence of Instruction – Cursive Writing

Lower case cursive letters fall in either of two groups based on the sequence of movements required for their formation. The letters in the basic group require less complicated movements than the letters in the families group. Letters in the families group are based on formations learned in the basic group.

Cursive lower case-basic groups

1. *i u t w*
2. *l e*
3. *n m*
4. *c o a*

Cursive lower case-families

5. *i*   family   *j p s r*
6. *l*   family   *b f h k*
7. *c*   family   *d g q*
8. *ɔ*   family   *v x y z*

Cursive upper case

9. *ɔ*   family   *M N W U V X Y Z*
                  H K   P R B
10. *c*   family   *C O A E D*
11. *l*   family   *S G L*
12. *l*   family   *I J*
13. *J*   family   *T F*

was justified. Slow the pace and provide additional monitored practice for those students who are having difficulty. Do not expect students to make the transition from manuscript to cursive writing quickly. Requiring the use of cursive writing before all letters are known may result in the formation of poor writing habits.

10. *Provide practice at the chalkboard.* It is easier to monitor four or five students who are working at the chalkboard than it is to monitor them while they write at their desks. Using black magic markers, draw parallel lines about two inches apart on one chalkboard. These lines last quite a long time and are helpful to students as they practice their letter formations.

Sample words for cursive writing practice

Cursive lower case-basic groups

1. i t u w   "swing up, then trace back down"

words using i, u, t, and w

it	wit	ti
		tut
		tutti
		tutu

2. l e   "swing up, then loop back down"
words using l and e and previous letters

l	*e*	*i*	*t*	*w*
let	eel	ill	tee	we
lie	ell	it'll	tell	well
lit	elite		tie	welt
little			tile	wet
lull			till	will
lute			tilt	wilt
			title	wit

phrases emphasizing i, u, t, w, l and e

let it wilt   we will tile it
it will tell   we will title it
will it tilt?   little wet eel
it will tilt   little ill eel
tie it well   little lie
it will wilt   we will wet it
we will tell   we will let it wilt
we will tie it   well, will it wilt?
title it   it'll wilt

3. n m   "forward and over the hill(s)"
words with n and m as first letter

n	*m*		
net	me	millet	mull
nettle	meet	mine	mullet
new	melt	mini	mute
newt	men	mint	mutt
nil	menu	minuet	
nit	met	minute	
nitwit	mettle	mite	
null	mew	mitt	
nut	mile	mitten	
	mill	mule	

words with n and m in random positions

n		*m*
in	tent	elm
inn	tin	emit
lent	tint	lime
lentil	tune	mime
line	until	time
lint	went	mum
nine	win	

nineteen   wine

nun

ten

phrases emphasizing n and m

nine men will tell	we went in
time will tell	nine ill men
it will melt	ten well men
we met in line	we will win
until we meet	let me win
we met ten little tin men	let me wet it
let me meet ten tin men	let me melt it
we met nineteen men	let me win it
until we win	in a minute
will nineteen men tell?	we went in tent

4. c o a   "swing up, go back down and around"
words with c, o, or a as first letter

c	o	a
cell	oil	ace
cent	omelet	aim
cite	omit	all
clue	on	alone
cull	once	allowance
cue	one	am
cut	out	an
cute	outline	animal
	owl	ate
	own	

words with c, o, and a in random positions

c	o	a
accent	locomotion	catamaran
account	lotto	mallet
calculate	moon	mammal
cancel	motion	mama
catcall	motto	manual
coconut	mountain	nation
cocoon	onion	tattoo
collect	ocelot	tattle
comic	total	wallet
mecca	women	wallow

sentences emphasizing c, o, and a

1. Ten clean comical clowns eat coconut at a cinema.
2. An ocelot ate an onion omelet at noontime.
3. At noontime, nine mice ate a coconut.
4. A comical clown will call a collie to eat.
5. Ten women want to come out on a little tan catamaran.
6. A nice niece will not tell a tattletale.

7. A nice tattoo on a clown will be cute.
8. A cow on a moon at noontime will eat a cocoon.
9. Ten women want to nominate one woman in an election.
10. A location on a tall mountain will be nice.

Cursive lower case–families

5. i family   i u t w   j p s r
   words with j, p, s, and r as first letter

j	*p*	*s*	*r*
jail	palace	sails	raccoon
jean	panic	scales	ration
jell	papoose	scouts	rattle
jest	peace	sense	react
jet	pest	sentences	reclaim
jewel	piece	smells	relation
join	place	smiles	remote
joint	plate	snails	roasts
jolt	plea	snowmen	roosts
jowl	plant	solution	route

words with j, p, s, and r in random positions

j	*p*	*s*	*r*
ajar	apple	scissors	error
eject	appear	sisters	erase
enjoy	apply	missiles	scrape
adjust	ripple	session	scream
adjective	supper	seasons	screen
rejoin	suppose	suspense	warrior
rejoice	support	stainless	terrace
juju	snapper	somersault	terrier
jujitsu	supermarket	possess	terror
pajamas	reappear	distress	mirror

sentences emphasizing j, p, s, and r

1. Put peas on a nice new plate please.
2. A snowman loses a smile as a sun appears.
3. A terrier smells a raccoon near a tree.
4. We want to somersault at a palace supper.
5. Use scissors to cut out a paper snowman.
6. A scout roasts a nice raccoon to eat at suppertime.
7. An error on a paper is not nice at all.
8. A roast for supper is at a supermarket.
9. A jetsetter is on a jet to a mountains.
10. One sister is in a missile on a trip to a moon.

6. l family: b f h k
   words with b, f, h, and k as first letter

b	*f*	*h*	*k*
batter	fable	habit	kitten
balance	false	hammer	kennel

better	famous	hamster	kerchief
blister	feature	harbor	kettle
bluff	flask	harmonica	kimono
bullet	fleet	horse	kitchen
bumper	forest	hollow	knee
burrow	fourth	hospital	knife
burst	fashion	human	knot
brilliant	follow	humble	know

words with b, f, h, and k in random positions

b	*f*	*h*	*k*
babble	cuff	champ	nickel
barber	cliff	phantom	polka
barbell	coffee	phone	knock
blubber	baffle	shallow	knuckles
barbells	fluff	shelter	khaki
bomb	raffle	shoe	knapsack
rabbit	ruffle	shuffle	knack
remember	staff	while	knickknack
robber	stiff	whiskers	knickers
terrible	waffle	witch	rocket

sentences emphasizing b, f, h, and k

1. The barber babbles while he swallows waffles.
2. The robber has a khaki knapsack full of knickers.
3. A champ horse swallows a shoe while in the shelter.
4. A wise human whistles while he shaves whiskers in the shower.
5. The batter must balance the bat and hit the ball better.
6. A hamster with a harmonica follows a human into a hospital.
7. That famous phantom phones for a fellow freak to join him.
8. A fashion show will feature a famous fearful foursome.
9. A rocket will blast off for the trip to another planet.
10. A white rabbit will remember to look for a new hutch.

7. c family: d g q
words with d, g, and q as first letter

d	*g*	*q*
dabble	gallon	quack
daffodil	gallop	quail
dancer	gamble	quake
dawn	garden	quarrel
dentist	glimmer	quarter
different	gobble	queen
difficult	goblet	question
dinosaur	grade	quick
dribble	graduation	quiet
dipper	grammar	quill

words with d, g, and q in random positions

d	*g*	*q*
adder	dagger	acquaint

fiddled	gaggle	acquire
griddled	garage	conquer
haddock	giggled	conquest
handicap	goggle	consequence
handled	gorgeous	equal
huddled	grudge	frequent
riddle	jiggled	jonquil
saddled	juggled	kumquat
salamander	suggest	sequel

sentences emphasizing d, g, and q

1. A gaggle of gorgeous geese gobbled grits and grain.
2. A dangerous gambler drew good cards with quick and quiet skill.
3. A juggler jiggled and juggled a group of bats and balls.
4. The queen quarrels with her subjects about equal rights.
5. The dentist's daughter has a difficult riddle.
6. The consequence of the conqueror's conquest is a quarrel.
7. A saddled salamander huddled against a difficult dinosaur.
8. The giant judge giggled when he saw the dangerous robber gagged.
9. A gallant knight galloped to the queen's castle on a dinosaur.
10. At graduation, we had a quarrel about a juggling contest.

8. 7 family: v x y z
words with v, x, y, or z as the first letter

v	x	y	z
vacation	xebec	yacht	zany
valentine	xenon	yardstick	zebra
vampire	xeric	yawn	zero
vegetable	xylem	yellow	zigzag
velvet	xylophone	yesterday	zillion
victory		yodel	zinc
violence		yogurt	zinnia
vision		yonder	zodiac
vocabulary		young	zoo
volunteer		youngster	zoom

words with v, x, y, or z in random positions

v	x	y	z
believe	ax	biology	blaze
cover	axle	berry	dazzle
develop	complex	dillydally	enzyme
evolution	exact	family	fizzle
government	exchange	gabby	freeze
gravity	exciting	geography	graze
gravy	exhaust	happy	jazz
heaven	exit	kayak	lazy
native	explode	pygmy	puzzle
valve	oxen	pyramid	quartz

sentences emphasizing v, x, y, and z

1. At valentine vacation, a velvet vampire volunteered to yodel.

2. Many good, green vegetables grow in the garden in spring.
3. Yonder by the river grows a happy, gabby pygmy family.
4. A zillion lazy zebras zigzag through the jungles.
5. Yesterday a dazzling blaze developed near the zoo.
6. Youngsters enjoy freezing as they build jazzy snowmen.
7. My family likes to dillydally around kayaks or yachts.
8. My geography homework is to find some zinc and quartz.
9. A xylophone player is happy when he can play some jazz.
10. The zoo exit is next to the zebra's jazzy new cage.

Cursive Upper Case

Use names of students in the classroom or countries of the world for practice on cursive upper case letters. Cursive upper case letters can be taught individually to students as they learn to write their own names. Gradually, as the lower case letters are mastered, upper case letters can be introduced in their family groups based on similarities in formation.

Appendix A
Resources for Classroom Use

Anthologies and bibliographies of children's literature, series titles available from libraries, and series titles available from educational publishers.

Anthologies and Bibliographies of Children's Literature

Anthology of Children's Literature, Fourth Edition, 1970
E. Johnson, E. Sickels, and F. Sayers
Houghton Mifflin

This anthology presents a sampling of the best of children's literature: nursery rhymes, nonsense rhymes, picture books, fables, folk tales, myths and legends, sacred writings, fantasy, fiction, and poetry. The book is a valuable resource for teachers.

The Bookfinder: A Guide to Children's Literature About the Needs and Problems of Youth Aged 2-15, 1977
Sharon Spredemann Dreyer
American Guidance Service

This guide describes and categorizes 1,031 current children's books according to more than 450 descriptors relevant to the physical and emotional growth of youth aged 2-15. The guide provides bibliographic information (author, publisher), a synopsis, and interest level for each book. This book is valuable in helping to find just the right book for a student who is experiencing some unhappiness or difficulty

Easy Reading
Michael F. Groves, Judith A. Boettcher, and Randall A. Ryder
International Reading Association

An annotated listing of book series and periodicals for less able readers.

"B" is for Betsy, 1939
Betsy and the Boys, 1945
Back to School with Betsy, 1943; and others
Carolyn Haywood
Harcourt, Brace, Jovanovich

The experiences of Betsy and her friends at home and school are presented in this series. Reading Level: 2–3. The Little Eddie *series is also appropriate for this reading level. Interest Level: 2–5.*

Amelia Bedelia, 1963
Amelia Bedelia and the Surprise Shower, 1966
Play Ball Amelia Bedelia, 1978
Come Back Amelia Bedelia, 1970
Peggy Parish
Harper & Row

Unfortunately, Amelia is quite literal-minded and this problem gets her into lots of trouble. Reading Level: 2–3. Interest Level: 2–5.

Little House in the Big Woods, 1953
Little House on the Prairie, 1975
and seven others
Laura Ingalls Wilder
Harper & Row

These books describe Laura's own life and family as they travel by covered wagon and settle in the midwest. Many details of pioneer life, as well as an abundance of descriptive detail are included. Reading Level: 3–4. Interest Level: 3–6.

Encyclopedia Brown: Boy Detective, 1978
Encyclopedia Brown Solves Them All, 1977
Encyclopedia Brown Finds the Clues, 1966;
and others
Donald J. Sobol
Thomas Nelson Company

Leroy Brown, a ten year old boy more commonly known as "Encyclopedia," frequently helped his father, the Chief of Police, solve the more difficult cases. The series is suitable for both boys and girls since a young girl detective frequently assists Encyclopedia. Reading Level: 3–4. Interest Level: 3–6.

Danny Dunn and the Anti-Gravity Paint, 1964
Danny Dunn and the Homework Machine, 1965
Danny Dunn and the Weather Machine, 1959
Danny Dunn and the Automatic House, 1979
Jay Williams and Raymond Abrashkin
McGraw Hill Book Company

Danny Dunn has a knack for getting into trouble. First he daydreams about space in school instead of doing his math; then he has to write the sentence, "Space flight is a hundred years away," three hundred times as punishment. Next he helps Professor Bullfinch discover anti-gravity paint which eventually allows them to take off into space in a rocket. Reading Level: 3–4. Interest Level: 3–7.

The Moffets
The Middle Moffets
Rufus M
Eleonor Estes
Harcourt, Brace Jovanovich, 1968

This series tell of the fun the Moffet family had in their home on New Dollar Street. Reading Level: 4. Interest Level: 4-6.

Homer Price, 1943
Centerburg Tales, 1951
Robert McCloskey
Viking Press

A series of stories about an all-American boy who manages to have many hilarious adventures. Reading Level: 4-5. Interest Level: 4-6.

Henry Huggins, 1979
Henry and Ribsy, 1954;
and other Henry books
Ramona the Pest, 1968
Ramona the Brave, 1975
Beverly Cleary
Morrow

Henry and his dog Ribsy find all kinds of adventure in their own neighborhood. Ramona manages to have a lot of humorous problems as she grows up. Reading level for both series: 4-5. Interest Level: 4-7.

The Great Brain, 1967
The Great Brain Does it Again, 1975
The Great Brain Reforms, 1973;
and others
John D. Fitzgerald
Dial Press

Tom Fitzgerald, self-proclaimed "Great Brain" outwits many people with his devilishly clever financial schemes, and most often he comes out of each adventure with money in his pocket. John Fitzgerald tells of his admiration and annoyance with his brother's antics. Reading Level: 4-5. Interest Level: 4-7.

King of the Wind, 1948
Brighty of the Grand Canyon, 1953
Misty of Chincoteague, 1947
Marguerite Henry
Rand McNally

King of the Wind *tells the story of a famous thoroughbred horse and a mute stable-boy's devotion to the horse.* Brighty *is a burro who helps to catch a murderer and* Misty *is a horse who lives on one of the islands off the coast of Virginia. Reading Level: 5. Interest Level: 3-9.*

Series Titles Available From Educational Publishers

The following titles are available from Fearon–Pitman Publishers, Inc., Belmont, California.

Laura Brewster Books
Lisa Eisenberg

Laura Brewster investigates insurance frauds in six different books. Reading Level: 3.0. Interest Level: 6-12.

Pacemaker Bestsellers I, II, III

Mystery, adventure, espionage, terror, war, and other topics are found in the thirty separate titles of the Bestseller Series. Reading Level: 3.0. Interest Level: 6-12.

Space Police Series
Galaxy 5 Series
Leo P. Kelley

The twelve titles in these two series explore space fantasy. Reading Level: 3.0. Interest Level: 6–12.

Spector
Anita Jackson

Easy to read thrillers filled with mystery and suspense. Reading Level: 3.0. Interest Level: 6–12.

Jim Hunter Books
Ben Butterworth and Bill Stockdale

British secret agent Jim Hunter travels around the world and uses all kinds of exotic gadgets in an effort to thwart the evil schemes of Bratt, his arch villain. Reading levels range from 1.0 to 3.0 in this series of twelve books. Interest Level: 6–12.

Pacemaker Classics

*The eight titles in this series (*Robinson Crusoe, Treasure Island, 20,000 Leagues Under the Sea, *and others) have been abridged and adapted to reading levels ranging from 2.1 to 2.8.*

Pacemaker Vocational Readers
Lynne Glasner and Marilyn Thypin

This series of ten titles features young adults in job-hunting and job-keeping situations. Photographs and an easy text make these books useful for students with reading problems. Reading Level: 1.2. Interest Level: 7–12.

Pacemaker True Adventures
Edward G. Jerrome

Well known historical characters and their adventures are featured in this eleven-book series. Reading levels range from 2.0 to 2.5.

The following series are available from Addison-Wesley Publishing Co., Inc.

Deep Sea Adventure Series
F. Berres, W. Brisco, V. Coleman, and F. Hewett

The twelve books in this series persent such topics as Treasure Under the Sea, Frogmen in Action, Danger Below, Enemy Agents, *and others. Reading Level Range: 1.8 to 5.0. Interest Level: 3–8.*

Morgan Bay Mysteries
V. Rambeau and N. Rambeau

A mysterious castle in Morgan Bay sets the scene for the beginning of this series Musical ghosts, gold, midnight visitors, and marble statues are featured in the series. Reading Level Range: 2.3 to 4.1. Interest Level: 5–12.

Checkered Flag Series
H. Bamman and R. Whitehead

This series of eight books features hot rods, race cars, dune buggies, antique cars, and motorcycles. Reading Level: 2.4 to 4.5. Interest Level: 5–12.

Wildlife Adventure Series
W. Briscoe and R. Leonard

Gatie the Alligator, Skipper the Dolphin, Tawny the Mountain Lion, and Arctos the

Grizzly *are among the titles in this series. Reading Level: 2.6 to 4.4. Interest Level: 3-7.*

The following titles are available from Garrard Publishing Company, Champaign, Illinois.

Target Books
Edited with commentary by Bennett Wayne

Biographies of interesting historical figures, sports stars, and others in America's past. The type size and spacing in these books is designed specifically for the older student with poor reading skills. Sample titles: Adventurers in Buckskin, Big League Pitchers and Catchers, Four Women of Courage, Indian Patriots of the Great West. *Reading Level: 3-4. Interest Level: 6-12.*

Sports Library Series

Thirty different titles on popular sports and famous athletes. Reading Level: 4. Interest Level: 6-12.

Americans All Series

Thirty biographies of famous Americans emphasize the unique contributions of individuals of all races, creeds, and national origins to the American way of life. Reading Level: 4. Interest Level: 6-12.

How They Lived

Documentaries of Early American life based on journals, diaries and other firsthand source materials. Sample titles: Mississippi Steamboat Days, Stagecoach Days and Stagecoach Kings, When the Rails Ran West. *Reading Level: 4. Interest Level 6-12.*

American Democracy

These nine books feature such government processes and symbols as Electing Our Presidents, The Statue of Liberty Comes to America, The FBI, *and others. Reading Level: 4. Interest Level: 6-12.*

Wonder of Wonders: Man
By Anne Terry White and Gerald S. Lietz

The human body is featured in this series. Sample titles: Man the Thinker, Secrets of the Heart and Blood, When Hunger Calls. *Reading Level: 4. Interest Level: 6-12.*

Collections of Student Writing and Thinking

Somebody Real: Voices of Real Children, 1973
Nicholas Anthony Duva, editor
American Faculty Press

Somebody Real *is an anthology of writings by twenty-four minority students in a sixth grade class in Jersey City. The students write about their life in the city and their awareness of violence, drugs, school, neighborhoods, and their expressions of love, death, life, loneliness, and other abstract ideas. Pictures of the writers are included. Reading Level: 5-6. Interest Level: 5-12.*

The Voice of Children, 1974
June Jordan and Terri Bush, editors
Holt, Rinehart and Winston

A collection of poetry and short prose pieces written by black and Puerto Rican children from Brooklyn about school, families, life in the city, and of their feelings about themselves. Reading Level: 5-6. Interest Level: 5-12.

Listen to Us: The Children's Express Report, 1978
Dorriet Kavanaugh, editor
Workman Publishing Company

More than 2,000 children present candid views on such topics as family relationships, family problems, school, friends, children with special problems (handicaps), children in trouble, sex, T.V., money, religion, feelings, adult treatment of kids, and others. The book was compiled by teenage editorial assistants who interviewed children all over the country.

"The underlying philosophy of Children's Express can be summed up in four words: 'Children Can Do It.'"

The Me Nobody Knows: Children's Voices From the Ghetto, 1969
Avon Books

Ghetto children write on such topics as "How I See Myself," "How I See My Neighborhood," "The World Outside." Some are poems, some are paragraphs, some are diary entries.

Writing Kits

Write to Communicate
Reader's Digest Services, Inc.

The Write to Communicate *program is available in four different kits appropriate for grades four through eight. Each kit includes ten units that develop specific skills in a writer's workshop format. The program takes students through three phases of writing: prewriting, writing, and rewriting. Each kit contains workbooks, activity cards, a printing press (a folder that contains non-smudging Mylar carbon), and cards with samples stories, poems, and reports.*

Interaction, Level 2
Interaction, Level 3
James Moffett, Senior Author
Houghton Mifflin

The Interaction *kits provide activities for writing, acting, listening, and discussing. The kit includes films, booklets, games, activity cards, cassettes, and a teacher's guide. These activities are designed to be used by small groups or individuals with a minimum of teacher instruction.*

SRA Composition
Science Research Associates

Designed for students in grades four to six, this kit presents forty-eight cassette centered lessons on basic writing skills. Includes such topics as writing topic sentences, writing reports, and building paragraphs.

Open Box: Ideas for Creative Expression
Encyclopedia Britannica Educational Corporation

This kit, which contains "shortstrips," cassettes, and picture cards, emphasizes the importance of talking and discussing before writing. Each shortstrip provides a stimulating writing activity designed for intermediate grade children.

Appendix B
Resources for Teacher Use

If You're Trying To Teach Kids How To Write, You've Gotta Have This Book!
Margery Frank
Incentive Publications

Margery Frank organizes her book around questions and comments about teaching writing frequently voiced by teachers. Some of the questions are, "Where Do I Begin?" "But Teaching Writing Is Such Hard Work," "My Kids Say They Can't Think of Anything to Write," "Help!" and others. Ms. Frank helps teachers to analyze their bias toward teaching writing, then proceeds to provide an abundance of creative writing ideas for use with students in the middle grades. A list of resource materials is also included in the book.

Reading, Writing and Rating Stories, 1976
Carol Sager
Curriculum Associates

Reading, Writing and Rating Stories is a writing program designed to improve the quality of writing in the middle grades. The program trains students to evaluate their own writing using a descriptive scale covering four areas: vocabulary, elaboration (the addition of ideas and details that enliven people, places, and events), organization, and structure (includes punctuation, sentence structure and variety). Students are asked to read short selections then to answer guide questions related to the four evaluation areas. The program employs a self-directing self-correcting approach although demonstration lessons by the teacher are encouraged.

Teaching Writing, K through 8, 1978
Jack Hailey
Instructional Lab, University of California

Teaching Writing is comprised of three major sections.
    Part One, "Looking at Student Writing," features a discussion of holistic assessment as one way to evaluate children's writing. Both rationale and procedures for this

writing assessment strategy that is currently receiving wide attention are presented.

Part Two, "Teaching Writing," includes one chapter on philosophy about composition teaching, and one chapter that presents nine paradigms for teaching writing. The first paradigm emphasizes the prewriting, writing, postwriting, and rewriting stages of the writing process. Other paradigms feature using different literary structures (such as rhymes, folktales, headlines, biographies); using themes; writing imitations of sentences or paragraphs taken from children's literature; combining sentences; writing generalizations after recording a collection of experiences.

Part Three, "Reviewing the Masters," reviews the philosophy and techniques for writing developed by James Moffett, James Britton, Francis Christensen, Josephine Miles, Walter Gibson, and Kenneth Macrorie.

The Language Arts Idea Book: Classroom Activities for Children, 1976
Joanne Schaff
Goodyear Publishing Co.

The Language Arts Idea Book *provides a collection of over three hundred activities that focus on listening, speaking, reading, and writing skills. Each activity has an indicated grade range (generally primary and/or elementary grades) for most appropriate use; however, most activities can be used outside the stated range. The creative writing activities (the largest section) include such activities as vocabulary development, sentence and paragraph construction, story writing, poetry writing, and book report writing.*

Slithery Snakes and Other Aids to Children's Writing, 1967
Walter T. Petty and Mary E. Bowens
Prentice-Hall

"Creativity occurs whenever isolated experiences and ideas are put into new combinations or patterns." The activities and suggestions in this book provide stimulation for creative writing in the primary and elementary grades and emphasize the importance of oral language experiences as a prerequisite to writing, along with appropriate teacher feedback.

Sparkling Words: Three Hundred and Fifteen Practical and Creative Writing Ideas, Revised Edition, 1979
Ruth Kearney Carlson
Paladin House

Creative writing is presented through an integrated language arts approach using a variety of prewriting activities that focus on multisensory experiences, literary examples (folktales, science fiction, and poetry), and vocabulary development. An appendix includes the "Carlson Analytic Scale for Measuring Originality of Children's Stories" with procedures and explanations of the levels of originality used in the scale. The bulk of the activities in this book are relevant for primary and elementary grades. Numerous samples of student writing are included.

Pumpkins, Pinwheels and Peppermint Packages, 1974
Imagene Forte, Mary Ann Pangle, and Robbie Tupa
Incentive Publications

This book features 28 learning centers and 350 activities in the areas of Language Arts, Art and Music, Social Studies and Science, and Math. The centers and activities are divided into themes arranged by months in the year and may be used for both group and individual learning in the primary or elementary grades.

Let Them Write Creatively, 1973
Grace K. Pratt-Butler
Charles E. Merrill

Creativity is not limited to writing alone. Creativity begins much earlier as children begin to listen, speak, move, play, sing, and use art materials. All of these experiences, along with teacher guidance and support, build the foundation for creative writing. This book provides ideas for prewriting activities for young children, which gradually leads into writing. The author uses a narrative style to present her philosophy and suggestions on teaching writing.

Writing Exercises from Exercise Exchange, 1976
Littleton Long, editor
National Council of Teachers of English

The writing exercises in this volume focus on both expository and creative writing and place emphasis on the need for prewriting and rewriting as part of the writing process. Chapters cover prewriting, diction (vocabulary use), paragraph structure, style, description, research, short story writing, and rewriting. The activities are most suited for junior high and high school students.

Write Now! Insights Into Creative Writing, 1973
Anne Wescott Dodd
Learning Trends, Inc.

This book leads students through a number of activities designed to develop creative abilities in writing. Activities focus on using concrete details to express abstract ideas, using the five senses as an aid to adding descriptive detail, and writing short stories, plays, poetry, and journals. While the book is designed for junior high grade range, it can also be used as a source of writing ideas by teachers in the elementary grades.

The Great Perpetual Learning Machine, 1976
Jim Blake and Barbara Ernst
Little, Brown

"A stupendous collection of ideas, games, experiments, activities, and recommendations for further explorations—with tons of illustrations." Although many academic areas are covered (Nature and Ecology, Science, Math, Arts and Crafts, Music and Movement, Ourselves, and Language) many of the activities encourage writing in some form: observing and recording, describing, explaining, charting, comparing, planning, and imagining.

Mud Puddles, Rainbows and Asparagus Tips, 1979
Bruce Raskin, editor
Education Today Company

"Our book title suggests the three dimensions of a comprehensive, viable, child-centered language arts program: mud puddles, *the down-to-earth, everyday uses of language;* rainbows, *the fanciful, exploratory aspects of expression;* asparagus tips, *the essentials—guidelines and rules that support confident and disciplined communication." Chapter titles are "Listening and Speaking," "Building Skills," "Writing: Everyday Applications," "Writing: Free Expression," and "Exploring Drama and Movement." Each chapter consists of a number of articles contributed to Learning Magazine.*

Language Arts Activities for the Classroom, 1978
Sidney W. Tiedt and Iris M. Tiedt
Allyn and Bacon

This book contains 1,099 suggestions for developing speaking, listening, reading, and writing skills. The authors emphasize that these skills are so strongly interrelated that they cannot be taught in isolation.

Reference Bibliography

Anastasiow, N. "The Picture Story Language Test." In Buros, O.K. (ed.) *The Seventh Mental Measurements Yearbook.* Highland Park, NJ: Gryphon Press, 1972.

Anderson, Velma R. and Thompson, Sheryl K. *Test of Written English* (TWE). Novato, CA: Academic Therapy Publications, 1979.

Arena, J. (ed.) *Building Spelling Skills in Dyslexic Children.* San Rafael, CA: Academic Therapy Publications, 1968.

Bateman, Donald and Zidonis, Frank. *The Effect of a Study of Transformational Grammar on the Writing of Ninth and Tenth Graders.* Champaign, IL: National Council of Teachers of English, 1966.

Bates, Jefferson D. *Writing With Precision.* Washington, DC: Acropolis Books, Ltd., 1978.

Beaven, M.H. "Individualized Goal Setting, Self-Evaluation, and Peer Evaluation." In Cooper, C. and Odell, L. (eds.) *Evaluating Writing: Describing, Measuring, Judging.* Urbana, IL: National Council of Teachers of English, 1977.

Bloom, B. *Handbook of Formative and Summative Evaluation.* New York: McGraw Hill, 1971.

Bloomington Public Schools. *Bloomington Writing Assessment 1977; Student Exercises, Teacher Directions, Scoring.* St. Paul, MN: Minnesota State Department of Education, 1977. (ED 155 692)

Bloomington Public Schools. *Bloomington Writing Assessment 1977: A Report to Students, Public and Teaching Staff.* St. Paul, MN: Minnesota State Department of Education, 1977.

Boder, E. "Developmental Dyslexia: Prevailing Diagnostic Concepts and A New Diagnostic Approach." In Myklebust, H. (ed.) *Progress in Learning Disabilities.* New York: Grune and Stratton, 1971.

Braddock, R., Lloyd-Jones, R., and Schoer, L. *Research in Written Composition.* Urbana, IL: National Council of Teachers of English, 1963.

Britton, J., Burgess, T., Martin, N., McLeod, A., and Rosen, H. *The Development of Writing Abilities (11–18).* London: Macmillan Education, 1975.

Bruce, B., et al. *A Cognitive Science Approach to Writing. Technical Report No. 89.* Washington, DC: National Institute of Education (DHEW), 1978. (ED 157 039)

Burgess, Carol, et al. *Understanding Children Writing.* Harmondsworth, Middlesex, England: Penguin Books, Ltd., 1973.

Buros, O.K. *The Seventh Mental Measurements Yearbook.* Highland Park, New Jersey: Gryphon Press, 1972.

Burrows, Alvina T., et al. *Children's Writing: Research in Composition and Related Skills.* Champaign, IL: National Council of Teachers of English, 1961. (ED 090 546)

Burrows, Alvina T. "Composition: Prospect and Retrospect". In Robinson, H., (ed.) *Reading and Writing Instruction in the United States: Historical Trends.* Newark, DE: International Reading Association, 1977.

Burrows, Alvina T., Jackson, D.C. and Saunders, D.O. *They All Want to Write: Written English in the Elementary School* (Rev. Ed.). Englewood Cliffs, New Jersey: Prentice-Hall, 1964.

Burrows, Alvina T. *What Research Says to the Teacher.* Washington, D.C.: National Education Association, 1966. (ED 017 482)

Carlson, R.K. *Sparkling Words: Two Hundred Practical and Creative Writing Ideas* (Rev. Ed.). Berkeley, CA: Wagner Printing Company, 1973.

Clegg, A.B. *The Excitement of Writing.* London Chatto and Windus, 1964.

Cohen, C. and Abrams, R. *Spellmaster. Spelling: Teaching and Learning, Book One.* Exeter, NH: Learnco Incorporated, 1976.

Cohen, C. and Abrams, R. *Spellmaster. Spelling: Teaching and Learning, Book Two.* Exeter, NH: Learnco Incorporated, 1976.

Committee on Writing Standards. "Standards for Basic Skills Writing Programs." Urbana, IL: National Council of Teachers of English, March, 1979.

Cooper, Charles, R. and Odell, Lee (eds.) *Evaluating Writing.* Urbana, IL: National Council of Teachers of English, 1977

Cooper, Charles R. and Odell, Lee. *Research on Composing, Points of Departure.* Urbana, IL: National Council of Teachers of English, 1978.

Diederich, Paul B. *Measuring Growth in English.* Urbana, IL: National Council of Teachers of English, 1974.

Dolch, Edward W. *A Manual for Remedial Reading.* Champaign, IL: Garrard Press, 1939.

Dubrow, H.C. *Learning to Write.* Cambridge, MA: Educators Publishing Service, 1968.

Eldridge, Cornelia C. "A Study of the Relationships Between the Oral and Written Composition of Third Grade Children." In English Curriculum Study Center, *Research in Cognate Aspects of Written Composition.* Athens, GA: University of Georgia, 1968. (ED 026 368)

English Curriculum Study Center. *A Curriculum in Written Composition, 4-6: A Guide for Teachers.* Athens, GA: University of Georgia, 1968. (ED 026 364)

English Curriculum Study Center. *Research in Cognate Aspects of Written Composition.* Athens, GA: University of Georgia, 1968. (ED 026 368)

English Curriculum Study Center. *Use of Literary Models in Teaching Written Composition, K-6.* Athens, GA: University of Georgia, 1968. (ED 026 365)

Evertts, Eldonna L. *Explorations in Children's Writing.* Urbana, IL: National Council of Teachers of English, 1970.

Ewing, June B. "A Study of the Influence of Various Stimuli on the Written Composition of Selected Third Grade Children." In English Curriculum Study Center, *Research in Cognate Aspects of Written Composition.* Athens, GA: University of Georgia, 1968. (ED 026 368)

Fader, D. *The New Hooked on Books.* Berkeley, CA: Berkeley Medallion Books, 1976.

Fadiman, C. and Howard, J. *Empty Pages: A Search for Writing Competency in School and Society.* Belmont, CA: Fearon-Pitman Publishers, Inc., 1979.

Finn, Patrick, J. "Computer Aided Description of Mature Word Choice in Writing." In C.R. Cooper and Odell, Lee (eds.). *Evaluating Writing.* Urbana, IL: National Council of Teachers of English, 1977.

Flesch, R. *The Art of Readable Writing.* New York: Macmillan, 1949.

Foley, J. "Evaluation of Learning in Writing". In Bloom, B., Hastings, T., and Madaus, G. (eds.). *Handbook on Formative and Summative Evaluation of Student Learning.* New York: McGraw Hill, 1971.

Gesell, A. and Ilg, F. *The Child From Five To Ten.* New York: Harper and Bros., 1946.

Geuder, P., Harvey, L., Wages, J., and Lloyd, D. *They Really Taught Us How To Write.* Urbana, IL: National Council of Teachers of English, 1974.

Golub, L. "Stimulating and Receiving Children's Writing: Implications for an Elementary Writing Curriculum". In Larson, R. (ed.) *Children and Writing in the Elementary School.* New York: Oxford University Press, 1975.

Golub, L. "Syntactical and Lexical Deviations in Children's Written Sentences." Unpublished paper, 1972. (ED 073 475)

Golub, L. "Written Language Development and Instruction of Elementary School Children." Paper presented to the National Conference on Research in English, 1973. (ED 073 474)

Graves, D. "Andrea Learns to Make Writing Hard." *Language Arts*, 1979, 56, (5): 569–576.

Graves, D. "A Six Year-Old's Writing Process: The First Half of First Grade". *Language Arts.* 1979, 56, (7): 829–835.

Graves, D. "What Children Show Us About Revision". *Language Arts.* 1979, 56, (3): 312–319.

Green H. and Petty, W. *Developing Language Skills in the Classroom* (5th Ed.). Boston: Allyn and Bacon, 1975.

Greene, Amsel. *Pullet Surprises.* Fullerton, CA: Sultana Press, 1969.

Grose, L.M., Metler, D., and Steinberg, E. *Suggestions for Evaluating Junior High School Writing.* Pittsburgh, PA: Association of English Teachers of Western Pennsylvania.

Hailey, J. *Teaching Writing K–8.* Berkeley, CA: Instructional Laboratory, University of California, 1978.

Hammill, D.D. and Bartel, N.R. *Teaching Children with Learning and Behavior Problems.* Boston: Allyn and Bacon, 1978.

Hammill, D.D. and Larsen, S.C. *Test of Written Language* (TOWL). Austin, TX: Pro-Ed, 1978.

Hanna, P.R. and Hanna, J.S. "Applications of Linguistics and Psychological Cues to the Spelling Course of Study." In Horn, T.D. (ed.) *Research on Handwriting and Spelling.* Champaign, IL: National Council of Teachers of English, 1966.

Harris, A.J. and Jacobson, M.D. *Basic Elementary Reading Vocabularies.* New York: MacMillan Co., 1972.

Hill, Edwin, C. and Hill, Margaret, K. *Written Language Development of Intermediate Grade Children.* Pittsburgh, PA: University of Pittsburgh, School of Education, 1966. (ED 010 059)

Hillerich, R. *A Writing Vocabulary of Elementary School Children.* Springfield, IL: Charles C Thomas, 1978.

Hillerich, R. "Developing Written Expression: How To Raise—Not Raze—Writers". *Language Arts*, 1979, 56: 769–777.

Hodges, R.E. "The Psychological Bases of Spelling". In Horn, T.D., *Research on Handwriting and Spelling.* Champaign, IL: National Council of Teachers of English, 1966.

Horn, Ernest. *A Basic Writing Vocabulary.* University of Iowa Monographs in Education, First Series, No. 4, 1926.

Horn, T.D. *Research on Handwriting and Spelling.* Champaign, IL: National Council of Teachers of English, 1966.

Horne, Rose N. "A Study of the Use of Figurative Language by Sixth Grade Children." In English Curriculum Study Center, *Research in Cognate Aspects of Written Composition.* Athens, GA: University of Georgia, 1968. (ED 026 368)

Hunt, K. *Grammatical Structures Written at Three Grade Levels.* Urbana, IL: National Council of Teachers of English, 1965.

Huntington Beach Union High School District. *The Test of Everyday Skills.* Monterey, CA: CTB/Mcgraw-Hill, 1978.

Jastak, J.F. and Jastak, S. *The Wide Range Achievement Test.* Wilmington, DE: Guidance Associates of Delaware, Inc., 1965.

Judine, Sister M. (ed.), *A Guide for Evaluating Student Composition.* Urbana, IL: National Council of Teachers of English, 1965.

Kaufman, H.S., and Biren, P.L., "Cursive Writing: An Aid to Reading and Spelling." *Academic Therapy.* 1979, 15 (2): 209–219.

Kincaid, Gerald, L. "Some Factors Affecting Variations in Quality of Students' Writing." In Braddock, R., Lloyd-Jones, R., and Schoer, L. (eds.) *Research in Written Composition.* Urbana, IL: National Council of Teachers of English, 1963.

Kinneavy, J.L. *A Theory of Discourse.* Englewood Cliffs, NJ: Prentice-Hall, 1971.

Larsen, R. and Hammill, D. *Test of Written Spelling (TWS).* San Rafael, CA: Academic Therapy Publications, 1976.

Larsen, Richard L. *Children and Writing in the Elementary School, Theories and Techniques.* New York: Oxford University Press, 1975.

Loban, W.D. *The Language of Elementary School Children.* Champaign, IL: National Council of Teachers, 1963.

Lundsteen, S. *Children Learn to Communicate: Language Arts Through Creative Problem Solving.* Englewood Cliffs, NJ: Prentice-Hall, Inc., 1976a.

Lundsteen, S. (ed.) *Help for the Teacher of Written Composition, New Directions in Research.* Urbana, IL: National Conference on Research in English, 1976b.

Macrorie, K. *Writing to Be Read* (Rev. 2nd Ed.) Rochelle Park, NJ: Hayden Book Co., 1968.

Mann, P., Suiter, P., and McClung, R. *Handbook in Diagnostic Prescriptive Teaching,* Second Edition. Boston, MA: Allyn and Bacon, 1979.

Marzano, R. and DiStefano, P. *DiComp: A Diagnostic System for Teaching Composition.* Indian Rocks Beach, FL: Relevant Productions, Inc., 1977.

Mellon, John C. *National Assessment and the Teaching of English.* Urbana, IL: National Council of Teachers of English, 1969.

Mellon, John C. *Transformational Sentence-Combining.* Urbana, IL: National Council of Teachers of English, 1969.

Moffett, J. and Wagner, B. *Student-Centered Language Arts and Reading, K–13,* Second Edition. Boston: Houghton Mifflin Company, 1976.

Moffett, James. *Teaching the Universe of Discourse.* Boston: Houghton Mifflin Company, 1968.

Murray, D. *A Writer Teaches Writing: A Practical Method of Teaching Composition.* Boston: Houghton Mifflin Company, 1968.

Myklebust, Helmer R. *Development and Disorders of Written Language, Volume One,*

Picture Story Language Test. New York: Grune and Stratton, 1965.

Myklebust, Helmer R. *Development and Disorders of Written Language, Volume Two, Studies of Normal and Exceptional Children.* New York: Grune and Stratton, 1973.

National Assessment of Educational Progress. *Explanatory and Persuasive Letter Writing: Selected Results from the Second National Assessment of Writing.* Denver, CO: Education Commission of the States, 1977.

National Assessment of Educational Progress. *Expressive Writing: Selected Results from the Second National Assessment of Writing.* Denver, CO: Education Commission of the States, 1976.

National Assessment of Educational Progress. *The Second National Assessment of Writing: New and Reassessed Exercises with Technical Information and Data.* Denver, CO: Education Commission of the States, 1978.

National Assessment of Educational Progress. *Write/Rewrite: An Assessment of Revision Skills. Selected Results from the Second National Assessment of Writing.* Denver, CO: Education Commission of the States, 1977.

National Assessment of Educational Progress. *Writing Mechanics, 1969–1974. A Capsule Description of Changing in Writing Mechanics.* Denver, CO: Education Commission of the States, 1977.

National Assessment of Educational Progress. *Writing: National Results—Writing Mechanics, Report 8.* Denver, CO: Education Commission of the States, 1972.

Neal, Edmund, R. "Writing in the Intermediate Grades." In Burrows, A. (ed.), *Children's Writing: Research in Composition and Related Skills.* Champaign, IL: National Council of Teachers of English, 1961. (ED 090 546)

Nebraska Curriculum Development Center. *A Curriculum for English.* Lincoln, NE: University of Nebraska Press, 1966. (ED 161 078)

New, J. and Leyba, R. "Miscue Analysis in Writing." Urbana, IL: National Council of Teachers of English, 1975. (ED 161 078)

Newkirk, T. "The Mass Testing of Writing: How Well Is It Being Done?" Report prepared at the University of New Hampshire, 1977. (ED 158 310)

O'Donnell, R.C., Griffin, W.J., and Norris, R.C. *Syntax of Kindergarten and Elementary School Children, Research Report 8.* Urbana, IL: National Council of Teachers of English, 1967.

O'Hare, Frank. *Sentence Combining: Improving Student Writing Without Formal Grammar Instruction.* Urbana, IL: National Council of Teachers of English, 1973.

O'Hare, Frank. *Sentence Craft: An Elective Course in Writing.* Lexington, MA: Ginn and Company, 1975.

Orton, S. *Reading and Writing and Speech Problems in Children.* New York: Norton, 1937.

Otto, W., McMenemy, R.A., and Smith, R.J. *Corrective and Remedial Teaching,* Second Edition. Boston: Houghton Mifflin Company, 1973.

Perkins, W.H. "The Picture Story Language Test." In Buros, O.K. (ed.), *The Seventh Mental Measurements Yearbook.* Highland Park, NJ: Gryphon Press, 1972.

Petty, W.T. "The Writing of Young Children". In Cooper, Charles R. and Odell, Lee (eds.). *Research on Composing, Points of Departure.* Urbana, IL: National Council of Teachers of English, 1978.

Piaget, J. *The Language and Thought of the Child.* New York: World Publishing Co., 1955.

Poteet, James A. "Characteristics of Written Expression of Learning Disabled and Non-Learning Disabled Elementary School Students". *Diagnostique.* 1979, 4, (1) Winter/Spring: 60–74. (Ed 159 830)

Pratt-Butler, G.K. *Let Them Write Creatively.* Columbus, OH: Charles E. Merrill Co., 1973.

Progoff, I. *At A Journal Workshop.* New York: Dialogue House Library, 1965.

Rinsland, H. *A Basic Vocabulary of Elementary School Children.* New York: The MacMillan Co., 1945.

Robinson, H. (ed.) *Reading and Writing Instruction in the United States: Historical Trends.* Newark, DE: International Reading Association, 1977.

Rosenthal, J.H. *The Neuropsychopathology of Written Language.* Chicago, IL: Nelson-Hall, 1977.

Rudorf, H.E. "Measurement of Spelling Ability". In Horn, T.D. (ed.), *Research on Handwriting and Spelling.* Champaign, IL: National Council of Teachers of English, 1966.

Sager, C. "Improving the Quality of Composition Through Pupil Use of A Rating Scale." Paper presented at the Annual Meeting of the National Council of Teachers, 1973. (ED 089 304)

Shaughnessy, Mina P. *Errors and Expectations, A Guide for the Teacher of Basic Writing.* New York: Oxford University Press, 1977.

Smith J.A. *Creative Teaching of the Language Arts in Elementary School.* Boston: Allyn and Bacon, 1973.

Strickland, R. "Evaluating Children's Compositions." In Burrows, A. (Ed.), *Children's Writing: Research in Composition and Related Skills.* Champaign, IL: National Council of Teachers of English, 1961. (ED 090 546)

Taylor, Karl K. "If not Grammar, What? Taking Remedial Writing Instruction Seriously." Paper prepared at Illinois Central College, 1978. (ED 159 668)

Thorndike, Edward L. and Lorge, Irving. *The Teacher's Word Book of 30,000 Words.* New York: Teachers College, Columbia University, 1944.

Vygotsky, L.S. *Thought and Language.* Cambridge, MA: MIT Press, 1962.

Wallace, G. and Larsen, S.C. *Educational Assessment of Learning Problems: Testing for Teaching.* Boston: Allyn and Bacon, 1978.

Wallace, G. and McLoughlin, J.A. *Learning Disabilities: Concepts and Characteristics.* Columbus, OH: Charles E. Merrill, 1979.

Weehawken Board of Education, *Individualized Language Arts.* Weehawken, NJ: Weehawken Board of Education, 1974.

Weiner, Eva. "The Diagnostic Evaluation of Writing Skills (DEWS): Application of DEWS Criteria to Writing Samples." *Learning Disability Quarterly.* 1980, 3, (2), Spring: 54–59.

Wiederholt, J.L. Hammill, D.D., and Brown, V. *The Resource Teacher: A Guide to Effective Practices.* Boston: Allyn and Bacon, 1978.

Wiener, Harvey, S. *Any Child Can Write.* New York: McGraw-Hill Book Company, 1978.

Wituche, V. "The Book Talk: A Technique for Bringing Together Children and Books." *Language Arts.* 1979, 56, (4): 413–417.

Wood, S. *An Evaluation of Published English Tests.* Madison, WI: Wisconsin Department of Public Instruction, 1967.

Zinsser, W. *On Writing Well, An Informal Guide to Writing Non-Fiction.* New York: Harper & Row, 1976.

Publishers' Addresses

Addison-Wesley Publishing Co.
Jacob Way
Reading, MA 01867

Allyn and Bacon, Inc.
470 Atlantic Avenue
Boston, MA 02210

American Faculty Press
44 Lake Shore Drive
Rockaway, NJ 07866

American Guidance Service, Inc.
Publisher's Building
Circle Pines, MN 55014

Art Education
28 E. Erie Street
Blauvelt, NY 10913

Atheneum Publications
122 E. 42nd Street
New York, NY 10017

Avon Books
959 Eighth Avenue
New York, NY 10019

Bantam Books, Inc.
666 Fifth Avenue
New York, NY 10019

Barnell-Loft, Ltd.
958 Church Street
Baldwin, NY 11510

Bradbury Press
2 Overhill Road
Scarsdale, NY 10583

Center for Humanities, Inc.
Communications Park, Box 100
White Plains, NY 10602

Century Communications, Inc.
5520 W. Touhy, Suite G
Skokie, IL 60077

Chelsea House Publishers
70 W. 40th Street
New York, NY 10018

Clarion Books
c/o Seabury Press
815 Second Avenue
New York, NY 10017

Coward, McCann and Geoghegan, Inc.
200 Madison Ave.
New York, NY 10016

Creative Teaching Associates
P.O. Box 7714
Fresno, CA 93727

Creative Teaching Press
5111 Hermosa Vista Avenue
Monterey Park, CA 91754

Curriculum Associates
5 Esquire Road
North Billerica, MA 01862

Thomas Y. Crowell Company
521 Fifth Avenue
New York, NY 10017

John Day Company
c/o Harper & Row Publishers
10 E. 53rd Street
New York, NY 10022

Delacorte Press
c/o Dell Publishing Co.
One Dag Hammarskjold Plaza
245 E. 47th Street
New York, NY 10017

Determined Productions
315 Pacific Avenue at Battery
P.O. Box 2150
San Francisco, CA 94126

Developmental Learning Materials
7440 Natchez Avenue
Niles, IL 60648

Dial Press
One Dag Hammarskjold Plaza
245 E. 47th Street
New York, NY 10017

Dormac, Inc.
P.O. Box 752
Beaverton, OR 97005

Doubleday & Co., Inc.
501 Franklin Avenue
New York, NY 11530

E.P. Dutton, Co., Inc.
2 Park Avenue
New York, NY 10016

Eastman Kodak Company
School and Youth Services
343 State Street
Rochester, NY 10583

Educational Progress Corporation
P.O. Box 45663
Tulsa, OK 74145

Education Today Company
530 University Avenue
Palo Alto, CA 94301

Encyclopedia Britannica Educational
  Corporation
425 North Michigan Avenue, 10th Floor
Chicago, IL 60611

Farrar, Straus & Giroux, Inc.
19 Union Square, W.
New York, NY 10003

Fearon-Pitman Publishers, Inc.
6 Davis Drive
Belmont, CA 94002

Follett Publishing Company
1010 West Washington Blvd.
Chicago, IL 60607

Four Winds Press
c/o Scholastic Book Services
904 Sylvan Avenue
Englewood Cliffs, NJ 07632

Garrard Publishing Company
1607 N. Market Street
Champaign, IL 61820

Globe Book Company, Inc.
175 Fifth Avenue
New York, NY 10010

Golden Press
c/o Western Publishing Company
850 Third Avenue
New York, NY 10022

Goodyear Publishing Company
1640 Fifth Street
Santa Monica, CA 90401

Greenwillow Books
c/o William Morrow and Company
105 Madison Avenue
New York, NY 10016

Guidance Associates
Communications Park, Box 300
White Plains, NY 10602

Harcourt Brace Jovanovich, Inc.
757 Third Avenue
New York, NY 10017

Harper and Row
10 East 53rd Street
New York, NY 10022

Harvey House Publishers
Waterside Plaza
New York, NY 10010

Hayden Book Company, Inc.
50 Essex Street
New Rochelle, NJ 07662

Holt, Rinehart and Winston
P.O. Box 3323
Grand Central Station
New York, NY 10017

Houghton Mifflin Company
One Beacon Street
Boston, MA 02107

Incentive Publications
P.O. Box 12522
Nashville, TN 37212

Instructional Laboratories
University of California
Berkeley, CA 94720

International Reading Association
800 Barksdale Road
P.O. Box 8139
Newark, DE 19711

Janus Book Publishers
2501 Industrial Parkway West
Hayward, CA 94545

King Features Syndicate
Education Division
235 East 45th Street
New York, NY 10017

Alfred A. Knopf
c/o Random House, Inc.
201 East 50th Street
New York, NY 10022

Learning Tree Filmstrips
P.O. Box 1590
Boulder, CO 80306

Learning Trends, Inc.
c/o Globe Book Company, Inc
175 Fifth Avenue
New York, NY 10010

Lerner Publications Company
241 First Avenue
North Minneapolis, MN 55401

J.B. Lippincott Company
521 Fifth Avenue
New York, NY 10017

Little, Brown and Company
34 Beacon Street
Boston, MA 02114

Lothrop, Lee and Shepard Company
c/o William Morrow and Company
105 Madison Avenue
New York, NY 10016

Macmillan Publishing Company
866 Third Street
New York, NY 10022

McDougal, Littell and Company
P.O. Box 1667
Evanston, IL 60204

McGraw-Hill Book Company
Webster Division
1221 Avenue of the Americas
New York, NY 10022

Meadowbrook Press
16648 Meadowbrook Lane
Wayzata, MN 55391

Miller Brody Productions
342 Madison Avenue
New York, NY 10017

Charles E. Merrill Publishing Co
1300 Alum Creek Drive
Columbus, OH 43216

Milton Bradley
Springfield, MA 01101

Modern Education Corporation
P.O. Box 721
Tulsa, OK 74101

William Morrow and Company, Inc.
105 Madison Avenue
New York, NY 10016

National Council of Teachers
   of English
1111 Kenyon Road
Urbana, IL 61801

National Information Center for
   Special Education Materials
University of Southern California
Research Park – RAN
Los Angeles, CA 90007

Tnomas Nelson, Inc.
407 Seventh Avenue
P.O. Box 946
Nashville, TN 37203

The New American Library, Inc
c/o The Times Mirror Company
1301 Avenue of the Americas
New York, NY 10019

Opportunities for Learning, Inc.
5024 Landershim Boulevard
North Hollywood, CA 91601

Paladin House
530 Lark Street
Geneva, IL 60134

Pantheon Books, Inc.
c/o Random House, Inc.
201 E. 50th Street, North
New York, NY 10022

Parent's Magazine Press
52 Vanderbilt Avenue
New York, NY 10017

The Perfection Form Company
8350 Hickman Road, Suite 15
Des Moines, IA 50322

Platt and Munk Publishers
c/o Grosset and Dunlap
51 Madison Avenue
New York, NY 10010

Prentice-Hall, Inc.
Route 9W
Englewood Cliffs, NJ 07632

Price/Stern/Sloan Publishers, Inc.
410 North La Cienega Boulevard
Los Angeles, CA 90048

Rand McNally and Company
P.O. Box 7600
Chicago, IL 60680

Random House, Inc.
201 E. 50th Street
New York, NY 10022

Reader's Digest Services, Inc.
Education Division
Pleasantville, NY 10570

Resources for the Gifted
3421 North 44th St.
Phoenix, AZ 85018

Scholastic Book Services
904 Sylvan Avenue
Englewood Cliffs, NJ 07632

Science Research Associates
259 East Erie Street
Chicago, IL 60025

Scott, Foresman and Company
1900 East Lake Avenue
Glenview, IL 60025

The Seabury Press
815 Second Avenue
New York, NY 10017

Simon and Schuster, Inc.
1230 Avenue of the Americas
New York, NY 10020

Society for Visual Education
1345 Diversey Parkway
Chicago, IL 60614

Spoken Arts
310 North Avenue
New Rochelle, NY 10801

Stemmer House Publishers, Inc.
22627 Caves Road
Owings Mill, MD 21117

Sterling Publishing Company
2 Park Avenue
New York, NY 10016

Sunburst Communications
39 Washington Avenue
Pleasantville, NY 10570

Teachers College Press
Columbia University
1234 Amsterdam Avenue
New York, NY 10027

Troll Associates
320 Route 17
Mahwah, NJ 17430

Vanguard Press, Inc.
424 Madison Avenue
New York, NY 10017

The Viking Press
625 Madison Avenue
New York, NY 10022

Frederick Warne and Company, Inc.
101 Fifth Avenue
New York, NY 10003

Franklin Watts, Inc.
c/o Grolier, Inc.
730 Fifth Avenue
New York, NY 10019

Windmill Books, Inc.
c/o E.P. Dutton Company, Inc.
2 Park Avenue
New York, NY 10016

Workman Publishing Company
One W. 39th Street
New York, NY 10018

Xerox Education Publications
1250 Fairwood Avenue
Columbus, OH 43216

Index

Achievement tests, weaknesses of, 4
Add the Ending activity, 163–165
Ads
    classified, as writing activity, 89–91
    job wanted, as writing activity, 87–89
    in writing activities, 83–84
Alligator Antics activity, 64
Alliteration, in writing activities, 134–135
Alphabet Antics activity, 134
Antonym Concentration activity, 121–124
Antonyms
    matching, 121–122
    pairs, list of, 122–124
Argument, pro and con, in writing
        activities, 83
Ask or Tell activity, 161
Ask, Tell, Exclaim! activity, 161–162
Auditory skills
    improving, 170
    and spelling, 170
Autobiography, as writing activity, 68–69

Bare Bear, The, activity, 171–175
Beginning, story
    in growth-level writing, 15
    in writing activities, 81–82
Bias, teacher, and writing evaluation, 5
Book reports, at growth level of writing,
        20
Broad or Narrow activity, 109–110
Building Compound Sentences activity,
        148–149
Building Simple Sentences activity, 139–
        141

Capital Contest activity, 154–156
Capitalization, 154
    informal evaluation of, 41
    in writing process, 3
Carlson Analytical Originality Scale, 6–7
Cartoon characters, in writing activities,
        75
Categorizing, 95–96
Character Description Grid, 72
Characters
    cartoon, in writing activities, 75
    in mastery-level writing, 16
    in writing activities, 72–74
Chart(s)
    of difficult words, for spelling im-
        provement, 171
    of mnemonic devices, for spelling, 170
Cliches
    list of, 129–131
    literal interpretation of, 129
Comic strips, in writing activities, 58–59
        (See also Cartoon characters)
Comparisons
    list of, 131–132
    original, writing, 113, 131–133
Complaints, as writing activity, 91–92
Complex sentences (See Sentences,
        complex)
Compound sentences (See Sentences,
        compound)
Concentration games, and spelling, 170
Conclusion, in writing activities, 106–107
Content
    in evaluating writing, 10–18

informal evaluation of, 35–36
Conversations
    activity, 162–163
    in limited-level writing, 11
    punctuation of, 162–163
Creatures, Monsters, and Dragons activity, 58

Descriptive Words activity, 127–128
Details
    arranging, in writing activities, 101
    concrete, and abstract words, 128
    descriptive
        combining, in sentence, 150
        in growth-level writing, 14
        and kernel sentences, 138–139
    identifying, in writing activities, 106–107
    irrelevant, in limited-level writing, 11
    listening and recalling, 108
    providing and arranging, 96
    spotting, in writing activities, 103–104
Diagnostic Evaluation of Writing Skills (Weiner), 4
DI-COMP, A Diagnostic System for Teaching Composition for Grades 10–14, 5
Diederich scale, 6
Directions, writing, as writing activity, 92–94
Dogs Eat activity, 138–139
Dolch Word List, 173–174

Editing, 3, 50
Endings, story
    in growth-level writing, 15
    trite, in limited-level writing, 11
Endings, verb, supplying, as writing activity, 163–164
Errors
    in growth-level writing, 9, 14, 29
    identifying and remediating, 153–154
    spelling
        dealing with, 169
        in growth-level writing, 32
        in limited-level writing, 30–32
        in mastery-level writing, 32
    vocabulary, in limited-level writing, 32
Essays, at growth level of writing, 20
Evaluating Writing: Describing, Measuring, and Judging (Cooper and Odell), 6
Evaluation, of writing skills (See Holistic evaluation; Informal evaluation; Peer evaluation; Self-evaluation; Teacher evaluation)
Exclamations, identifying, 161–162
Expanded sentences (See Sentences, expanded)

Fables, in writing activities, 70–71
Fact
    vs. fiction, in writing activities, 111–112
    vs. opinion, in writing activities, 112–113
Fact or Fiction activity, 111–112
Feedback, and writing, 1–2
Fiction, vs. fact, in writing activities, 111–112
First draft, 50
    manuscript handwriting for, 178
    writing levels in, 9
First National Assessment of Writing, 20
First person point of view, in writing activities, 76–78
Flashcards, and spelling, 170
Foolish Questions activity, 160–161

Generalizations
    in growth-level writing, 14
    hasty
        eliminating, 96
        identifying, 110–111
    supporting, in writing activities, 109
Grading, variations in, 5
Grocery List activity, 96–99
Growth level, of writing skills, described, 9, 12–13, 14–16, 19–21
Growth Sequence (Moffett), 10

Handwriting
    cursive
        instruction sequence, 179
        lower case exercises, 179–185
        transition to, 177
        upper case exercises, 185
    evaluating and improving, 177–185
    in growth-level writing, 33–34
    in limited-level writing, 33
    manuscript, 177–178
        for first drafts, 178
    in mastery-level writing, 34
    samples, in writing evaluation, 42–45
    in writing process, 3
Happy as a Lark activity, 131–132
Hasty Generalization activity, 110–111
Help activity, 152
Hidden Sentences activity, 158–159
Hillerich word frequency list, 21–22
Hoarse Horse, The, activity, 175–177
Holistic evaluation, of writing skills, 5
Homonyms, vs. homophones, 171–172
Homophones, 171
    in limited-level writing, 32
    list of, 175–177
Horn word frequency list, 21

I, We, He, She, They, It activity, 165–167

Ideas: *continued*
    in evaluating writing, 10–18
    in growth-level writing, 15, 19–2·
    main
        arranging, in writing activities, 101
        identifying, in writing activities,
            106–107
        stating, 96
    in mastery-level writing, 16–18
    related, sequencing, 101
Informal evaluation, of writing skills,
    9–10
    components, 10–34
    procedures, 34–45
Information, in growth-level writing, 20
Interpretation, in mastery-level writing, 18
Interviews, spelling, 171
Irrelevant Sentences activity, 100
Is That So? activity, 112–113

Jokes, jumbled, in writing activities, 99–
    100
Journals, as writing activity, 66–68
Jumbled Jokes activity, 99–100

Kernel sentences (*See* Sentences, kernel)
Kernel Sentences activity, 136–139

Language skills, in writing, 3
Letters (of the alphabet)
    cursive lower case
        basic groups, 179–182
        families, 182–185
    cursive upper case, 185
    omission of, in spelling, 170
    substitution of, in spelling, 170
Letters (communications)
    complaint, as writing activity, 91–92
    to editor, as writing activity, 91
    writing, as writing activity, 85–87
Limited level, of writing skill, described,
    9, 10–11, 12–13, 18–19
Listen for the Details activity, 108
Lists, in limited-level writing, 14

Make It Parallel activity, 151–152
Make It Real activity, 128
Mary Had a Little Lamb activity, 126–
    127
Mastery level, of writing skill, described,
    9, 12–13, 16–18
Memory, visual, and spelling skills, 171
Metaphors, recognizing and writing, 132–
    133
Mixed Up Stories activity, 101–102
    for pronoun inconsistency, 168–169
Mnemonic devices, for spelling, 170
Moods, character, in writing activities,
    74–75
Moral, in mastery-level writing, 18

Narrative, personal, in limited-level
    writing, 14
National Assessment of Educational
    Progress, 20
News
    eyewitness, in writing activities, 82, 84
    sports, in writing activities, 82–84, 165
Notebooks, for spelling, 169
Notetaking, 96
Nouns, specific, use of, 114–116

Opinion(s)
    vs. fact, in writing activities, 112–113
    in mastery-level writing, 18
    writing letter to editor, 91
Oral language sample, in writing evalu-
    ation 39–40
Organization
    informal evaluation of, 36
    in limited-level writing, 18–19
    in mastery-level writing, 21
    in prewriting stage, 3
    skills, 95–113
Outline
    making factual paragraph from, 108–
        109
    in writing activities, 96
Outline Match activity, 108–109

Paragraph
    dictation, in writing evaluation, 41–42
    factual, from outline, 108–109
    organization, in writing evaluation, 40–
        41
    structure, in growth-level writing, 19
Pass It On activity, 147–148
Peer evaluation, of writing skills, 7
Phonics, in writing and reading activities,
    169
Picture file, in writing activities, 53
Picture stimulus, in writing evaluation,
    34–38
Picture Story Language Test (Myklebust),
    4
Planning
    in growth-level writing, 19
    in limited-level writing, 19
Plot development, in mastery-level
    writing, 16
Poems, "sound," 133–134
Point of view, in writing activities, 75–78
Prewriting stage, elements of, 3
Pro and Con activity, 83
Pronouns
    inconsistency, detecting, 168–169
    in writing activities, 165–167
Proofreading, 9, 50, 153, 171
    in limited-level writing, 32
    and spelling errors, 169
Prove It! activity, 109

Punctuation
    in growth-level writing, 29
    of hidden sentences, 158-159
    identifying, in ictated material, 163
    informal evalua ion of, 42
    of questions, 160-161
    table of, 155
    in writing process, 3
Punctuation Dictation activity, 163

Questions
    foolish, 160-161
    identifying, 161-162
    restating as statements, 107-108
    vs. statements, as writing activity, 161
Questionnaire, on student reading, 52

Rating scales, 6-7
Reading, Writing, and Rating Stories
        (Sager), 7
Reducing Expanded Sentences activity,
        146-147
Repetitive Words activity, 125-126
Revision, 3, 9, 50
Rhyme, and spelling problems, 170
Run-On Sentences activity, 156-157

Scene I, Scene II, Scene III activity,
        60-61
Self-evaluation, of writing skills, 7
Sentence(s)
    combining, 149-151
    complex, 25-27
    compound, building, 148-149
    compound-complex, 28
    excessively worded, as writing activity,
        152
    expanded
        building, 143-146
        identifying components in, 141-
        143
        reducing, 146-147
        writing, 147-148
    fragments, 157
    hidden, 158-159
    irrelevant, in writing activities, 100
    kernel, 136-139
        lists of, 137-138
    parallel structure in, 151-152
    run-on, 28, 156-157
    scrambled, 159-160
    simple, 27-28
        building, 139-141
        lists of, 140-141
    topic, deriving from questions, 107-
        108
    types
        in growth-level writing, 28-29
        in mastery-level writing, 29-30
    zany

building, 143
    list of, 144
Sentence Building activity, 140-141
Sentence Collage activity, 157-158
Sentence Combining activity, 149-150
Sentence Fragments activity, 157
Sentence Scramble activity, 159-160
Sentence Sort activity, 101
Sentence structure
    developing skills, 135-136
    in growth-level writing, 28-29
    informal evaluation of, 37-38
    in limited-level writing, 27-28
    in mastery-level writing, 29-30
Sequence of events
    in growth-level writing, 15
    in writing activities, 60-61
Sequence Words activity, 102-103
Sequencing, 96
    in growth-level writing, 19
    in writing activities, 100, 101
Setting Grid, 79
Settings activities, 78-81
Sight words, and spelling, 169
Simple sentences (See Sentences, simple)
Slide-tape show, in writing activities,
        59-60
Sound Poems activity, 133-134
Sounds, confusion of, and spelling errors,
        170
Sparkling Words (Carlson), 7
Spelling
    auditory problems and, 170
    activities, 171-177
    in growth-level writing, 32
    improving, 169-170
    informal evaluation of, 38
    interviews, 171
    in limited-level writing, 30-32
    in mastery-level writing, 32
    phonics vs. sight words, 169
    skills, in writing, 3, 30
Spelling Interviews activity, 171
Spelling Mastery Contest, 171
Sports News activity, 82-84
    verb tense, 165
Spotting Details activity, 103
Statements
    identifying, 161-162
    vs. questions, as writing activity, 161
Stories
    beginning, in writing activities, 81
    mixed-up, in writing activities, 101-
        102
    zany, in writing activities, 69-70
Story starters
    in writing activities, 61-63
    in writing evaluation, 38-39
Storyboard, in writing activities, 55-56
Storybooks, in writing activities, 54-55

Strange as It Seems activity, 128–131
Structure, parallel, in writing activities, 151–152 (See also Sentence structure)
Student writing checklist, 45, 48
Style, personal
in growth-level writing, 16
in mastery-level writing, 16
Substitution activity, 124–125
Sun Is a Golden Earring, The, activity, 132–133
Synonym Call activity, 120–121
Synonym Pass and Sort activity, 121
Synonyms
adjectives, list of, 118–120
identifying meaning, 120–121
sorting by meaning, 121
verbs, list of, 116–118

Target groups, identifying, in writing activities, 84–85
Task analysis, in writing activities, 104–105
Teacher evaluation, of writing skills, 5
Telephone conversations, in writing activities, 64–66
Telephone messages, writing down, as writing activity, 85, 86
Tenses, verb, in writing activities, 163–165
Test of Everyday Writing Skills, 5
Test of Written Language (Hammill and Larsen), 4
Tests (See also Achievement tests)
at growth level of writing, 20
of writing skills, 2–5
Theme, in growth-level writing, 19
Thinking, in prewriting stage, 3
Time Machine Past activity, 105–106
Time sequence, words representing, 102
Titles, Topics, and Twisters activity, 63–64
Topic Imposed Words, 21
Topic sentence, as restatement of question, 107–108
Topics, narrowing, in writing activities, 109–110
T-unit, 25

Verbs
adding omitted tense endings, as writing activity, 163–164
specific, use of, as writing activity, 114–115
synonyms, list of, 116–118
tenses, use of, as writing activity, 165

Visual Dictation activity, 171
Visual memory, and spelling skills, 171
Visual skills
improving, 170
and spelling, 170
Vocabulary (See also Words)
in growth-level writing, 24–25
in limited-level writing, 23–24
in mastery-level writing, 25
specific, 113–115
use, informal evaluation of, 36–37

Want ads, as writing activity, 89–91
What's the Big Idea? activity, 106–107
What's Going On? activity, 141–143
"When," "where," "why" phrases, combining, in sentences, 151
"Who," "did what," "when," "where," "why," in expanded sentences, 141–146
Word cards, and spelling, 170
Word frequency lists, 21–23, 171–174
Words (See also Vocabulary)
abstract, 113
concrete details for, 128
choice of, and spelling, 169
descriptive, 113–114
identifying, 127–128
difficult, and spelling interviews, 171
excessive
deliberate use of, in writing activities, 152
eliminating, 149–150
invented, 21
playing with, 113
repetitive, substituting specific for, 125–127
sequence, in writing activities, 102–103
specific, substituting for general, 124–127
Topic Imposed, 21
Writing
creative, activities, 51–94
elements in, 3
mechanics of, 154–169
and other curriculum areas, 51
process
complexity of, 1–2, 3
encouraging, 47–51
qualitative vs. quantitative features, 2

Zaner-Bloser Scale, 33
Zany Sentences activity, 143–146
Zany Stories activity, 143–146

A

S

S